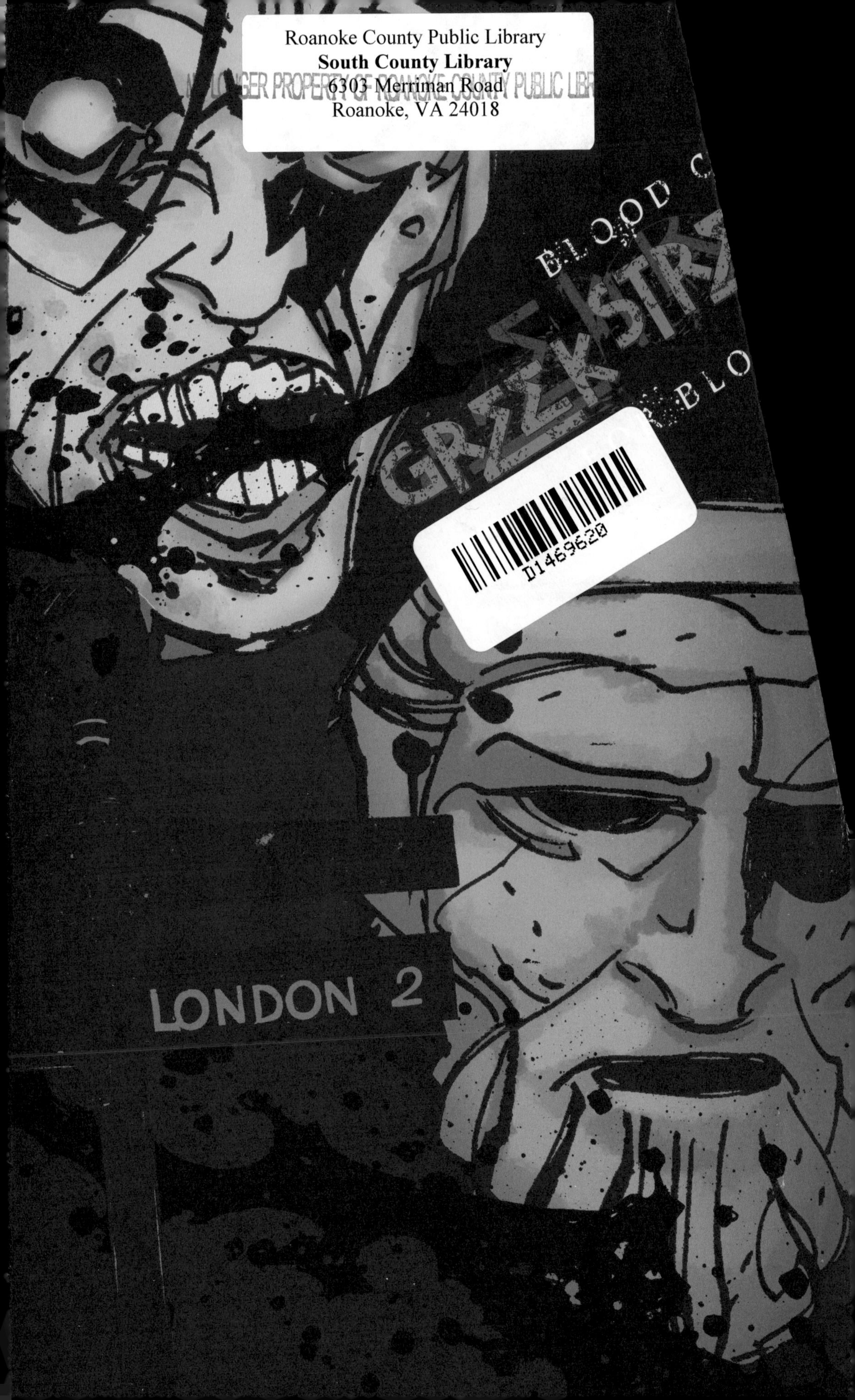
BLOOD
LONDON 2

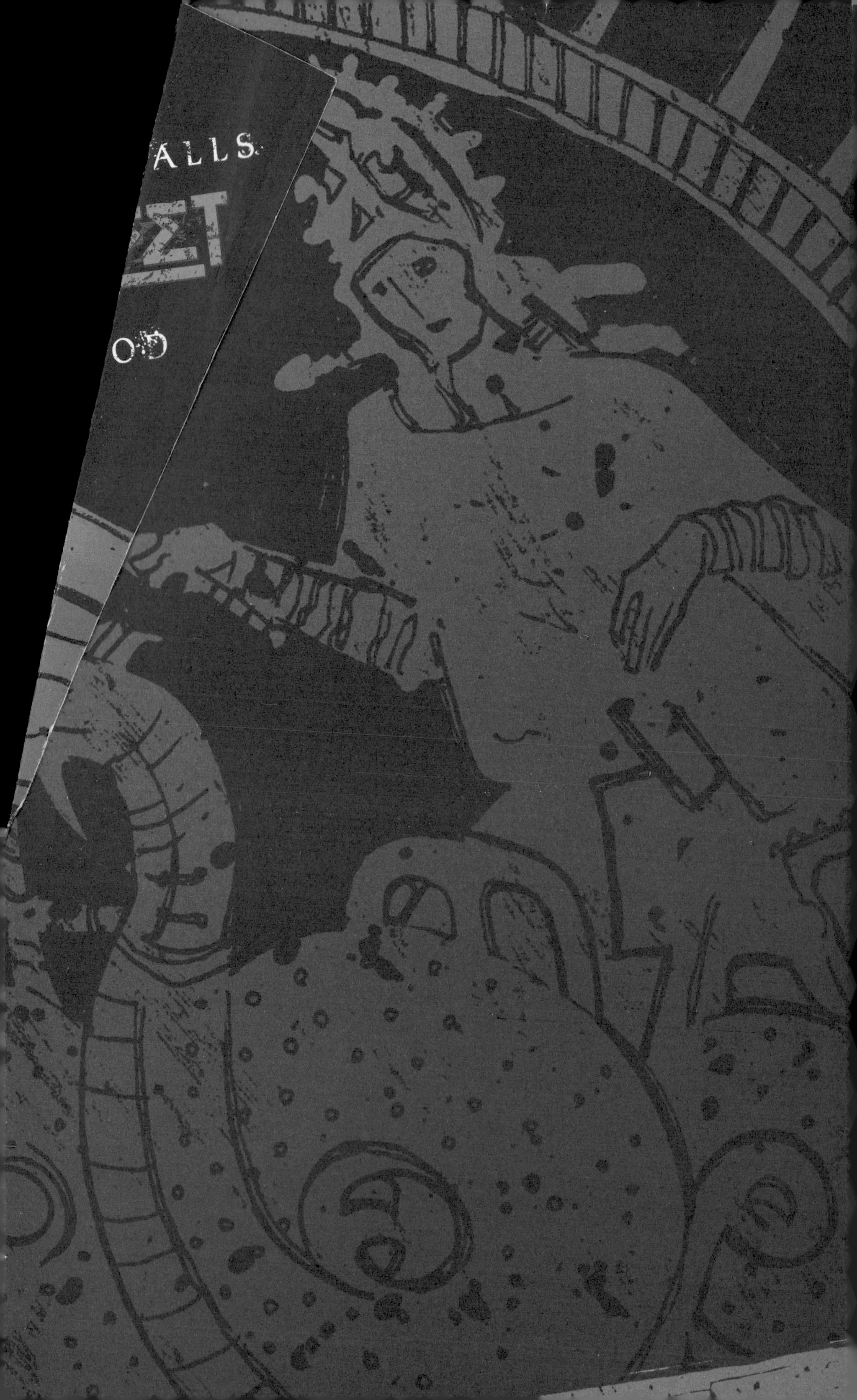

GREEK STREET

BLOOD CALLS FOR BLOOD

PETER MILLIGAN
WRITER

DAVIDE GIANFELICE
ARTIST

PATRICIA MULVIHILL
COLORIST

CLEM ROBINS
LETTERER

KAKO
JOCK
ORIGINAL SERIES COVERS

GREEK STREET
CREATED BY PETER MILLIGAN
AND DAVIDE GIANFELICE

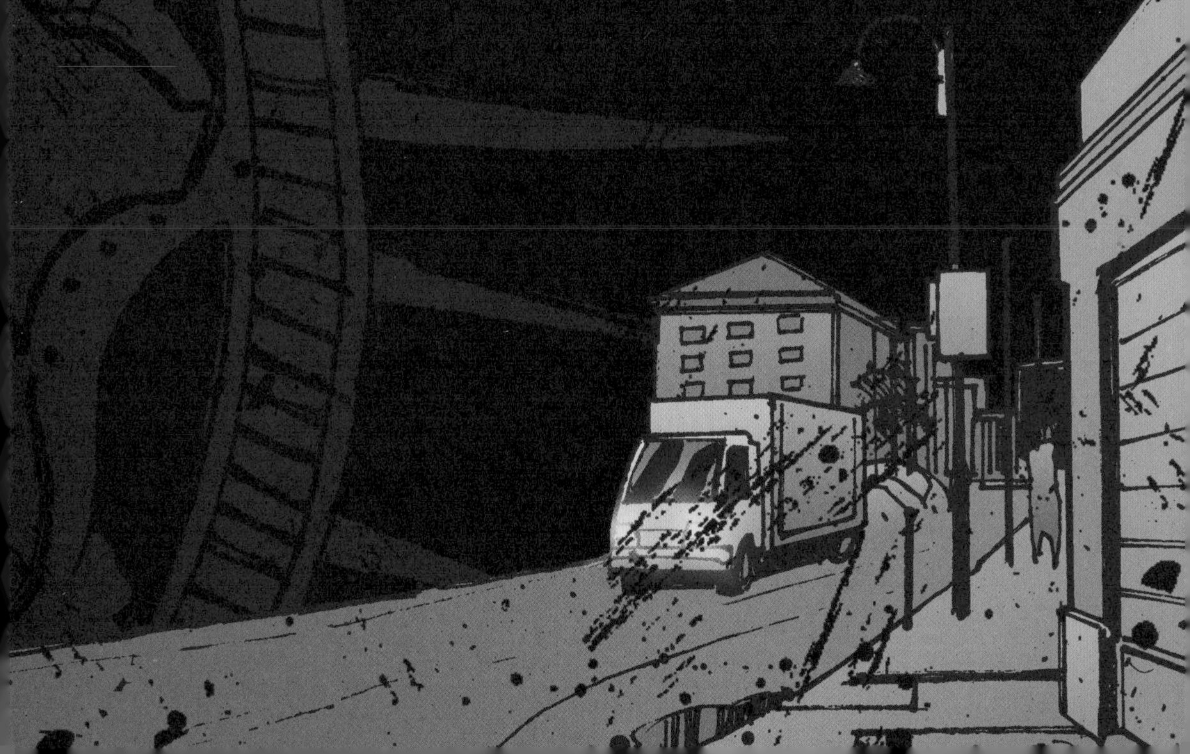

KAREN BERGER SVP – Executive Editor
WILL DENNIS Editor – Original Series
MARK DOYLE Assistant Editor – Original Series
GEORG BREWER VP – Design & DC Direct Creative
BOB HARRAS Group Editor – Collected Editions
SCOTT NYBAKKEN Editor
ROBBIN BROSTERMAN Design Director – Books

DC COMICS
PAUL LEVITZ President & Publisher
RICHARD BRUNING SVP – Creative Director
PATRICK CALDON EVP – Finance & Operations
AMY GENKINS SVP – Business & Legal Affairs
JIM LEE Editorial Director – WildStorm
GREGORY NOVECK SVP – Creative Affairs
STEVE ROTTERDAM SVP – Sales & Marketing
CHERYL RUBIN SVP – Brand Management

Cover art by Kako.
Publication design by Robbie Biederman.

GREEK STREET: BLOOD CALLS FOR BLOOD

DC Comics, 1700 Broadway, New York, NY 10019
A Warner Bros. Entertainment Company.
Printed in Canada. First Printing.
ISBN: 978-1-4012-2573-5

SUSTAINABLE
FORESTRY
INITIATIVE

Certified Fiber Sourcing
www.sfiprogram.org

Fiber used in this product line meets the
sourcing requirements of the SFI program.
www.sfiprogram.org PWC-SFICOC-260

BLOOD CALLS FOR BLOOD

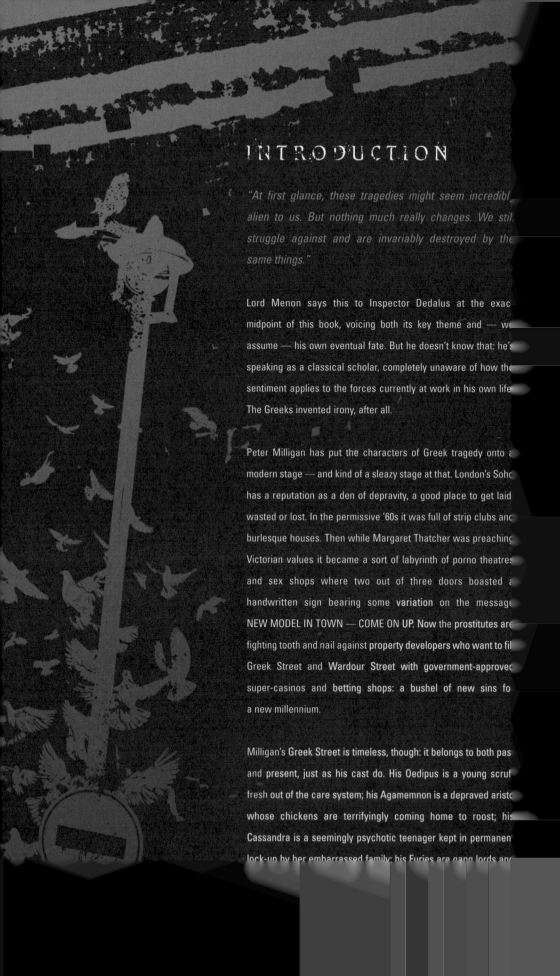

INTRODUCTION

*"At first glance, these tragedies might seem incredibl_
alien to us. But nothing much really changes. We stil_
struggle against and are invariably destroyed by the
same things."*

Lord Menon says this to Inspector Dedalus at the exac_
midpoint of this book, voicing both its key theme and — we
assume — his own eventual fate. But he doesn't know that: he's
speaking as a classical scholar, completely unaware of how the
sentiment applies to the forces currently at work in his own life_
The Greeks invented irony, after all.

Peter Milligan has put the characters of Greek tragedy onto a
modern stage — and kind of a sleazy stage at that. London's Soho
has a reputation as a den of depravity, a good place to get laid
wasted or lost. In the permissive '60s it was full of strip clubs and
burlesque houses. Then while Margaret Thatcher was preaching
Victorian values it became a sort of labyrinth of porno theatres
and sex shops where two out of three doors boasted a
handwritten sign bearing some variation on the message
NEW MODEL IN TOWN — COME ON UP. Now the prostitutes are
fighting tooth and nail against property developers who want to fil_
Greek Street and Wardour Street with government-approved
super-casinos and betting shops: a bushel of new sins fo_
a new millennium.

Milligan's Greek Street is timeless, though: it belongs to both pas_
and present, just as his cast do. His Oedipus is a young scruf_
fresh out of the care system; his Agamemnon is a depraved aristo_
whose chickens are terrifyingly coming home to roost; his
Cassandra is a seemingly psychotic teenager kept in permanen_
lock-up by her embarrassed family; his Furies are gang lords and

But that's just background, really; just grace notes. What Milligan is really doing, it seems to me, is rolling up his sleeves and dipping his hands into the blood and guts and agony that is true tragedy. He's showing us lives skidding out of control, hitting the wall, going up in flames. And — just as Aeschylus and Sophocles did — he's opening up to our gaze, with remorseless clarity, the forces within and around us that make it happen.

There's a central paradox in Greek tragedy, which is this: the tragic hero brings about his own downfall because of some terrible flaw or fracture in his own nature — pride, or lust, or moral blindness. But at the same time, he's destroyed because the gods, or some subset of the gods, decide to stitch him up good and proper. Fate and hubris go hand in hand. So destiny gets to pull the trigger, but you pretty much have to paint the target on your own chest first — and the horror of your downfall is precisely equal to the scale of your fuck-up. Ordinary mortals watch and wonder.

That's the world as the ancients saw it, and Milligan goes to some pains to prove that that model applies to all of us, lords and lowbrows and lap dancers alike. "This is the old dance," one of his choric strippers says at the outset. "This is the old story." If it still has the power to surprise and disturb us, that comes down to two things: it's a damn good story, and a storyteller at the top of his game.

Actually, I should have said three things: the art team on the book also bring their own overflowing amphora to the table. Davide Gianfelice's stark lines and Trish Mulvihill's perfectly judged color palette make this Soho look like a world teetering at the brink of the abyss, the interiors lurid and threatening or filled with unfathomable shadows, the street shots bleak and alienating. It's an uncomfortable world, but you're made to inhabit it, and that's what tragedy is all about — getting us in as close as possible to the blinded Oedipus, the trapped and slaughtered Agamemnon, the raving Cassandra, so that we feel shaken and awed by their fate and a rat's whisker away from having shared it.

And that's what you'll get on Greek Street, if you choose to walk there: that vivid, disquieting sense of engagement; that irresistible invitation to identify with monsters and sacrifices, the not-so-beautiful and the definitely damned. You'll look at your own life differently when you come out the far end, and really, you can't ask for more out of a book than that.

So come and dance the old dance. You'll find you already know the steps.

— Mike Carey,
London, 2009

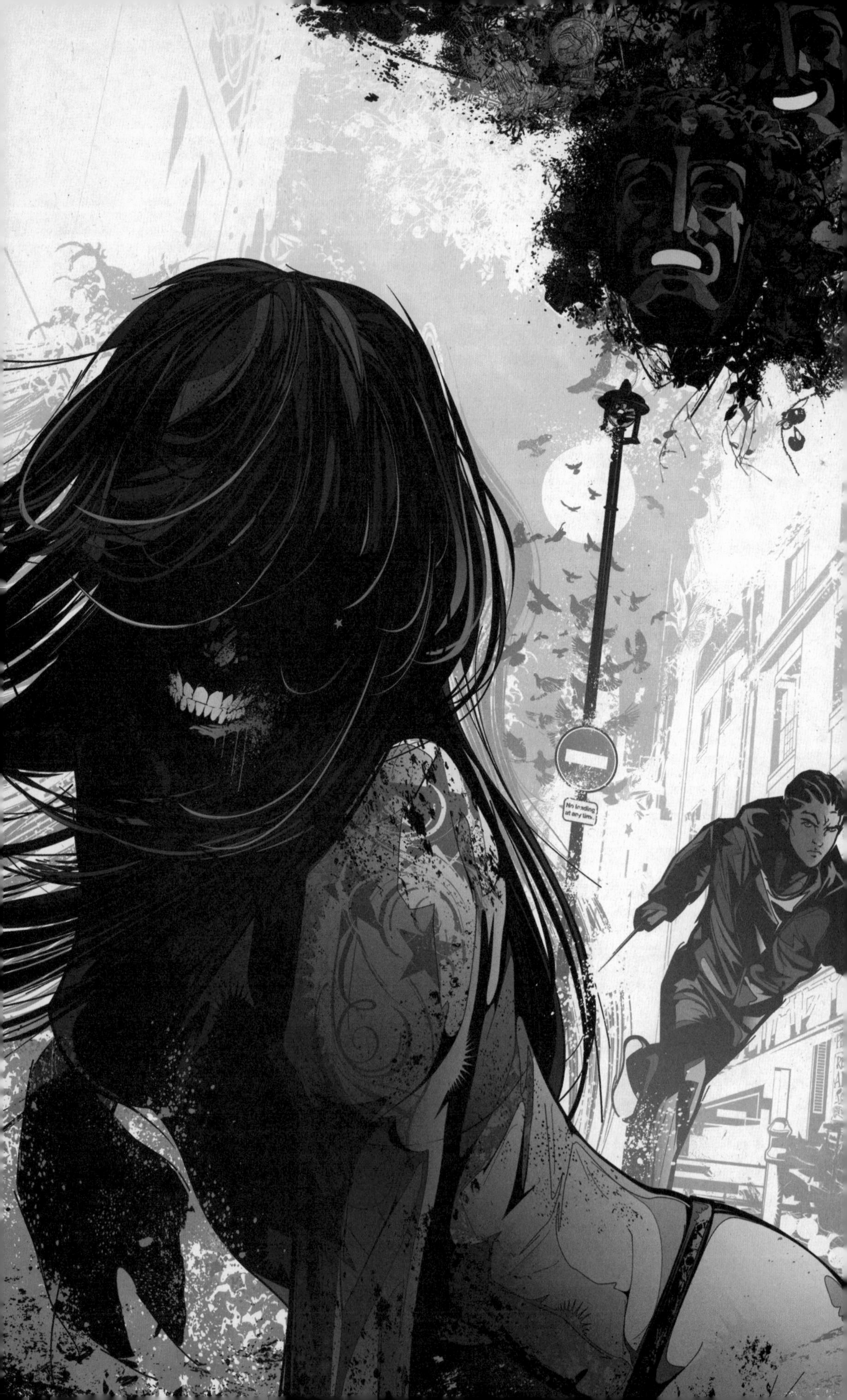

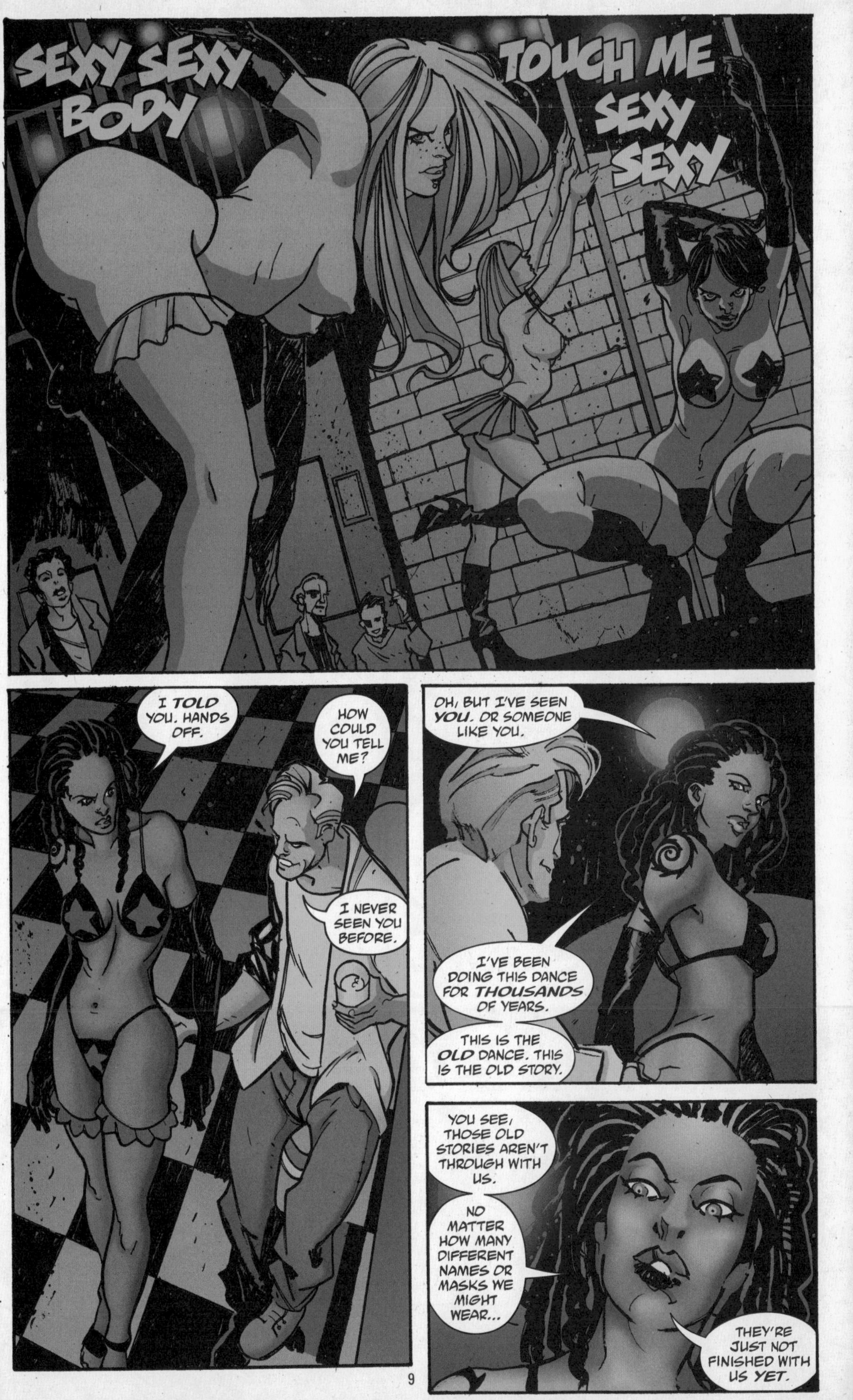
SEXY SEXY BODY
TOUCH ME SEXY SEXY
I TOLD YOU. HANDS OFF.
HOW COULD YOU TELL ME?
I NEVER SEEN YOU BEFORE.
OH, BUT I'VE SEEN YOU. OR SOMEONE LIKE YOU.
I'VE BEEN DOING THIS DANCE FOR THOUSANDS OF YEARS.
THIS IS THE OLD DANCE. THIS IS THE OLD STORY.
YOU SEE, THOSE OLD STORIES AREN'T THROUGH WITH US.
NO MATTER HOW MANY DIFFERENT NAMES OR MASKS WE MIGHT WEAR...
THEY'RE JUST NOT FINISHED WITH US YET.

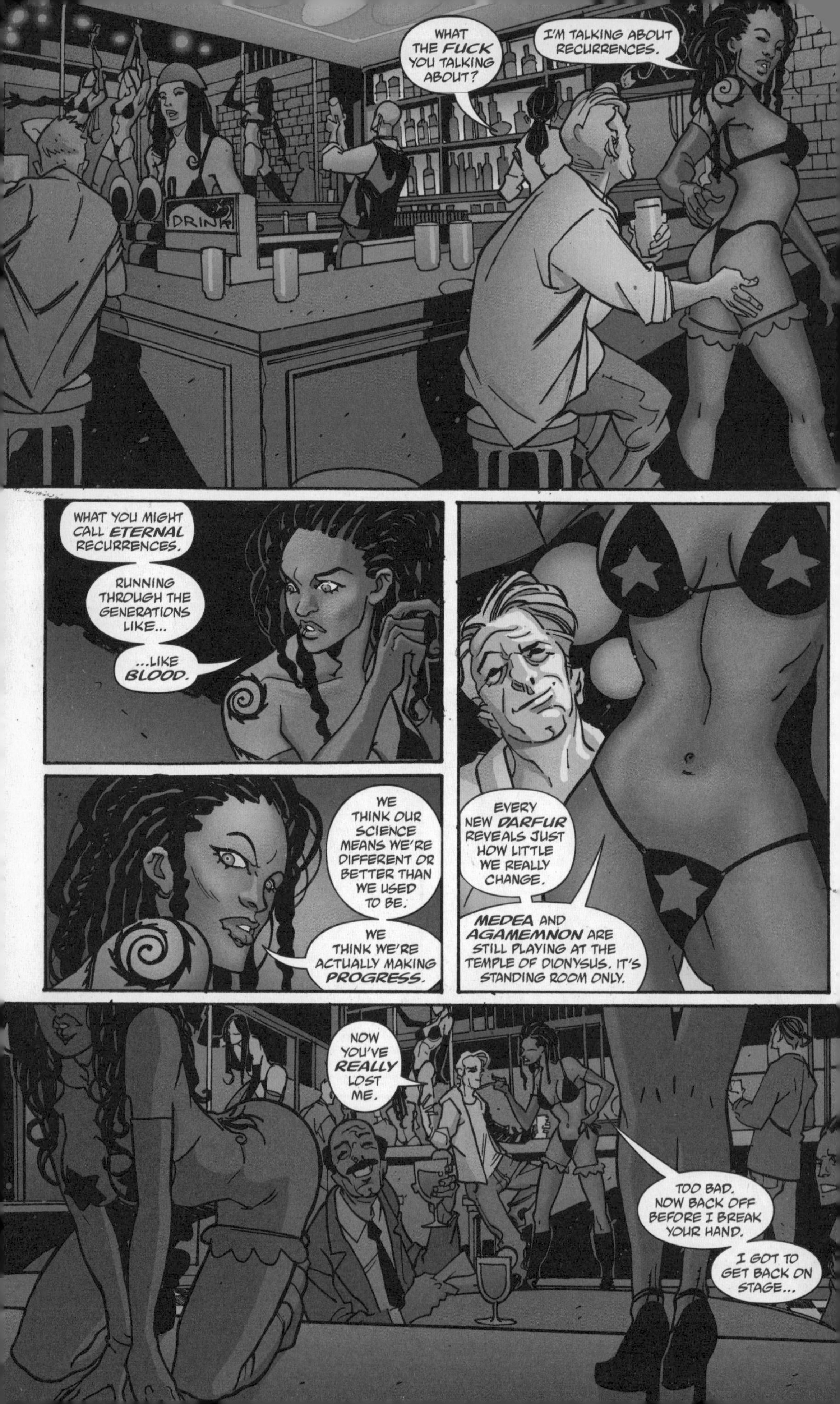
WHAT THE FUCK YOU TALKING ABOUT?
I'M TALKING ABOUT RECURRENCES.
DRINK
WHAT YOU MIGHT CALL ETERNAL RECURRENCES.
RUNNING THROUGH THE GENERATIONS LIKE...
...LIKE BLOOD.
EVERY NEW DARFUR REVEALS JUST HOW LITTLE WE REALLY CHANGE.
MEDEA AND AGAMEMNON ARE STILL PLAYING AT THE TEMPLE OF DIONYSUS. IT'S STANDING ROOM ONLY.
WE THINK OUR SCIENCE MEANS WE'RE DIFFERENT OR BETTER THAN WE USED TO BE.
WE THINK WE'RE ACTUALLY MAKING PROGRESS.
NOW YOU'VE REALLY LOST ME.
TOO BAD. NOW BACK OFF BEFORE I BREAK YOUR HAND.
I GOT TO GET BACK ON STAGE...

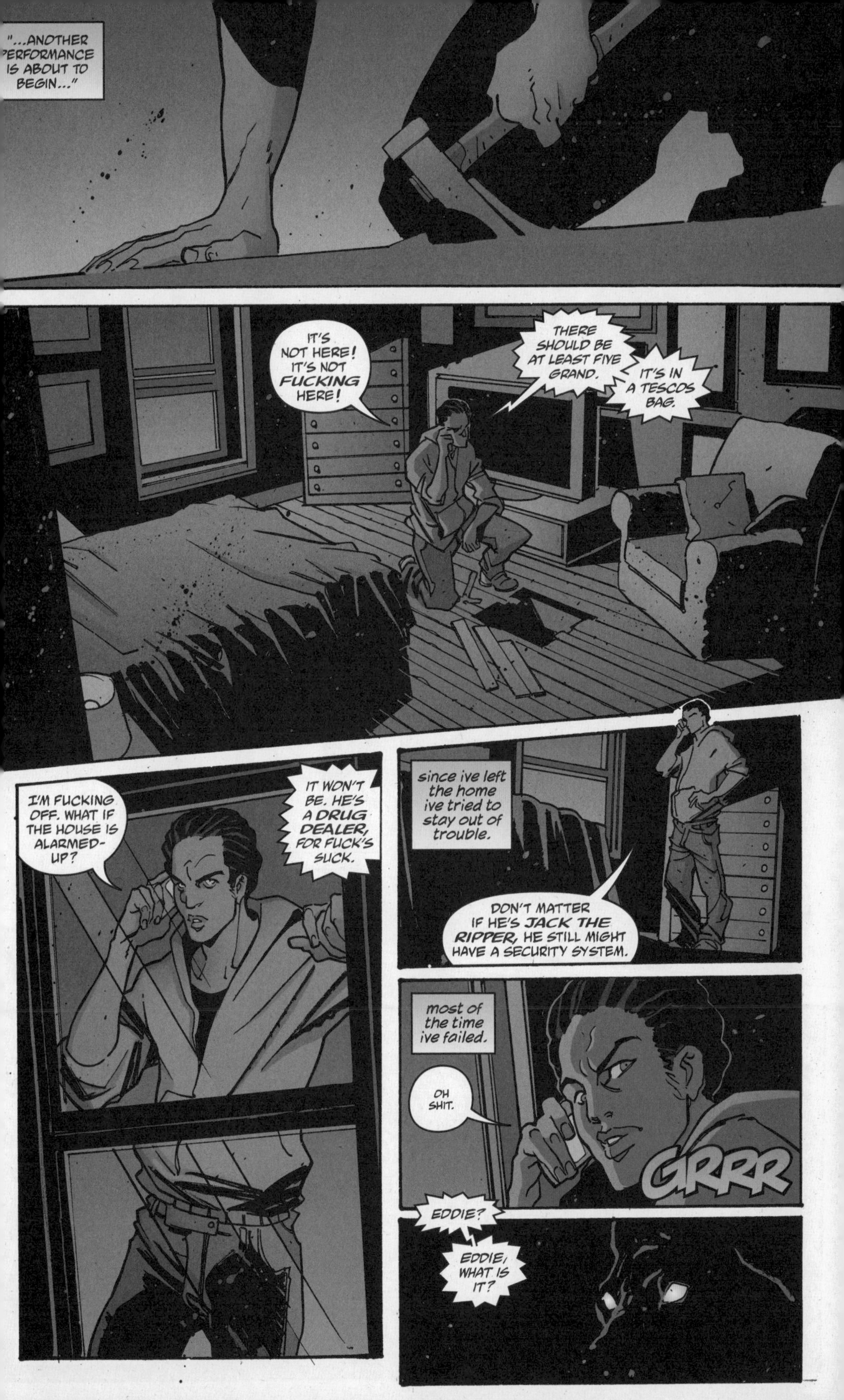
"...ANOTHER PERFORMANCE IS ABOUT TO BEGIN..."
IT'S NOT HERE! IT'S NOT FUCKING HERE!
THERE SHOULD BE AT LEAST FIVE GRAND.
IT'S IN A TESCOS BAG.
I'M FUCKING OFF. WHAT IF THE HOUSE IS ALARMED-UP?
IT WON'T BE. HE'S A DRUG DEALER, FOR FUCK'S SUCK.
since ive left the home ive tried to stay out of trouble.
DON'T MATTER IF HE'S JACK THE RIPPER, HE STILL MIGHT HAVE A SECURITY SYSTEM.
most of the time ive failed.
OH SHIT.
GRRR
EDDIE?
EDDIE, WHAT IS IT?

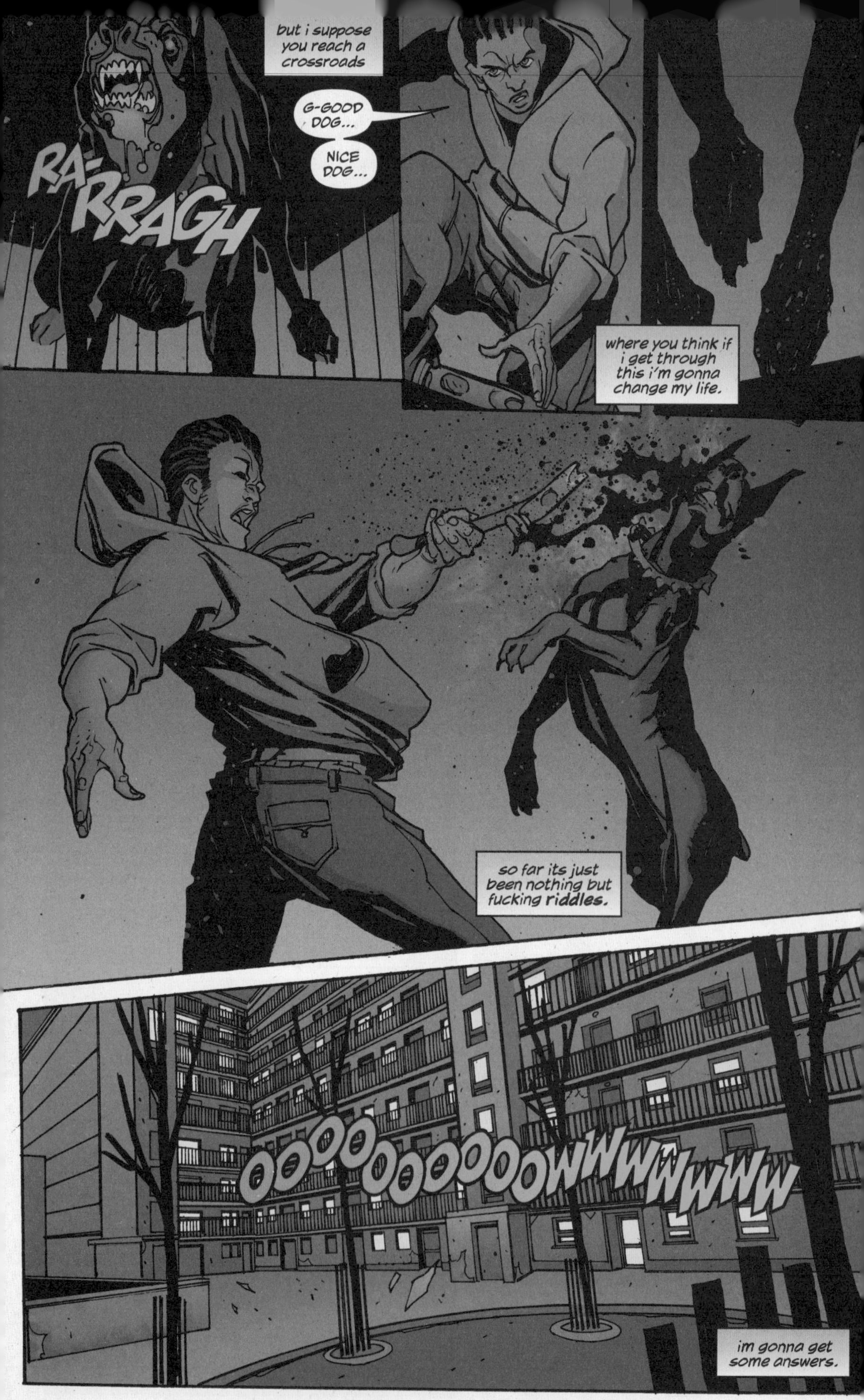

but i suppose you reach a crossroads
G-GOOD DOG...
NICE DOG...
RA-RRAGH
where you think if i get through this i'm gonna change my life.
so far its just been nothing but fucking **riddles.**
OOOOOOOOOOOOWWWWWWWW
im gonna get some answers.

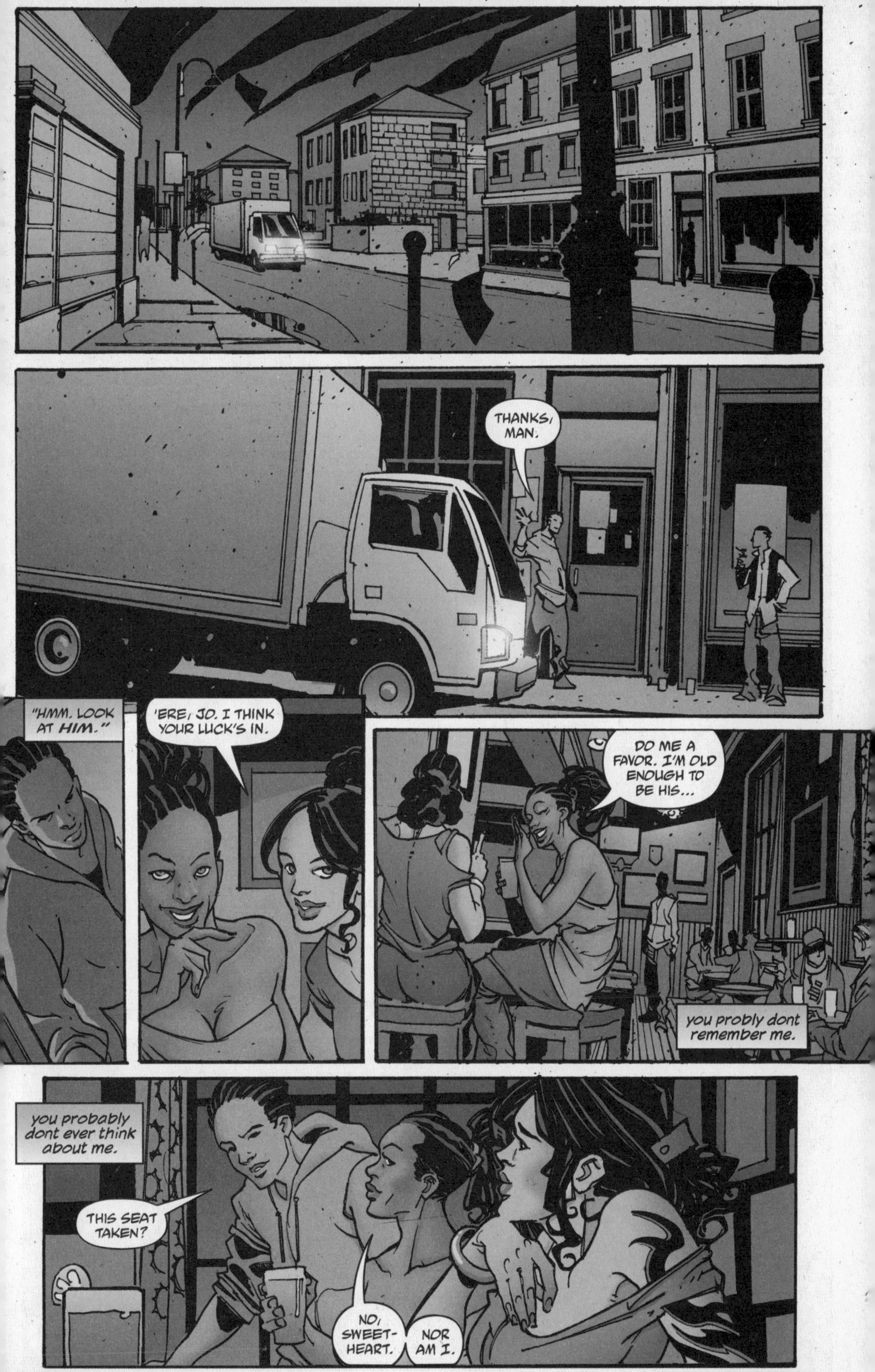
THANKS, MAN.
"HMM. LOOK AT **HIM**."
'ERE, JO. I THINK YOUR LUCK'S IN.
DO ME A FAVOR. I'M OLD ENOUGH TO BE HIS...
you probly dont remember me.
you probably dont ever think about me.
THIS SEAT TAKEN?
NO, SWEET-HEART.
NOR AM I.

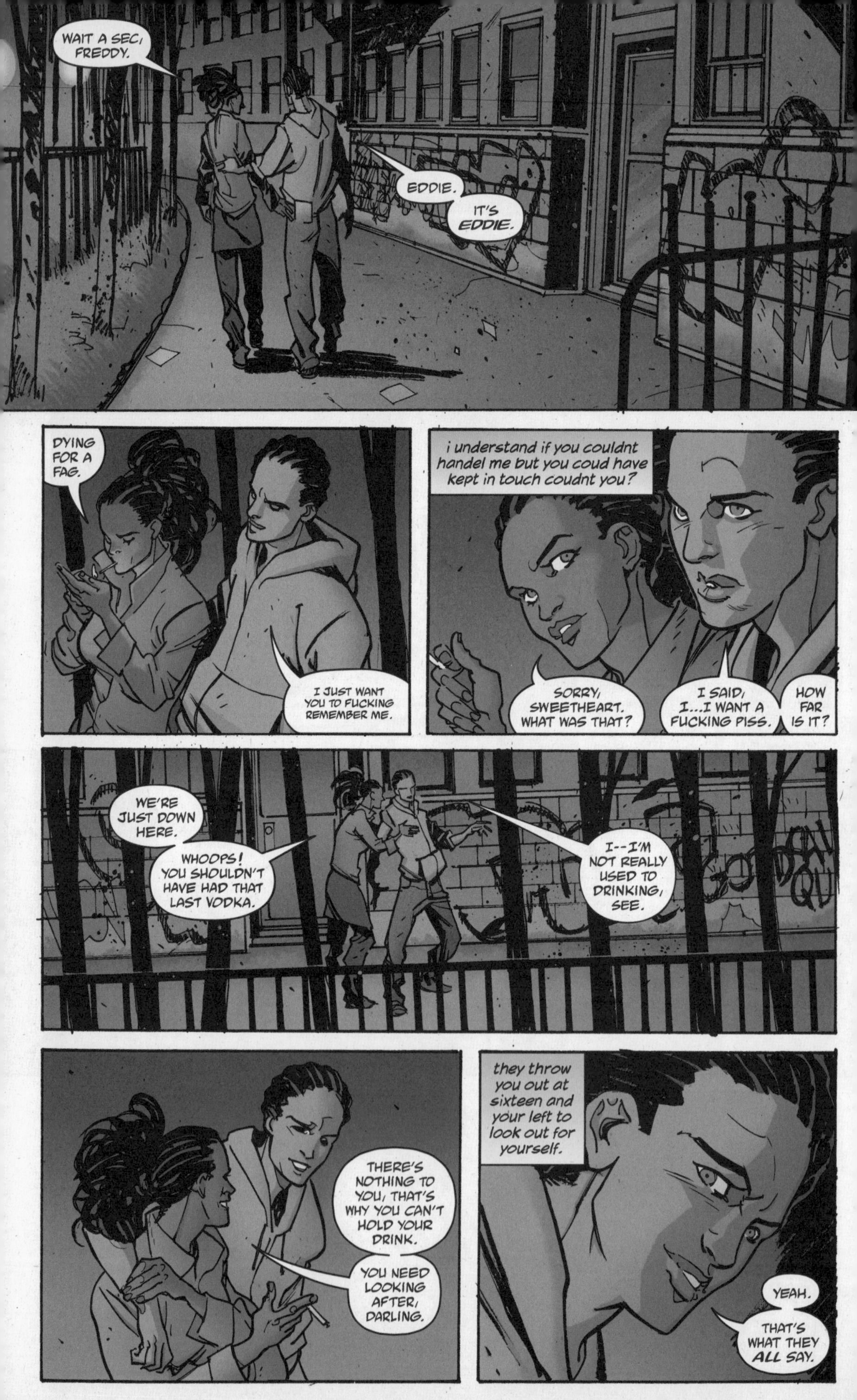

WAIT A SEC, FREDDY.
EDDIE.
IT'S EDDIE.
DYING FOR A FAG.
I JUST WANT YOU TO FUCKING REMEMBER ME.
i understand if you couldnt handel me but you coud have kept in touch coudnt you?
SORRY, SWEETHEART. WHAT WAS THAT?
I SAID, I...I WANT A FUCKING PISS.
HOW FAR IS IT?
WE'RE JUST DOWN HERE.
WHOOPS! YOU SHOULDN'T HAVE HAD THAT LAST VODKA.
I--I'M NOT REALLY USED TO DRINKING, SEE.
THERE'S NOTHING TO YOU, THAT'S WHY YOU CAN'T HOLD YOUR DRINK.
YOU NEED LOOKING AFTER, DARLING.
they throw you out at sixteen and your left to look out for yourself.
YEAH.
THAT'S WHAT THEY ALL SAY.

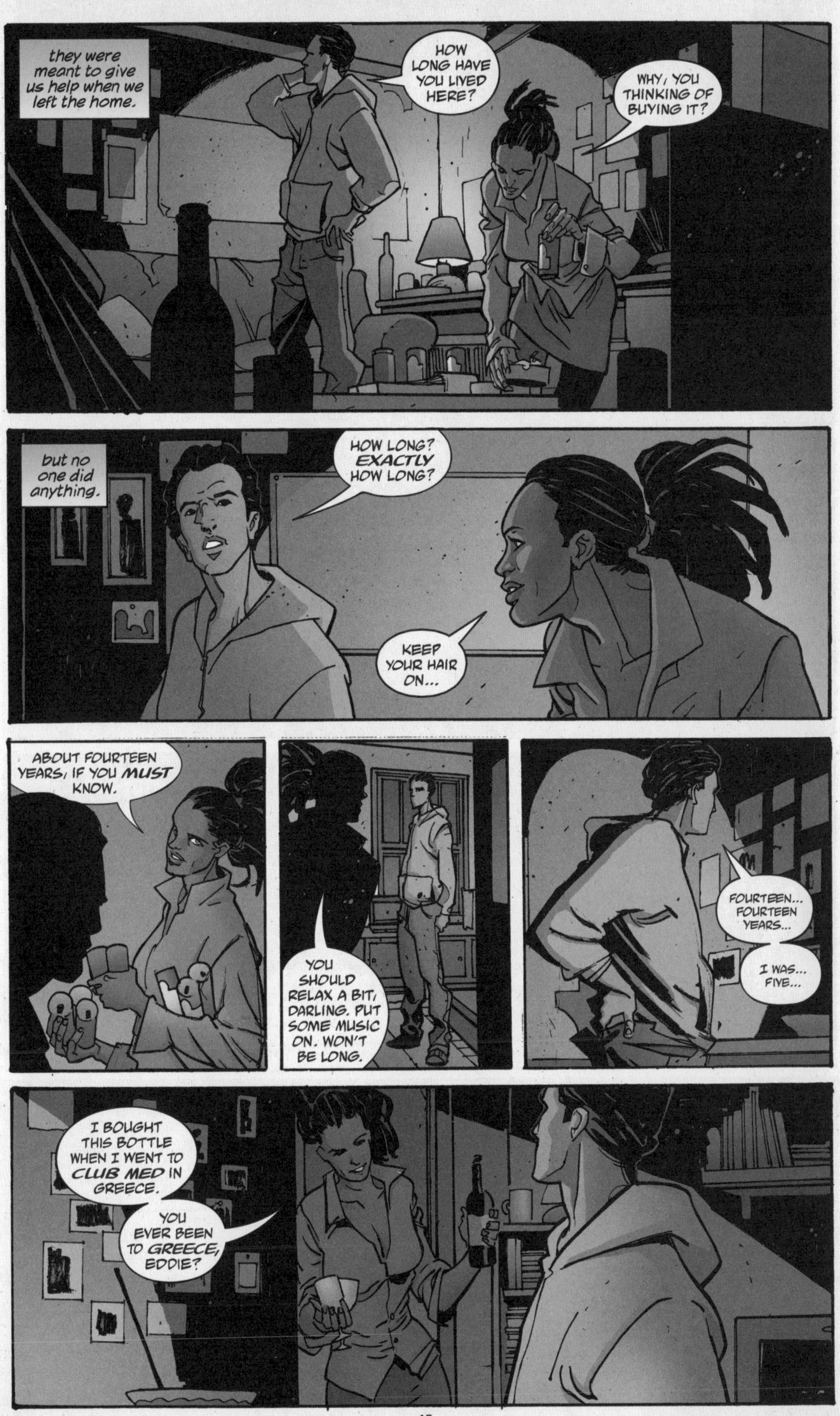
they were meant to give us help when we left the home.
HOW LONG HAVE YOU LIVED HERE?
WHY, YOU THINKING OF BUYING IT?
but no one did anything.
HOW LONG? EXACTLY HOW LONG?
KEEP YOUR HAIR ON...
ABOUT FOURTEEN YEARS, IF YOU MUST KNOW.
YOU SHOULD RELAX A BIT, DARLING. PUT SOME MUSIC ON. WON'T BE LONG.
FOURTEEN... FOURTEEN YEARS...
I WAS... FIVE...
I BOUGHT THIS BOTTLE WHEN I WENT TO CLUB MED IN GREECE.
YOU EVER BEEN TO GREECE, EDDIE?

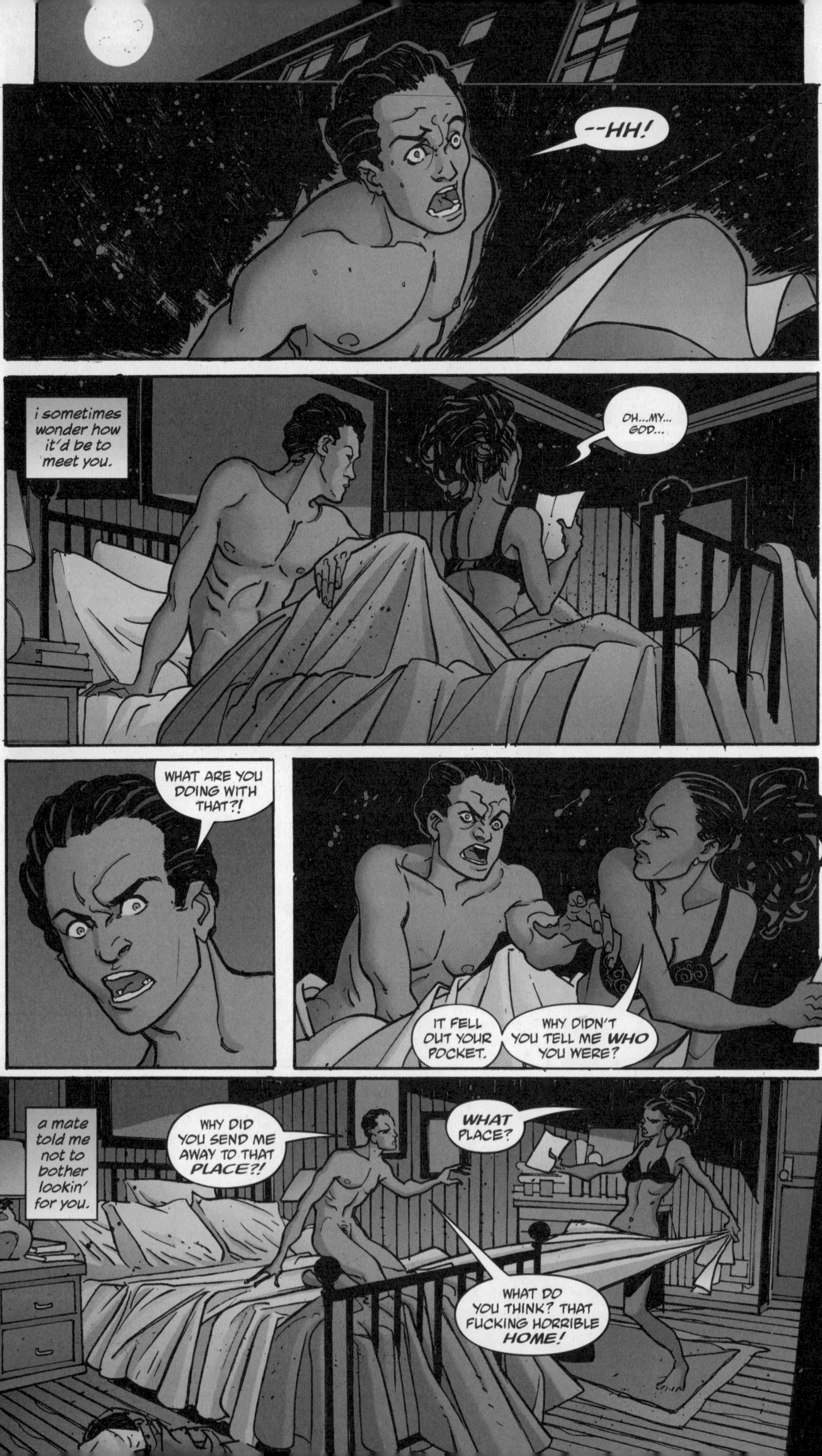
--HH!
i sometimes wonder how it'd be to meet you.
OH...MY... GOD...
WHAT ARE YOU DOING WITH THAT?!
IT FELL OUT YOUR POCKET.
WHY DIDN'T YOU TELL ME WHO YOU WERE?
a mate told me not to bother lookin' for you.
WHY DID YOU SEND ME AWAY TO THAT PLACE?!
WHAT PLACE?
WHAT DO YOU THINK? THAT FUCKING HORRIBLE HOME!

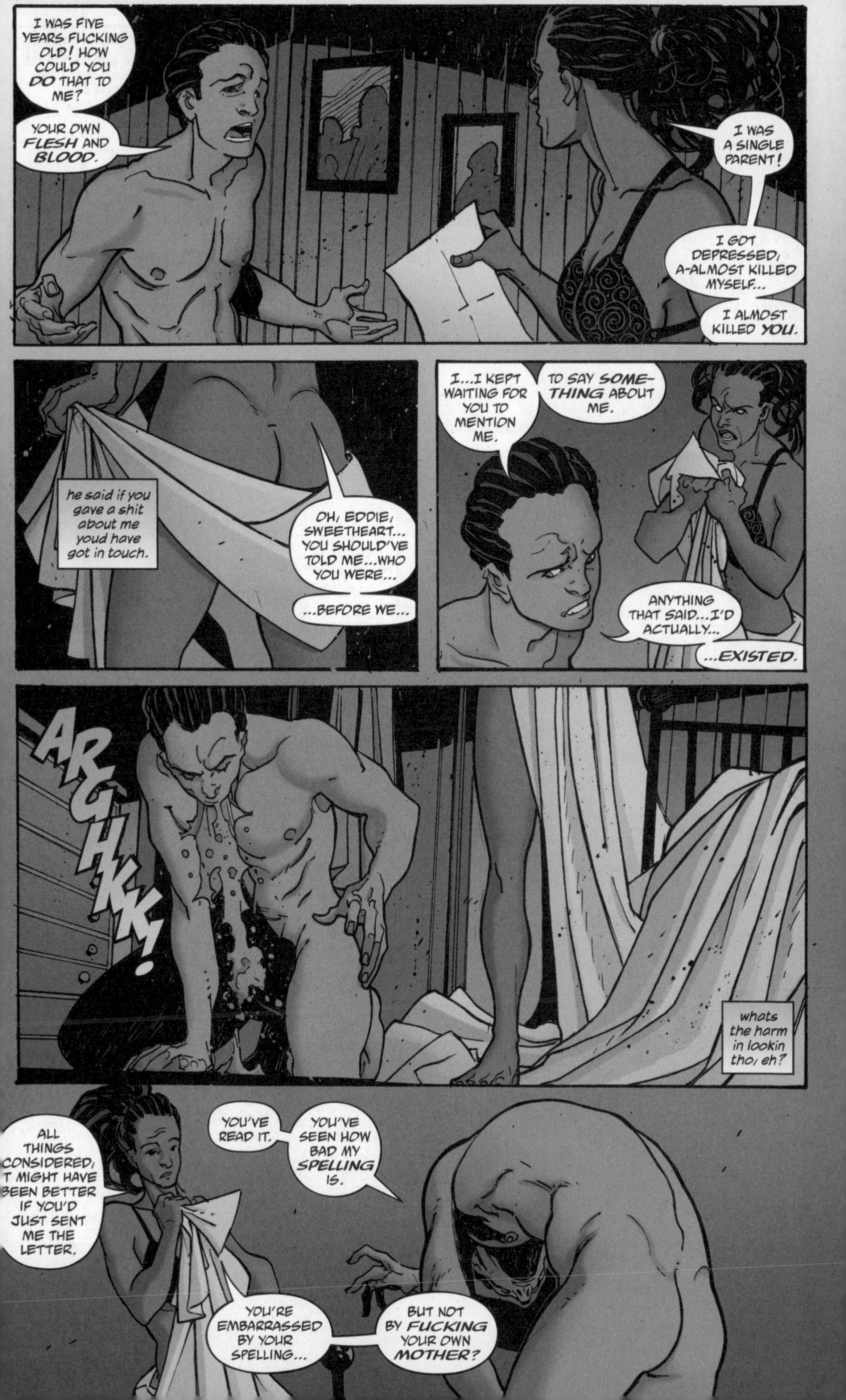

I WAS FIVE YEARS FUCKING OLD! HOW COULD YOU DO THAT TO ME?
YOUR OWN FLESH AND BLOOD.
I WAS A SINGLE PARENT!
I GOT DEPRESSED, A-ALMOST KILLED MYSELF...
I ALMOST KILLED YOU.
he said if you gave a shit about me youd have got in touch.
OH, EDDIE, SWEETHEART... YOU SHOULD'VE TOLD ME...WHO YOU WERE...
...BEFORE WE...
I...I KEPT WAITING FOR YOU TO MENTION ME.
TO SAY SOMETHING ABOUT ME.
ANYTHING THAT SAID...I'D ACTUALLY...
...EXISTED.
ARGHKK!
whats the harm in lookin tho, eh?
ALL THINGS CONSIDERED, T MIGHT HAVE BEEN BETTER IF YOU'D JUST SENT ME THE LETTER.
YOU'VE READ IT.
YOU'VE SEEN HOW BAD MY SPELLING IS.
YOU'RE EMBARRASSED BY YOUR SPELLING...
BUT NOT BY FUCKING YOUR OWN MOTHER?

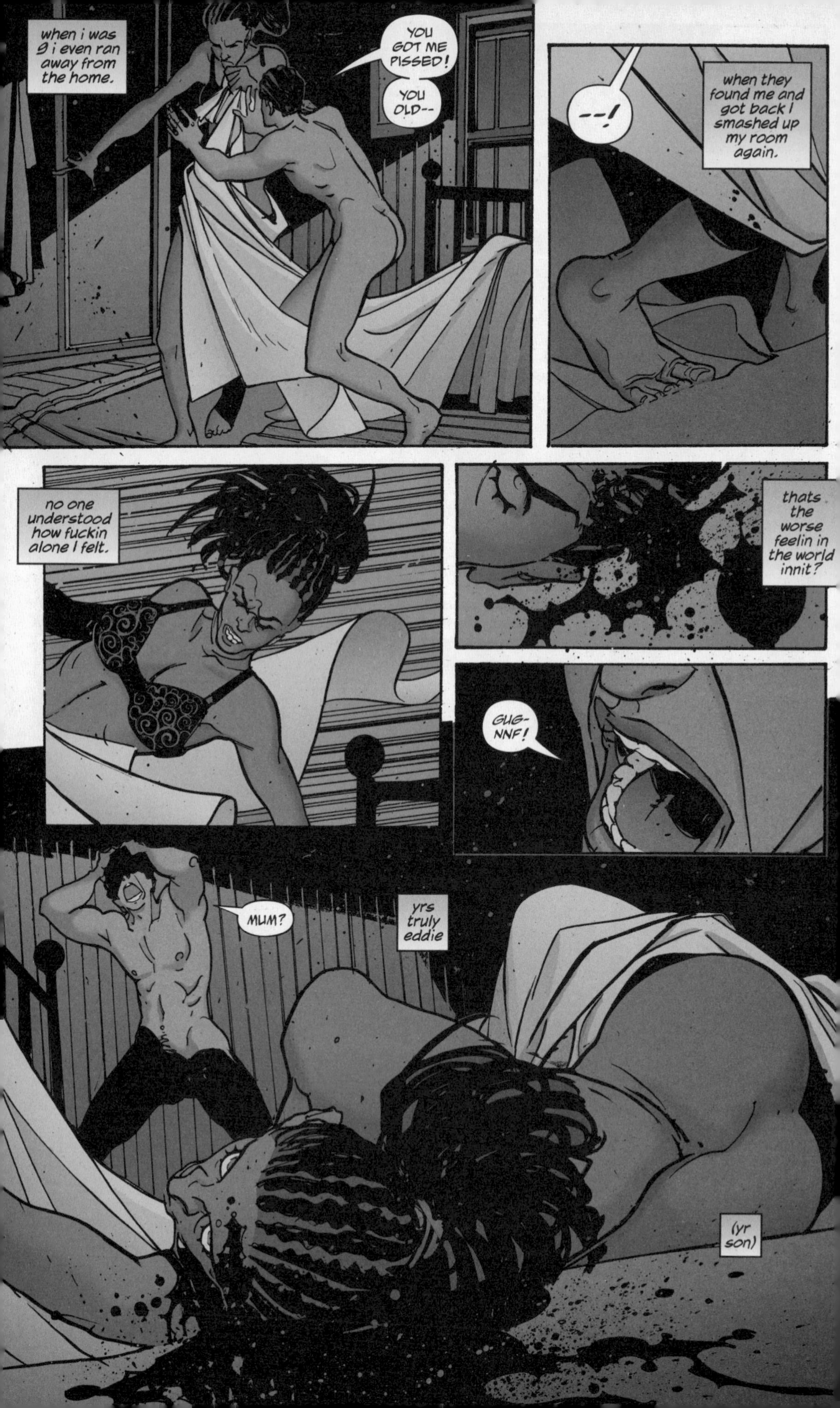
when i was 9 i even ran away from the home.
YOU GOT ME PISSED!
YOU OLD--
--!
when they found me and got back I smashed up my room again.
no one understood how fuckin alone I felt.
thats the worse feelin in the world innit?
GUG-NNF!
MUM?
yrs truly eddie
(yr son)

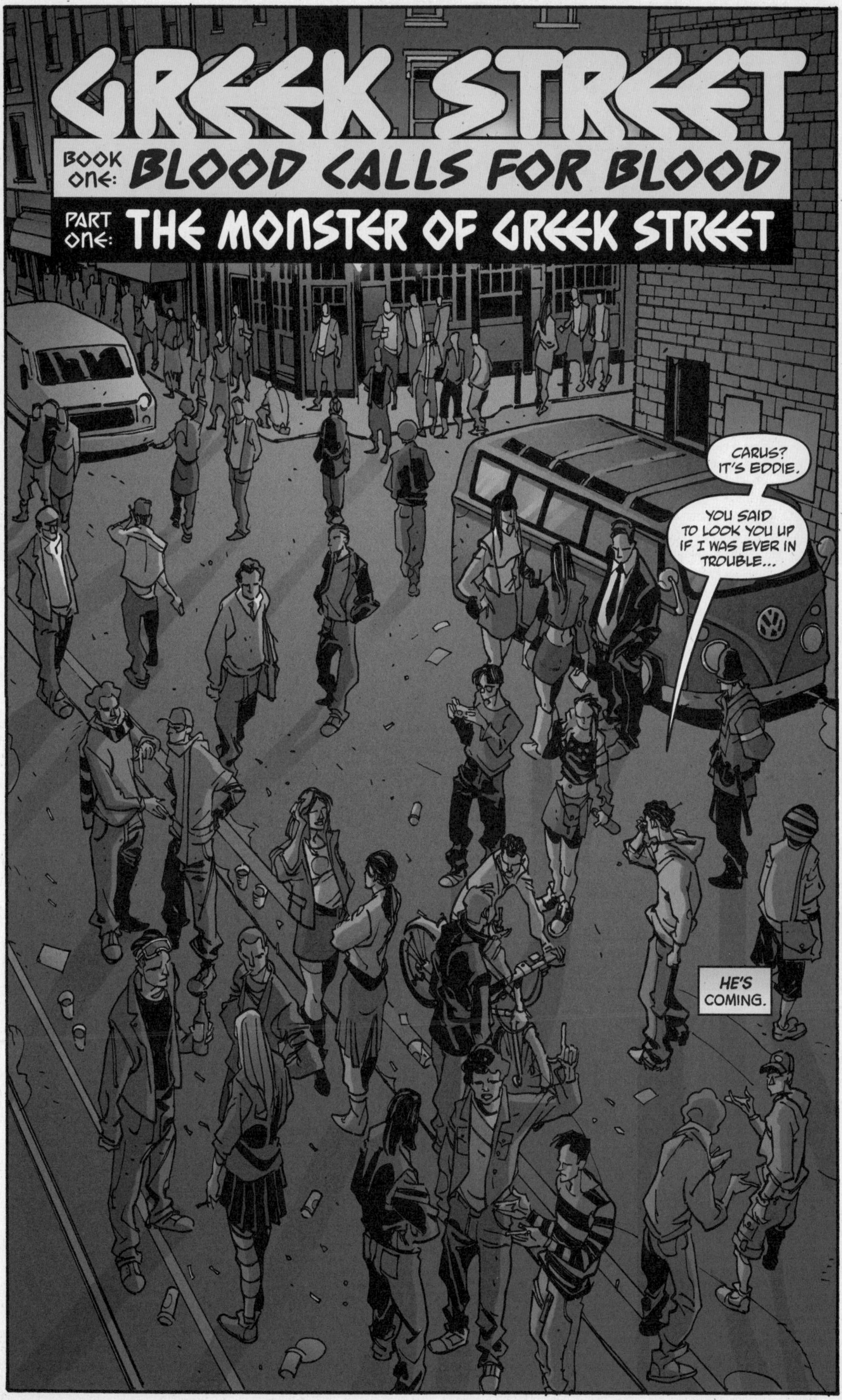
GREEK STREET
BOOK ONE: BLOOD CALLS FOR BLOOD
PART ONE: THE MONSTER OF GREEK STREET
CARUS? IT'S EDDIE.
YOU SAID TO LOOK YOU UP IF I WAS EVER IN TROUBLE...
HE'S COMING.

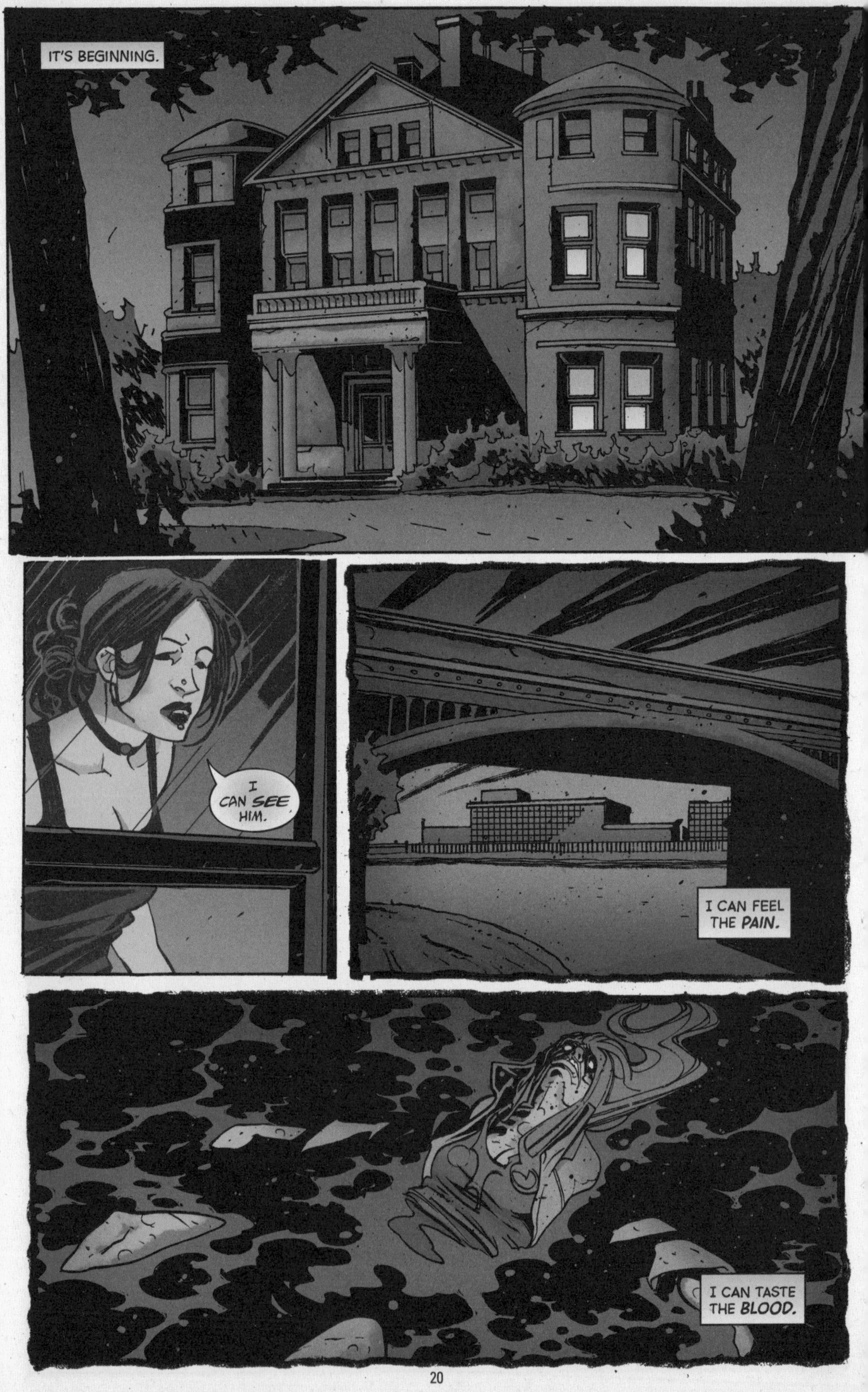
IT'S BEGINNING.
I CAN SEE HIM.
I CAN FEEL THE PAIN.
I CAN TASTE THE BLOOD.

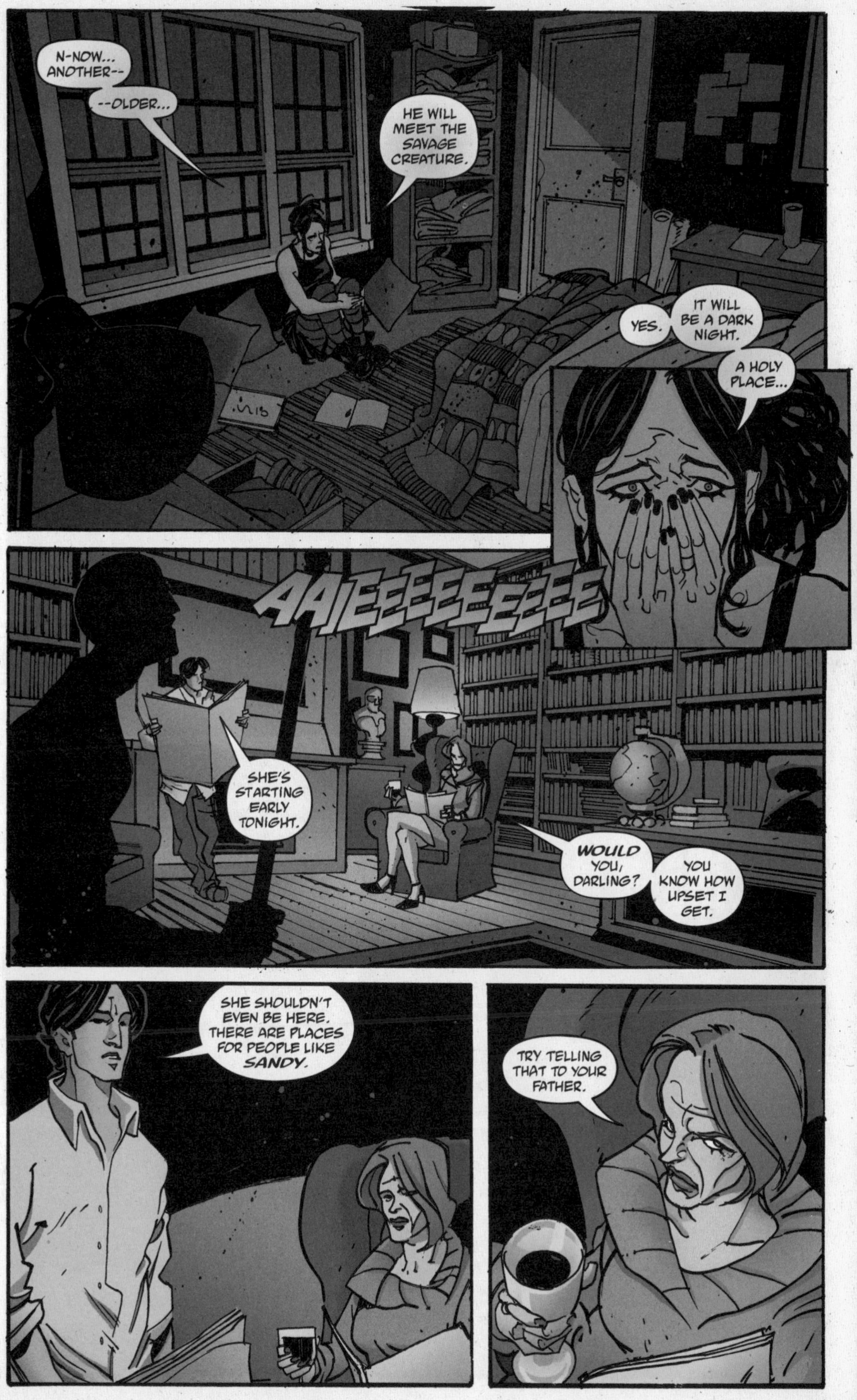
N-NOW... ANOTHER--
--OLDER...
HE WILL MEET THE SAVAGE CREATURE.
YES.
IT WILL BE A DARK NIGHT.
A HOLY PLACE...
AAIEEEEEEEEEE
SHE'S STARTING EARLY TONIGHT.
WOULD YOU, DARLING?
YOU KNOW HOW UPSET I GET.
SHE SHOULDN'T EVEN BE HERE. THERE ARE PLACES FOR PEOPLE LIKE SANDY.
TRY TELLING THAT TO YOUR FATHER.

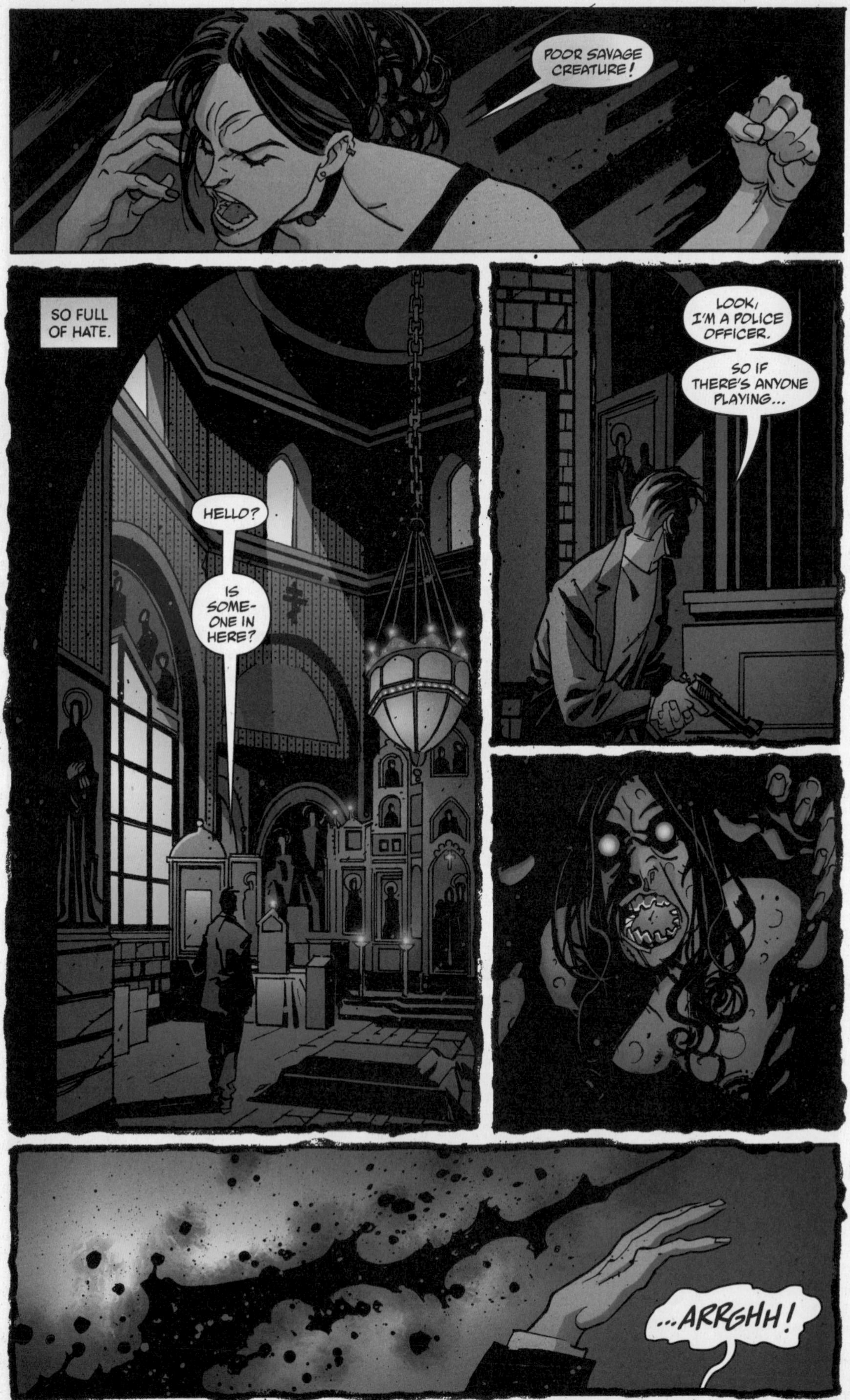
POOR SAVAGE CREATURE!
SO FULL OF HATE.
HELLO?
IS SOME-ONE IN HERE?
LOOK, I'M A POLICE OFFICER.
SO IF THERE'S ANYONE PLAYING...
...ARRGHH!

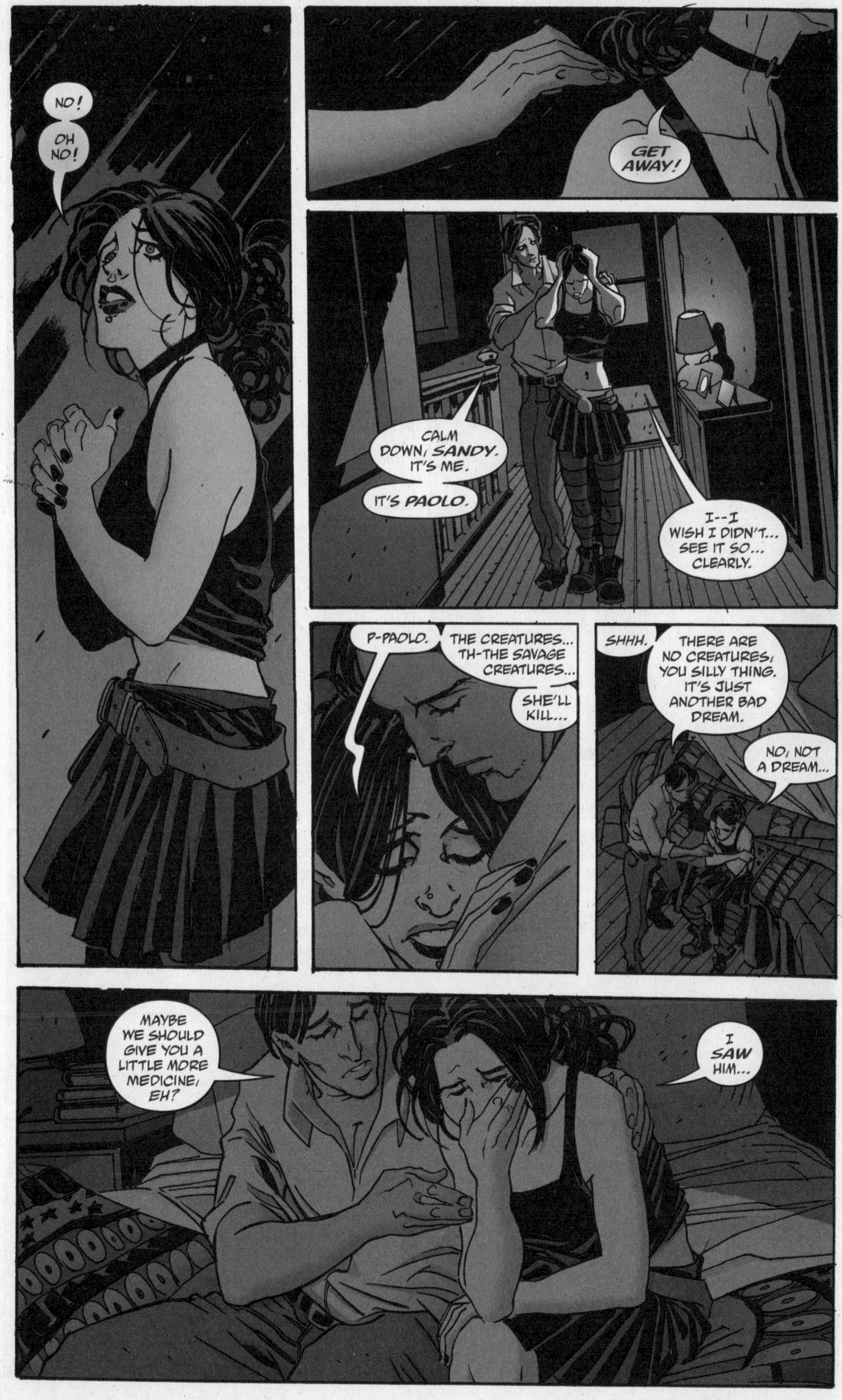
NO!
OH NO!
GET AWAY!
CALM DOWN, SANDY. IT'S ME.
IT'S PAOLO.
I--I WISH I DIDN'T... SEE IT SO... CLEARLY.
P-PAOLO.
THE CREATURES... TH-THE SAVAGE CREATURES...
SHE'LL KILL...
SHHH.
THERE ARE NO CREATURES, YOU SILLY THING. IT'S JUST ANOTHER BAD DREAM.
NO, NOT A DREAM...
MAYBE WE SHOULD GIVE YOU A LITTLE MORE MEDICINE, EH?
I SAW HIM...

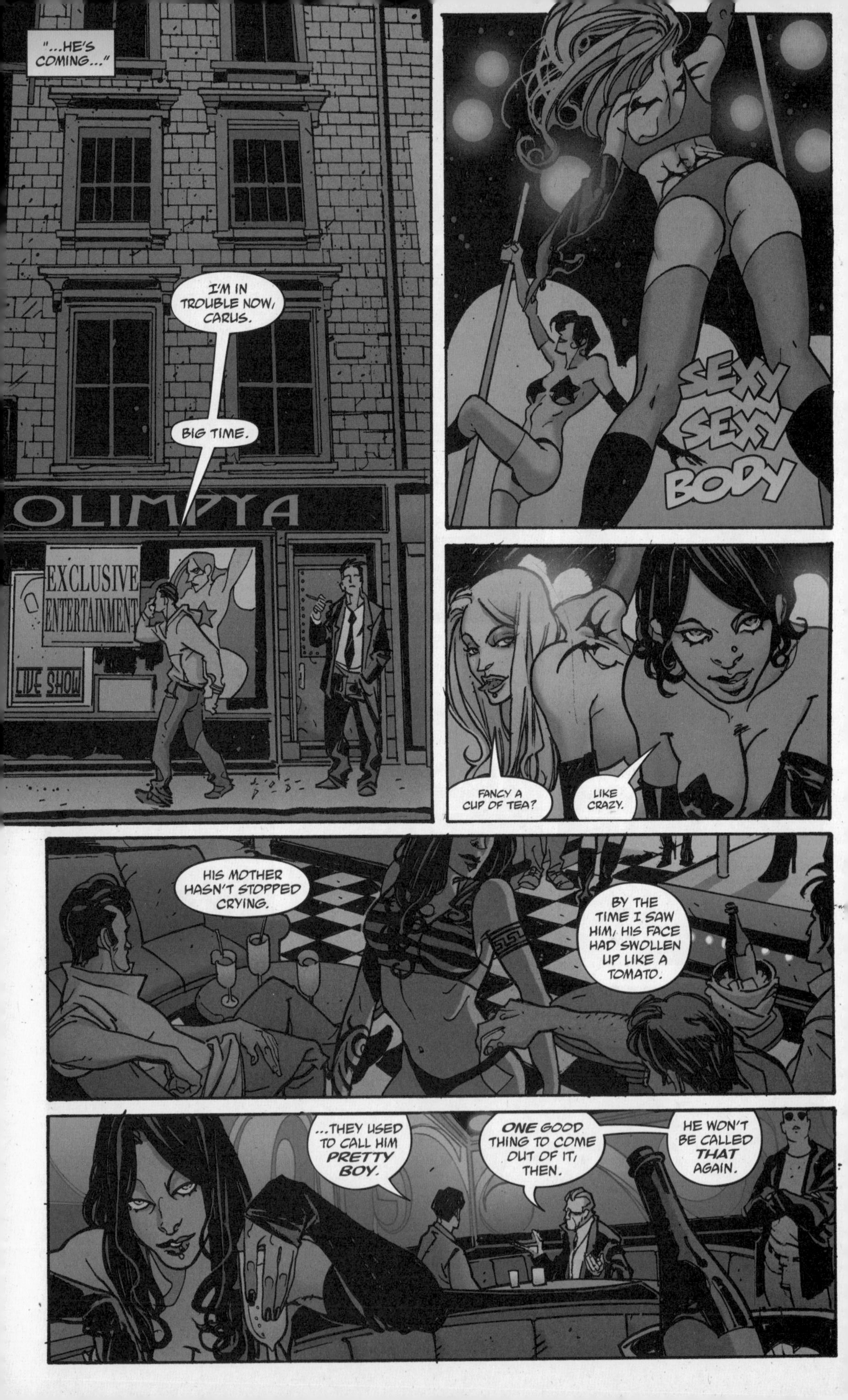
"...HE'S COMING..."
I'M IN TROUBLE NOW, CARUS.
BIG TIME.
OLIMPYA
EXCLUSIVE ENTERTAINMENT
LIVE SHOW
SEXY SEXY BODY
FANCY A CUP OF TEA?
LIKE CRAZY.
HIS MOTHER HASN'T STOPPED CRYING.
BY THE TIME I SAW HIM, HIS FACE HAD SWOLLEN UP LIKE A TOMATO.
...THEY USED TO CALL HIM PRETTY BOY.
ONE GOOD THING TO COME OUT OF IT, THEN.
HE WON'T BE CALLED THAT AGAIN.

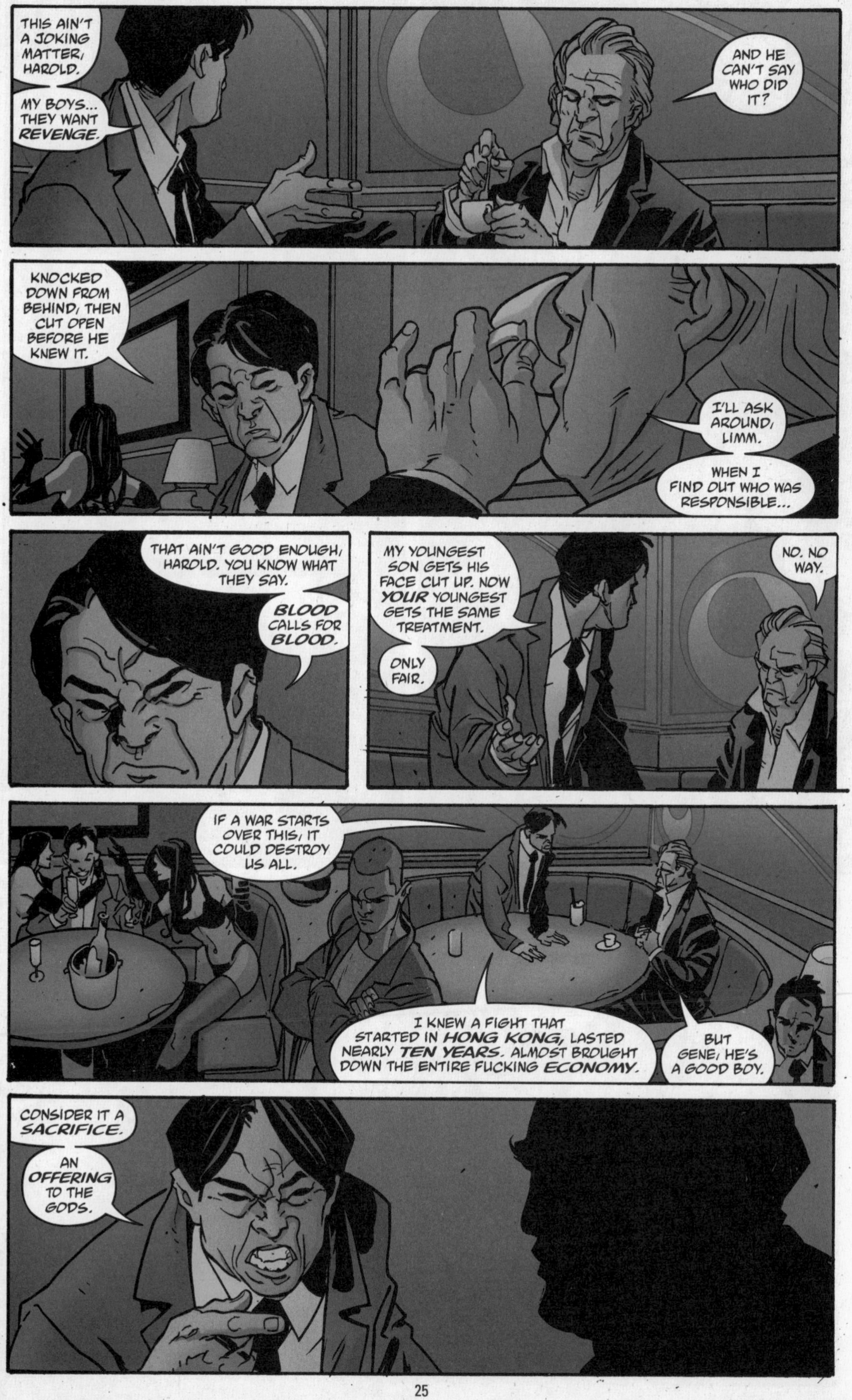
THIS AIN'T A JOKING MATTER, HAROLD.
MY BOYS... THEY WANT REVENGE.
AND HE CAN'T SAY WHO DID IT?
KNOCKED DOWN FROM BEHIND, THEN CUT OPEN BEFORE HE KNEW IT.
I'LL ASK AROUND, LIMM.
WHEN I FIND OUT WHO WAS RESPONSIBLE...
THAT AIN'T GOOD ENOUGH, HAROLD. YOU KNOW WHAT THEY SAY.
BLOOD CALLS FOR BLOOD.
MY YOUNGEST SON GETS HIS FACE CUT UP. NOW YOUR YOUNGEST GETS THE SAME TREATMENT.
ONLY FAIR.
NO. NO WAY.
IF A WAR STARTS OVER THIS, IT COULD DESTROY US ALL.
I KNEW A FIGHT THAT STARTED IN HONG KONG, LASTED NEARLY TEN YEARS. ALMOST BROUGHT DOWN THE ENTIRE FUCKING ECONOMY.
BUT GENE, HE'S A GOOD BOY.
CONSIDER IT A SACRIFICE.
AN OFFERING TO THE GODS.

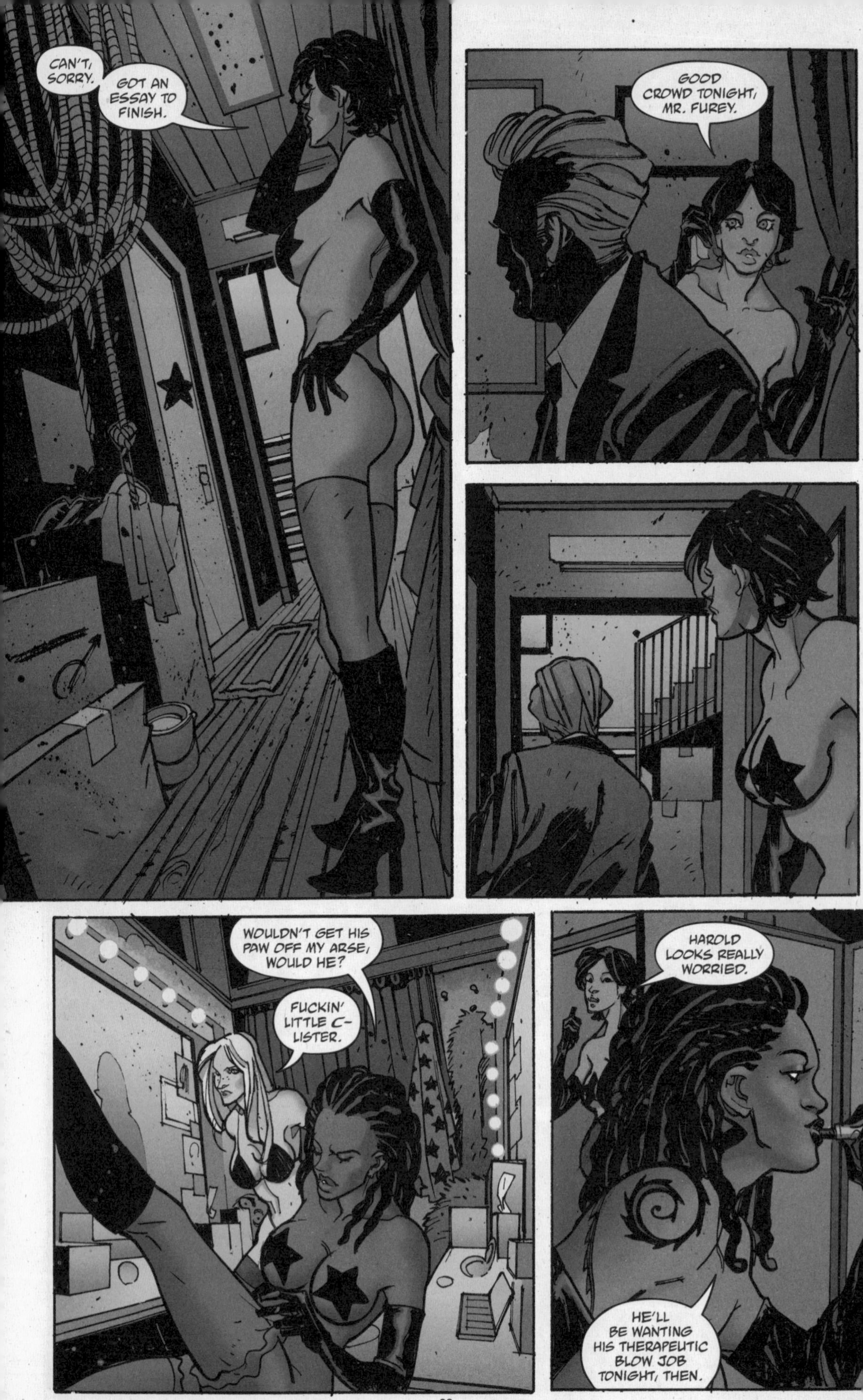
CAN'T, SORRY.
GOT AN ESSAY TO FINISH.
GOOD CROWD TONIGHT, MR. FUREY.
WOULDN'T GET HIS PAW OFF MY ARSE, WOULD HE?
FUCKIN' LITTLE C-LISTER.
HAROLD LOOKS REALLY WORRIED.
HE'LL BE WANTING HIS THERAPEUTIC BLOW JOB TONIGHT, THEN.

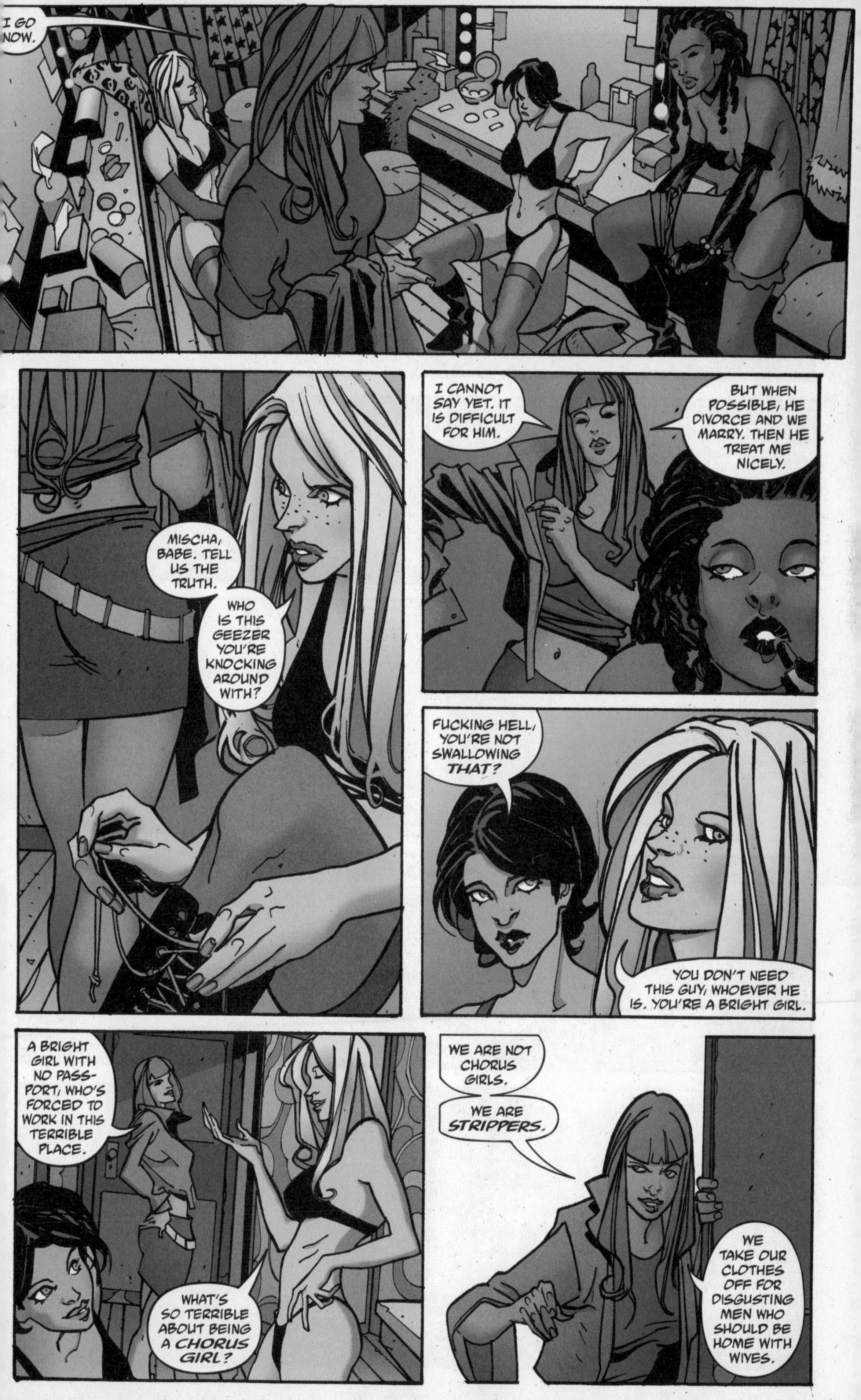

I GO NOW.
MISCHA, BABE. TELL US THE TRUTH.
WHO IS THIS GEEZER YOU'RE KNOCKING AROUND WITH?
I CANNOT SAY YET. IT IS DIFFICULT FOR HIM.
BUT WHEN POSSIBLE, HE DIVORCE AND WE MARRY. THEN HE TREAT ME NICELY.
FUCKING HELL, YOU'RE NOT SWALLOWING THAT?
YOU DON'T NEED THIS GUY, WHOEVER HE IS. YOU'RE A BRIGHT GIRL.
A BRIGHT GIRL WITH NO PASS-PORT, WHO'S FORCED TO WORK IN THIS TERRIBLE PLACE.
WHAT'S SO TERRIBLE ABOUT BEING A CHORUS GIRL?
WE ARE NOT CHORUS GIRLS.
WE ARE STRIPPERS.
WE TAKE OUR CLOTHES OFF FOR DISGUSTING MEN WHO SHOULD BE HOME WITH WIVES.

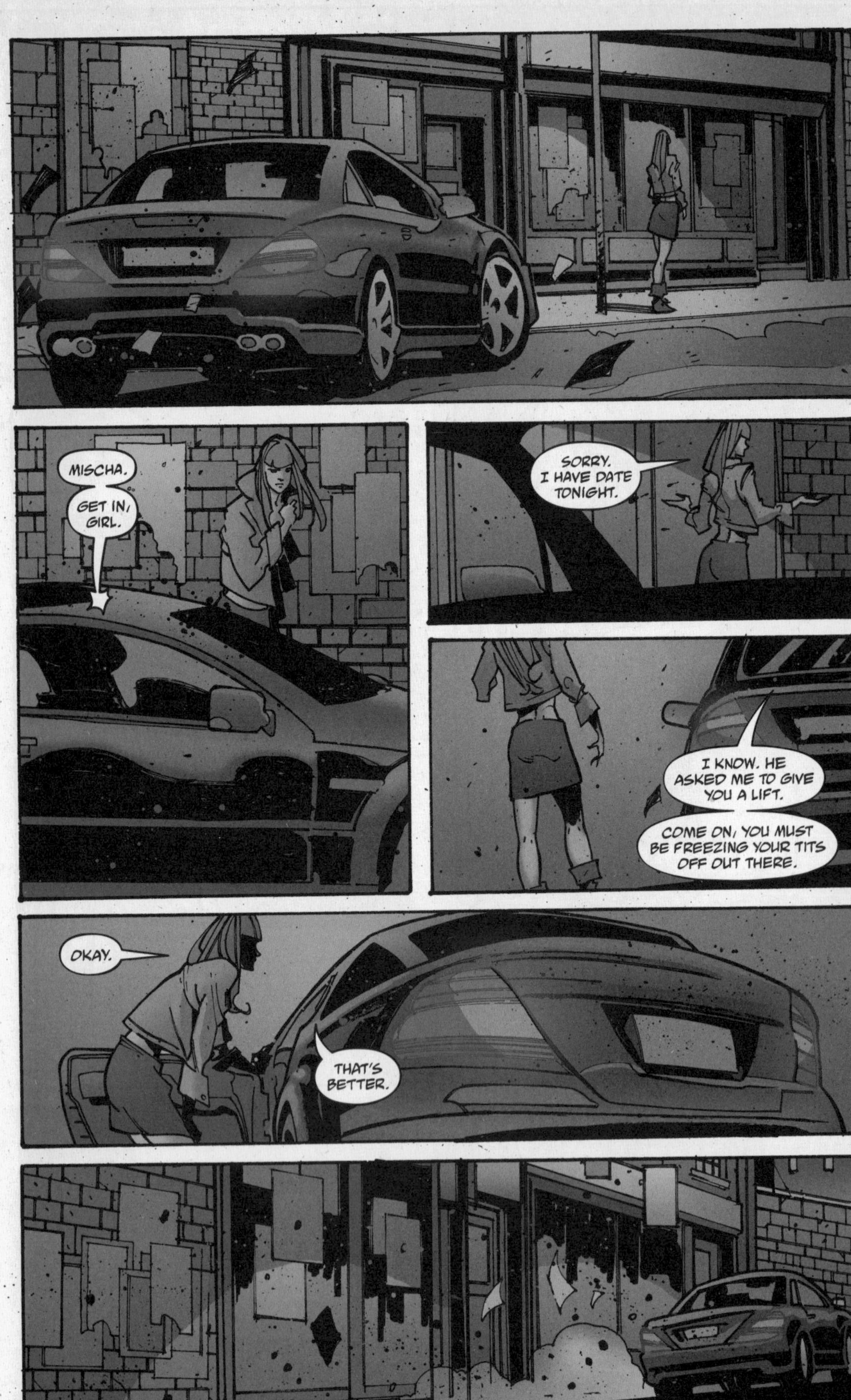
MISCHA.
GET IN, GIRL.
SORRY. I HAVE DATE TONIGHT.
I KNOW. HE ASKED ME TO GIVE YOU A LIFT.
COME ON, YOU MUST BE FREEZING YOUR TITS OFF OUT THERE.
OKAY.
THAT'S BETTER.

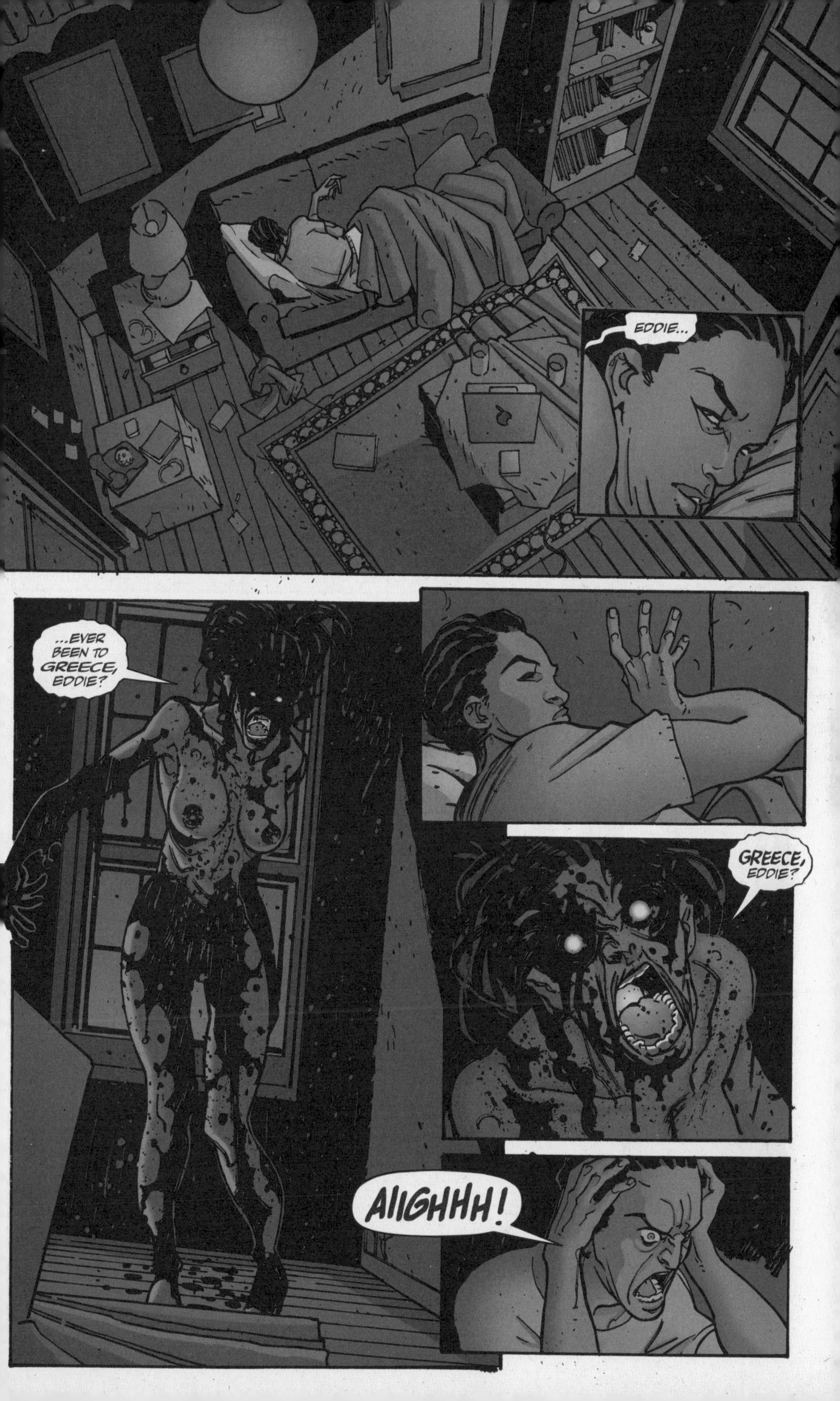
EDDIE...
...EVER BEEN TO GREECE, EDDIE?
GREECE, EDDIE?
AIIGHHH!

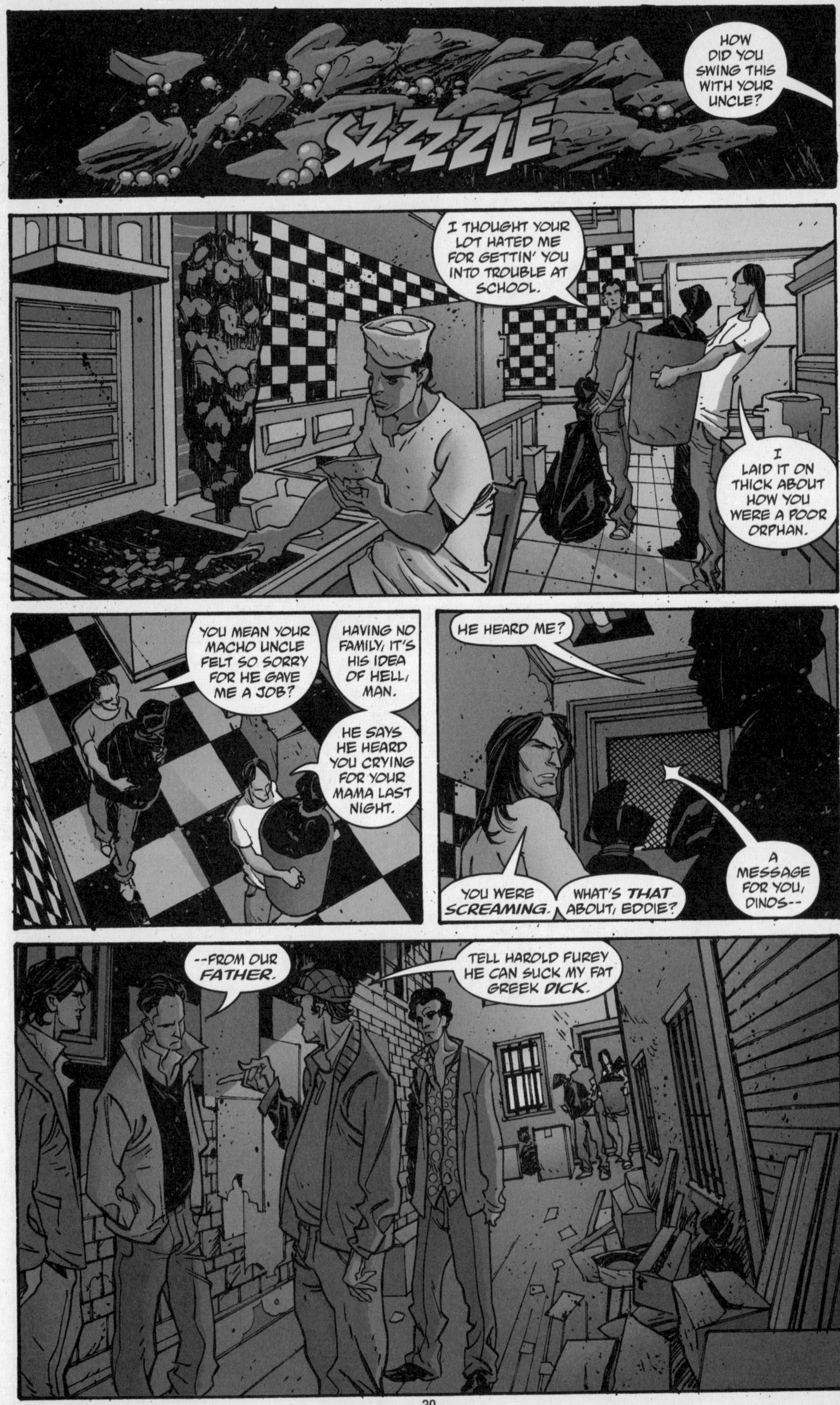
SZZZZLE
HOW DID YOU SWING THIS WITH YOUR UNCLE?
I THOUGHT YOUR LOT HATED ME FOR GETTIN' YOU INTO TROUBLE AT SCHOOL.
I LAID IT ON THICK ABOUT HOW YOU WERE A POOR ORPHAN.
YOU MEAN YOUR MACHO UNCLE FELT SO SORRY FOR HE GAVE ME A JOB?
HAVING NO FAMILY, IT'S HIS IDEA OF HELL, MAN.
HE SAYS HE HEARD YOU CRYING FOR YOUR MAMA LAST NIGHT.
HE HEARD ME?
YOU WERE SCREAMING.
WHAT'S THAT ABOUT, EDDIE?
A MESSAGE FOR YOU, DINOS--
--FROM OUR FATHER.
TELL HAROLD FUREY HE CAN SUCK MY FAT GREEK DICK.

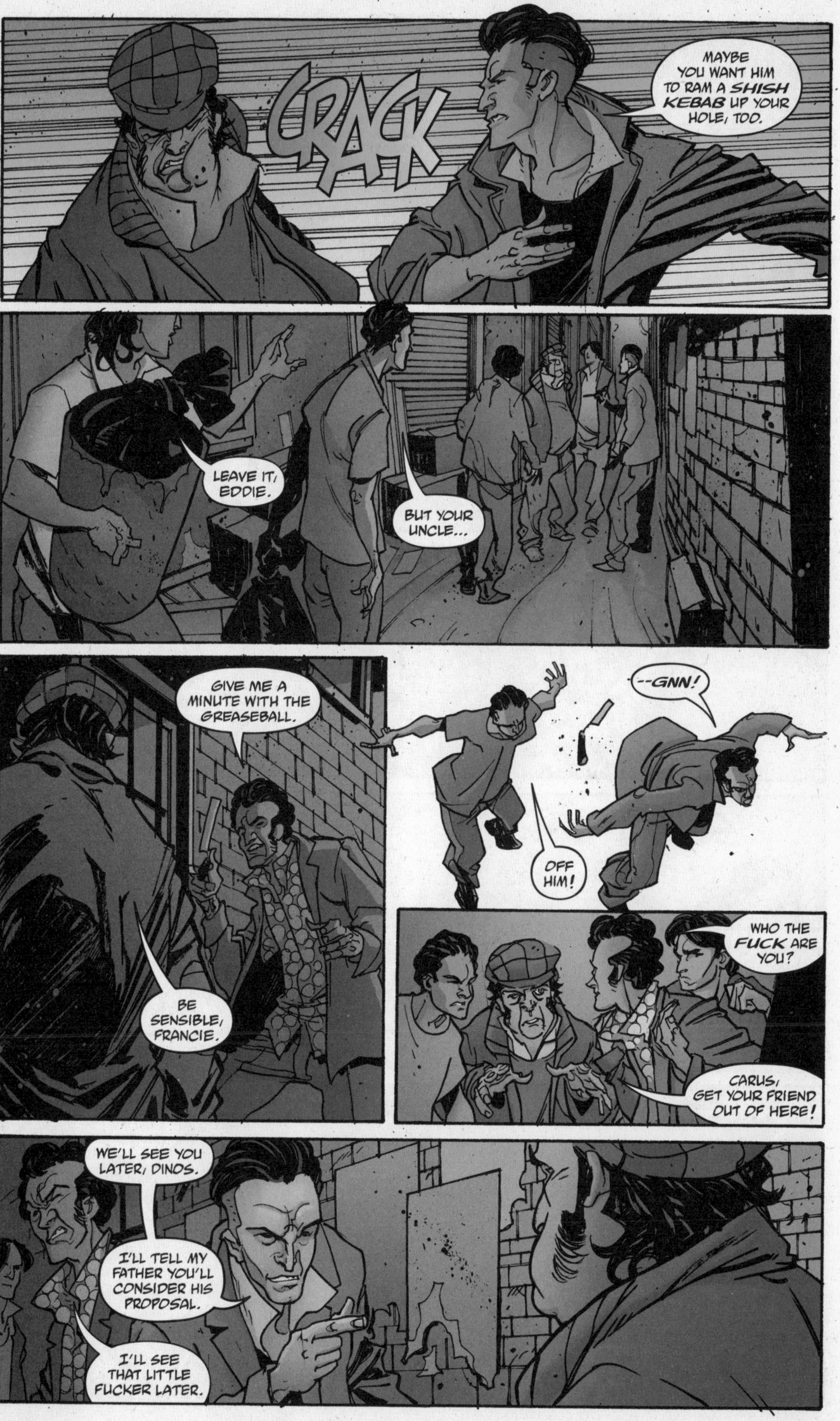
CRACK
MAYBE YOU WANT HIM TO RAM A SHISH KEBAB UP YOUR HOLE, TOO.
LEAVE IT, EDDIE.
BUT YOUR UNCLE...
GIVE ME A MINUTE WITH THE GREASEBALL.
BE SENSIBLE, FRANCIE.
--GNN!
OFF HIM!
WHO THE FUCK ARE YOU?
CARUS, GET YOUR FRIEND OUT OF HERE!
WE'LL SEE YOU LATER, DINOS.
I'LL TELL MY FATHER YOU'LL CONSIDER HIS PROPOSAL.
I'LL SEE THAT LITTLE FUCKER LATER.

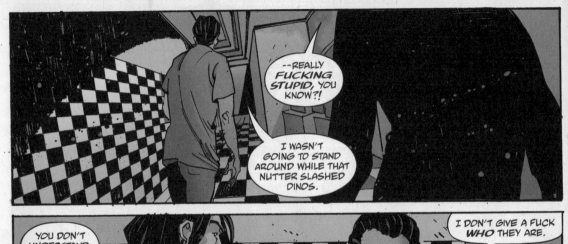

--REALLY *FUCKING* STUPID, YOU KNOW?!

I WASN'T GOING TO STAND AROUND WHILE THAT NUTTER SLASHED DINOS.

YOU DON'T UNDERSTAND. THEY'RE THE *FUREYS*.

I DON'T GIVE A FUCK *WHO* THEY ARE.

YOUR UNCLE WAS GOOD ENOUGH TO GIVE ME A *JOB*...

...MAYBE NOW HE'LL GIVE ME A *RAISE*.

SLAP

FUCKING *IDIOT*!

BUT...H-HE WOULD HAVE *CUT* YOU!

HIS BROTHERS WOULD HAVE STOPPED THEM. THEY WOULDN'T HAVE HURT ME *TOO* BAD.

IT'S HOW YOU DO BUSINESS WITH THEM. THEY GET NASTY. YOU ACT SCARED. LIFE GOES ON.

IT'S A KIND OF...*DANCE*, INNIT?

DANCE?

I WOULDN'T GET TOO CLOSE TO YOUR FRIEND, CARUS. HE'S MADE AN ENEMY OUT OF THE *FUREYS*.

THAT BOY'S *CURSED*.

YES...

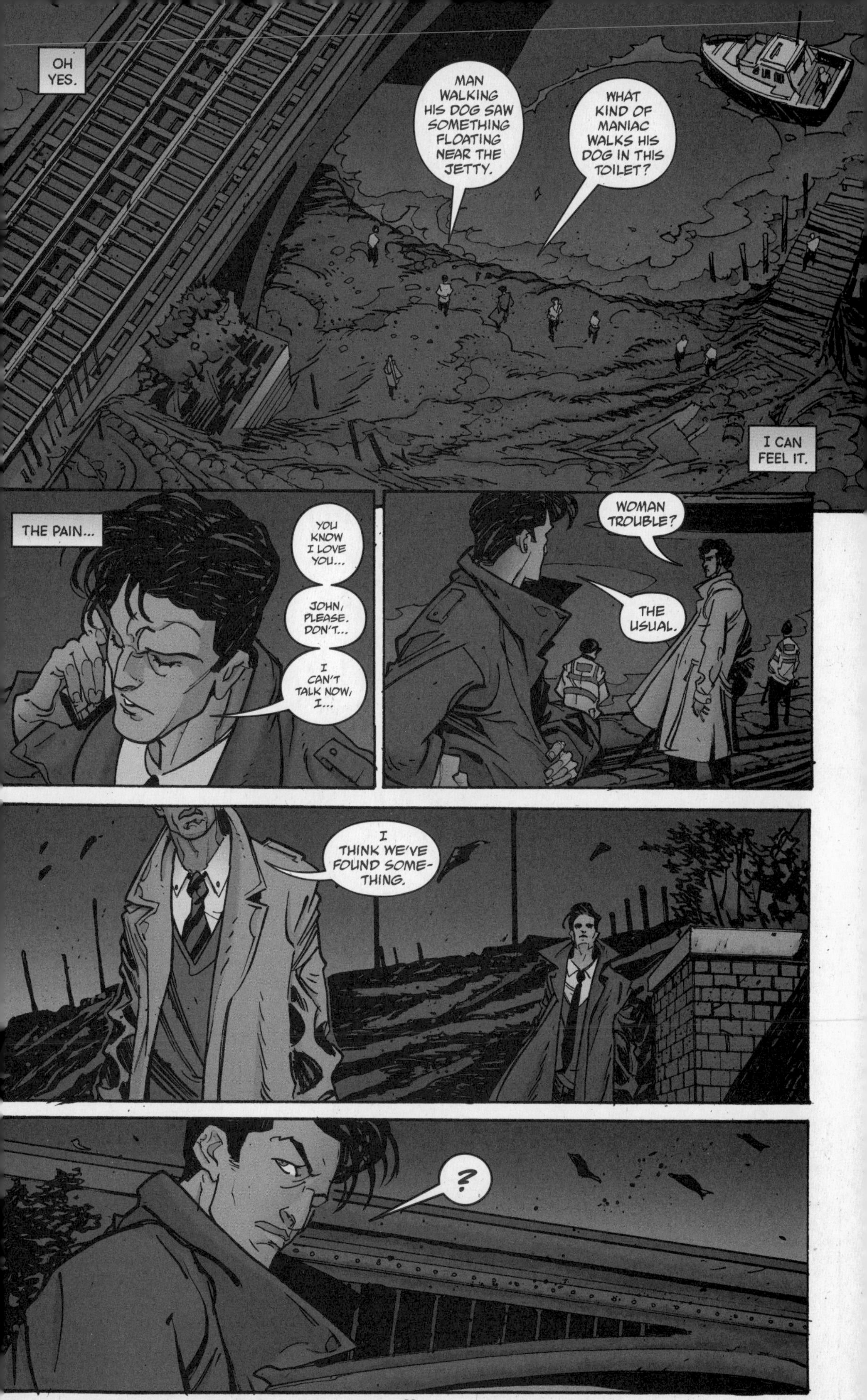
OH YES.
MAN WALKING HIS DOG SAW SOMETHING FLOATING NEAR THE JETTY.
WHAT KIND OF MANIAC WALKS HIS DOG IN THIS TOILET?
I CAN FEEL IT.
THE PAIN...
YOU KNOW I LOVE YOU...
JOHN, PLEASE. DON'T...
I CAN'T TALK NOW, I...
WOMAN TROUBLE?
THE USUAL.
I THINK WE'VE FOUND SOME-THING.
?

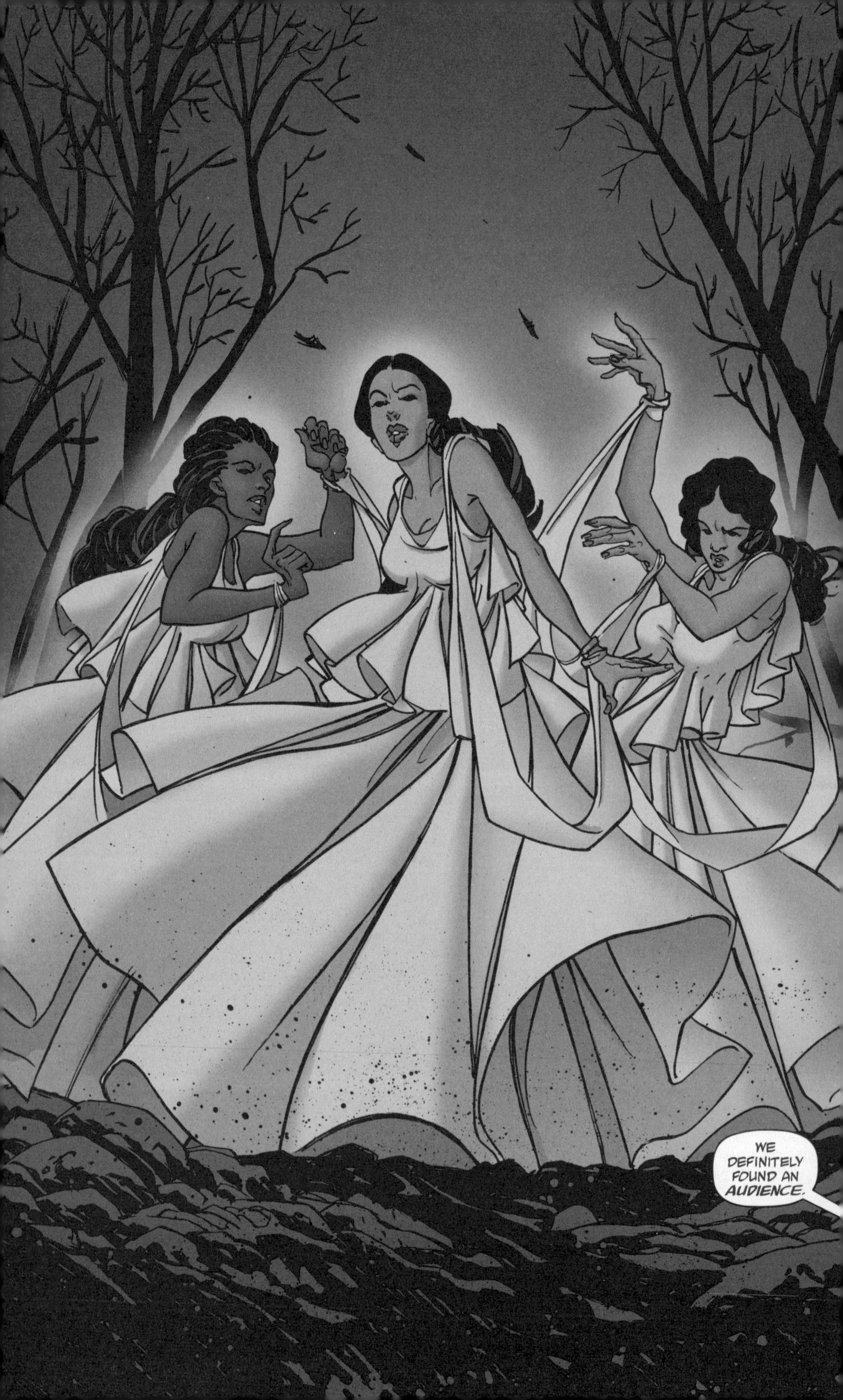
WE DEFINITELY FOUND AN AUDIENCE.

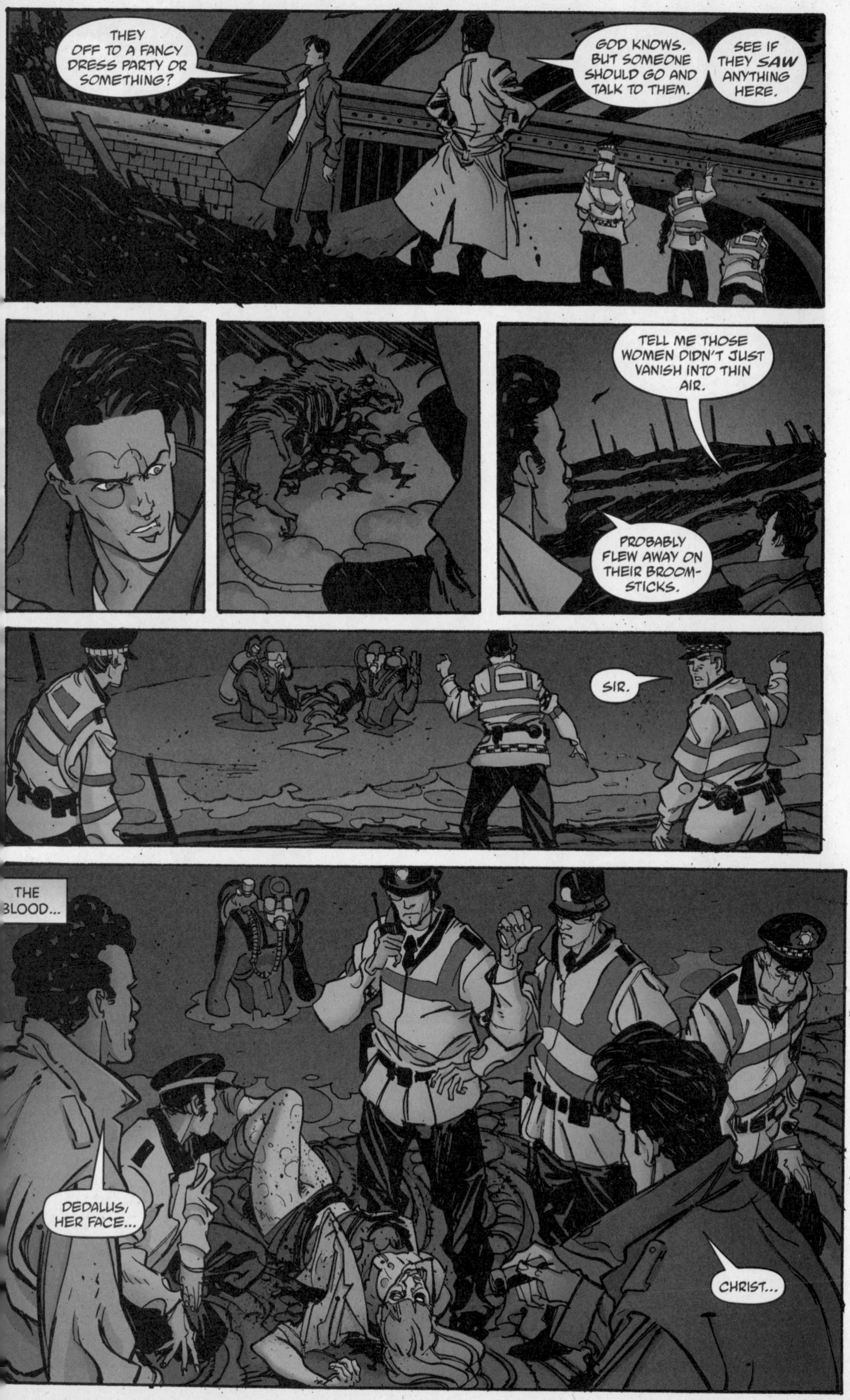
THEY OFF TO A FANCY DRESS PARTY OR SOMETHING?
GOD KNOWS. BUT SOMEONE SHOULD GO AND TALK TO THEM.
SEE IF THEY *SAW* ANYTHING HERE.
TELL ME THOSE WOMEN DIDN'T JUST VANISH INTO THIN AIR.
PROBABLY FLEW AWAY ON THEIR BROOM-STICKS.
SIR.
THE BLOOD...
DEDALUS, HER FACE...
CHRIST...

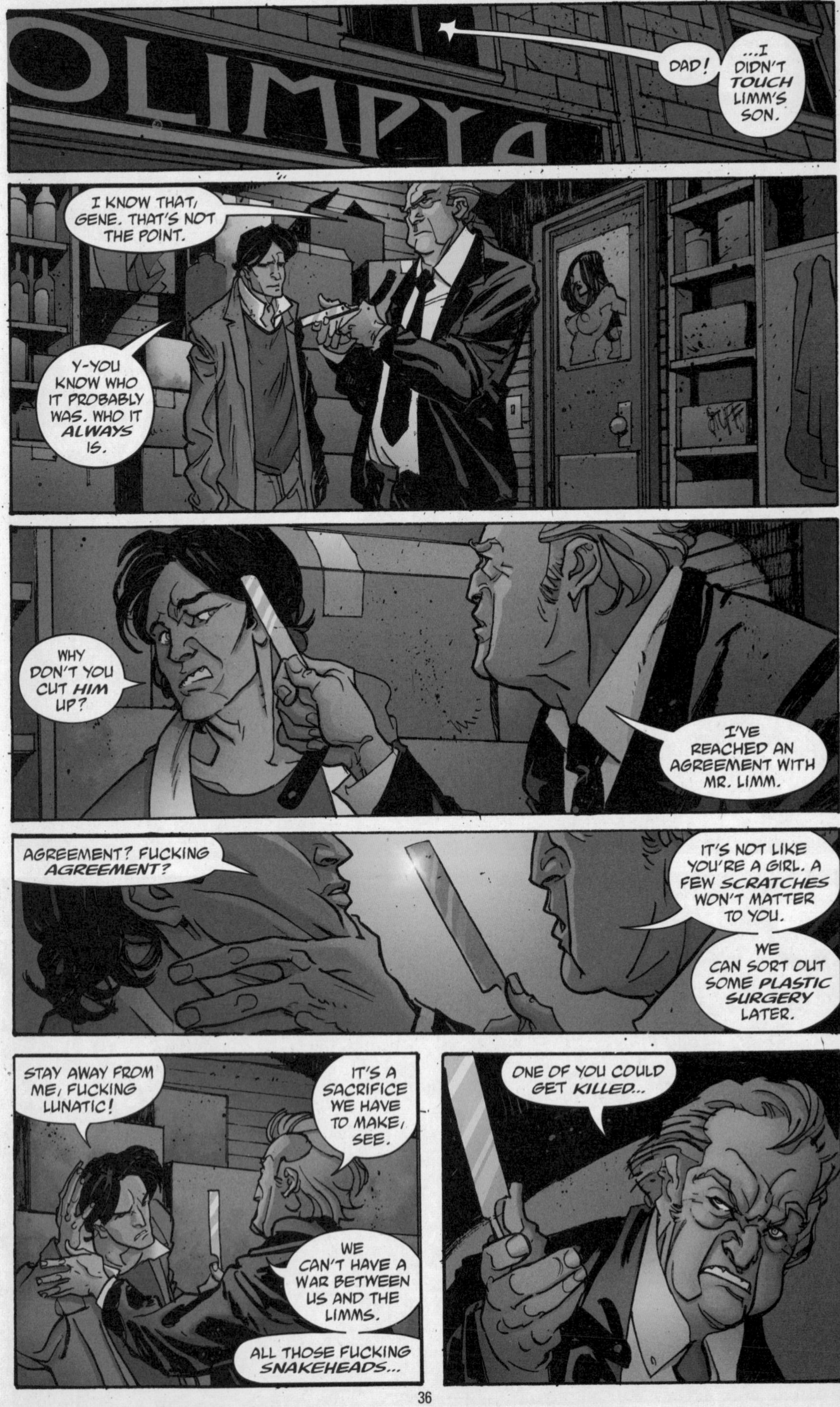
OLIMPYA
DAD!
...I DIDN'T TOUCH LIMM'S SON.
I KNOW THAT, GENE. THAT'S NOT THE POINT.
Y-YOU KNOW WHO IT PROBABLY WAS. WHO IT ALWAYS IS.
WHY DON'T YOU CUT HIM UP?
I'VE REACHED AN AGREEMENT WITH MR. LIMM.
AGREEMENT? FUCKING AGREEMENT?
IT'S NOT LIKE YOU'RE A GIRL. A FEW SCRATCHES WON'T MATTER TO YOU.
WE CAN SORT OUT SOME PLASTIC SURGERY LATER.
STAY AWAY FROM ME, FUCKING LUNATIC!
IT'S A SACRIFICE WE HAVE TO MAKE, SEE.
WE CAN'T HAVE A WAR BETWEEN US AND THE LIMMS.
ALL THOSE FUCKING SNAKEHEADS...
ONE OF YOU COULD GET KILLED...

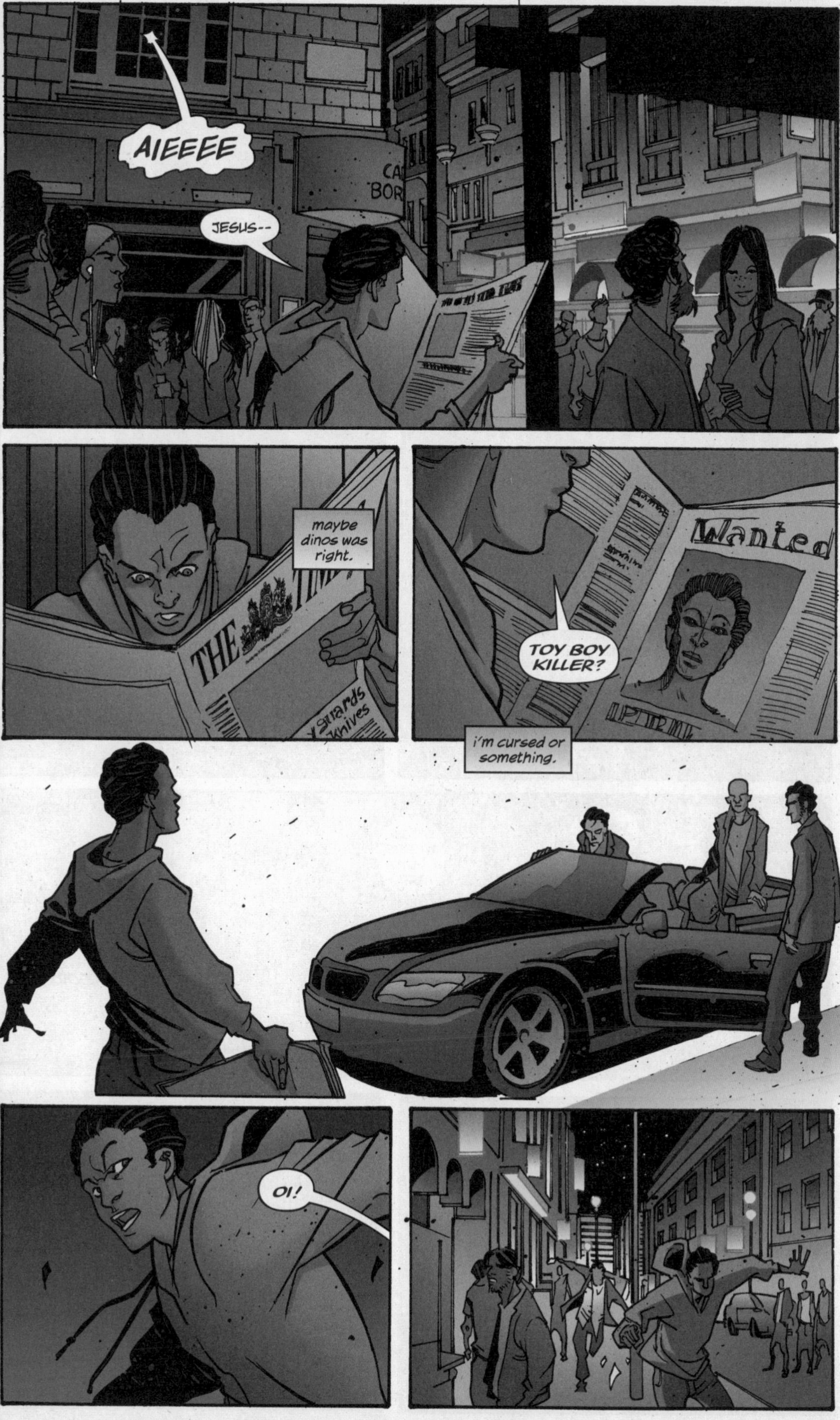

AIEEEE
JESUS--
maybe dinos was right.
Wanted
TOY BOY KILLER?
i'm cursed or something.
OI!

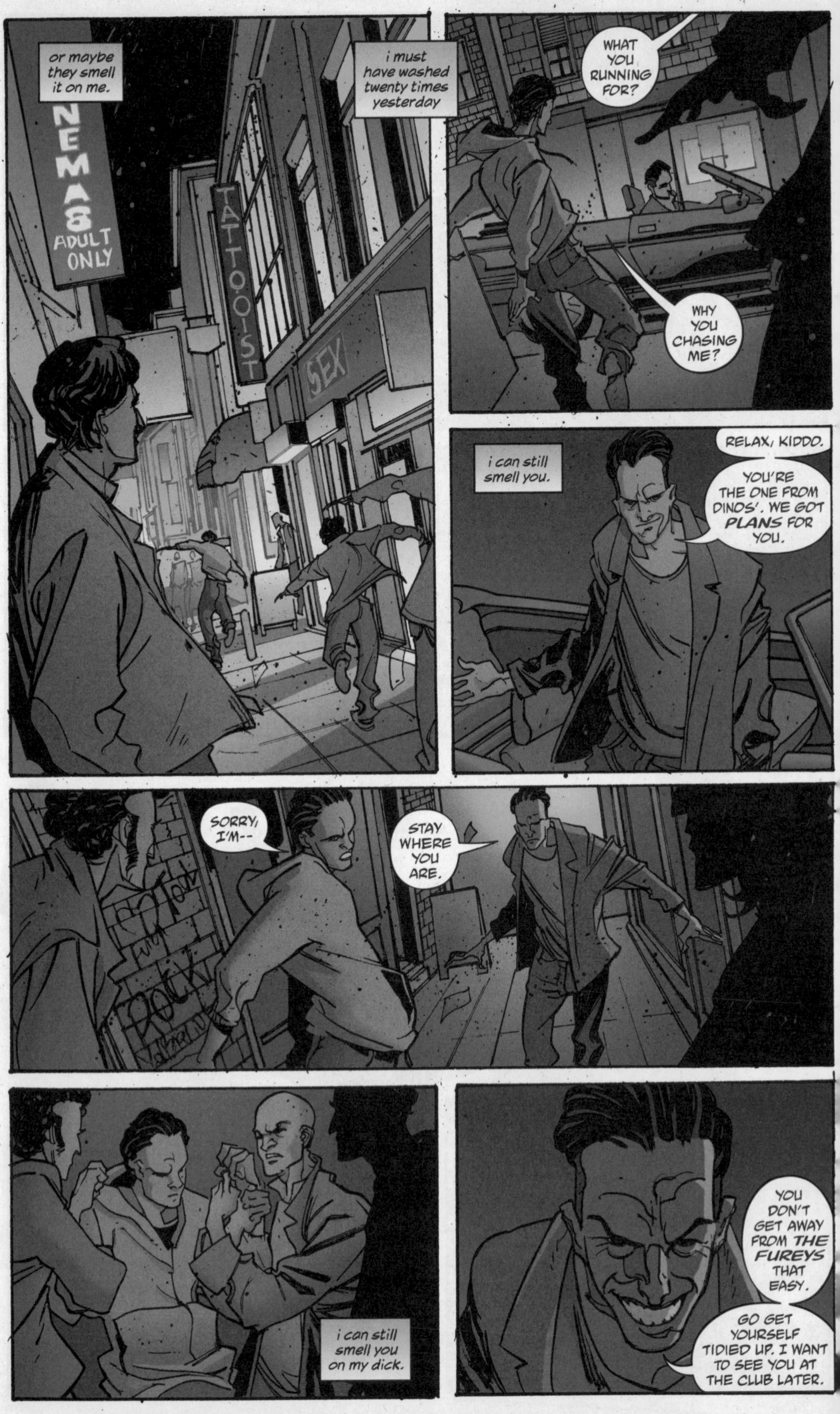

or maybe they smell it on me.
NEMA 8 ADULT ONLY
TATTOOIST
SEX
i must have washed twenty times yesterday
WHAT YOU RUNNING FOR?
WHY YOU CHASING ME?
i can still smell you.
RELAX, KIDDO.
YOU'RE THE ONE FROM DINOS'. WE GOT PLANS FOR YOU.
SORRY, I'M--
STAY WHERE YOU ARE.
i can still smell you on my dick.
YOU DON'T GET AWAY FROM THE FUREYS THAT EASY.
GO GET YOURSELF TIDIED UP. I WANT TO SEE YOU AT THE CLUB LATER.

you reach a point in your life when you wonder

you really ask yourself.

who the fuck am i?

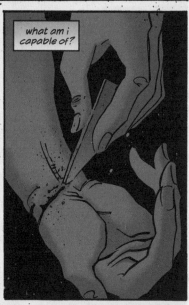

what am i capable of?

you reach a crossroads...

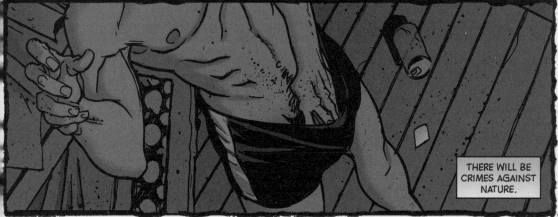

THERE WILL BE CRIMES AGAINST NATURE.

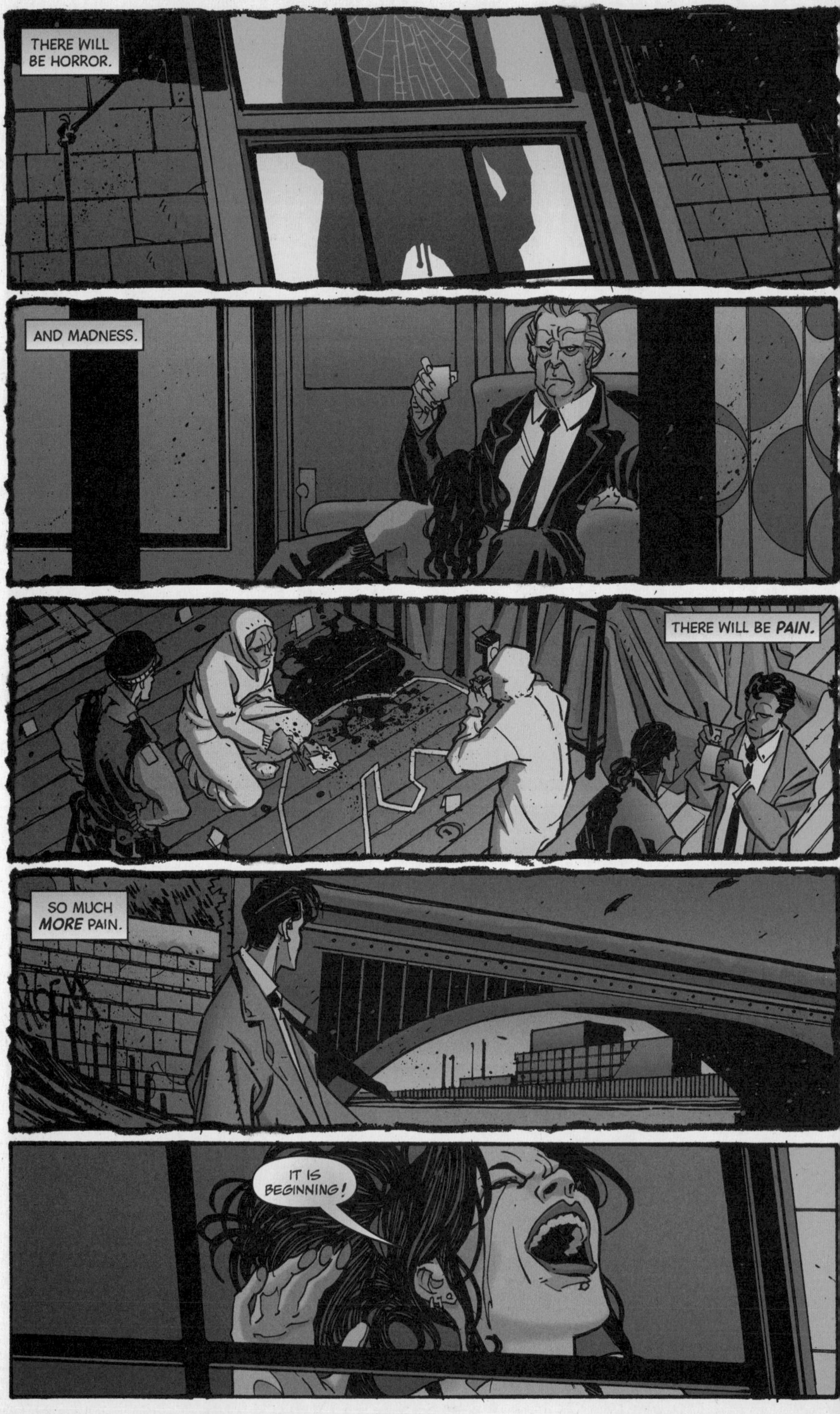
THERE WILL BE HORROR.
AND MADNESS.
THERE WILL BE PAIN.
SO MUCH MORE PAIN.
IT IS BEGINNING!

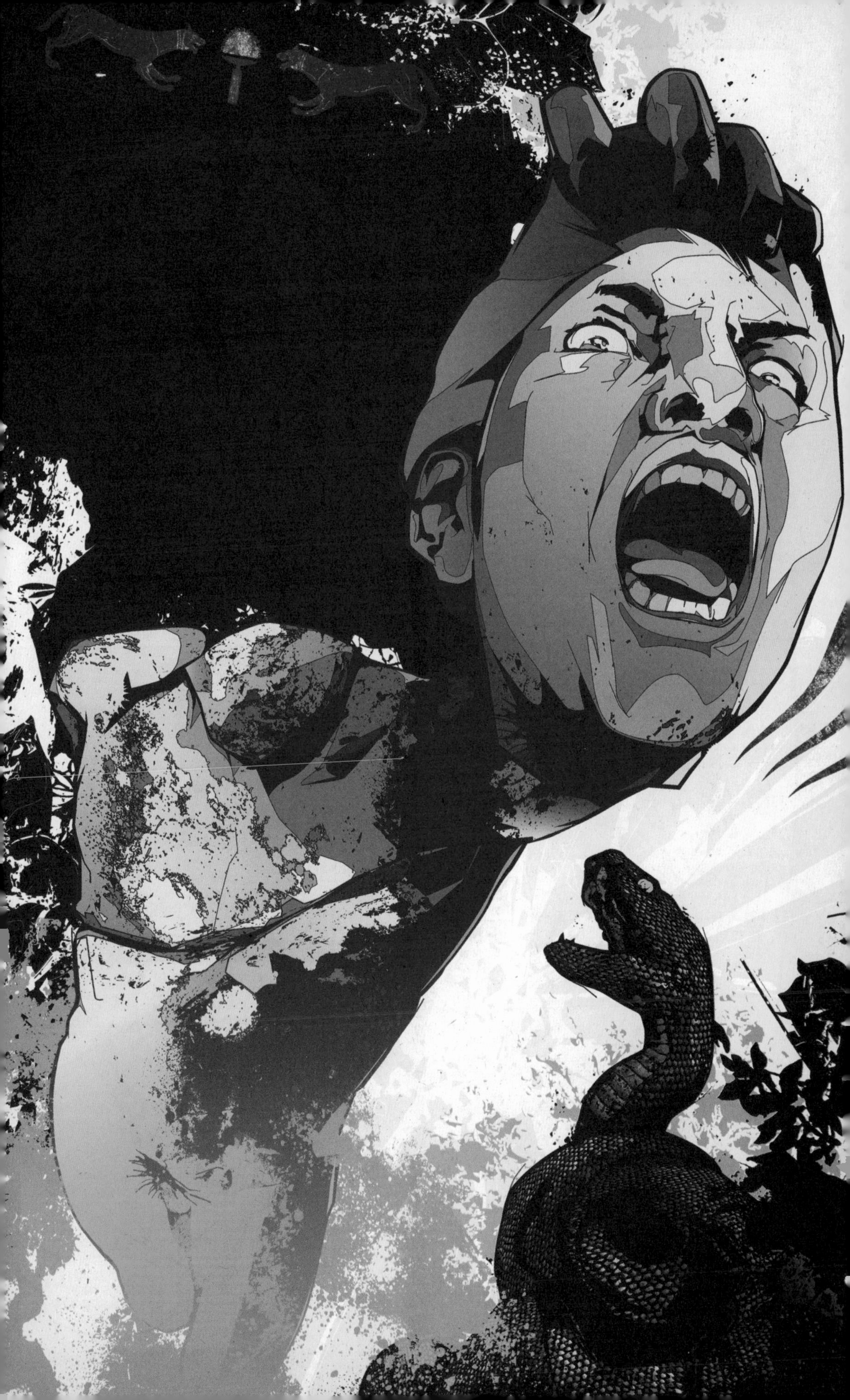

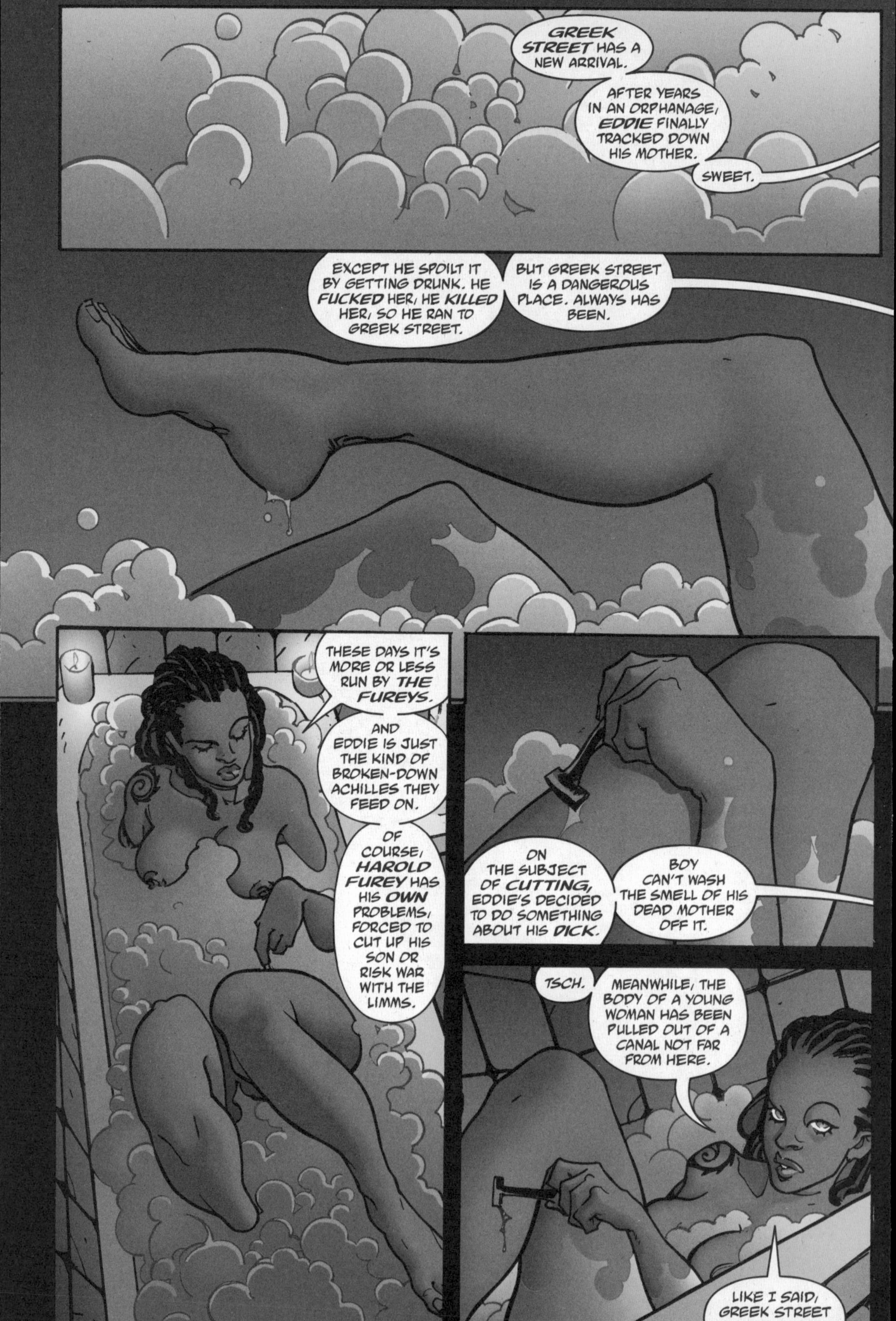
GREEK STREET HAS A NEW ARRIVAL.
AFTER YEARS IN AN ORPHANAGE, EDDIE FINALLY TRACKED DOWN HIS MOTHER.
SWEET.
EXCEPT HE SPOILT IT BY GETTING DRUNK. HE FUCKED HER, HE KILLED HER, SO HE RAN TO GREEK STREET.
BUT GREEK STREET IS A DANGEROUS PLACE. ALWAYS HAS BEEN.
THESE DAYS IT'S MORE OR LESS RUN BY THE FUREYS.
AND EDDIE IS JUST THE KIND OF BROKEN-DOWN ACHILLES THEY FEED ON.
OF COURSE, HAROLD FUREY HAS HIS OWN PROBLEMS, FORCED TO CUT UP HIS SON OR RISK WAR WITH THE LIMMS.
ON THE SUBJECT OF CUTTING, EDDIE'S DECIDED TO DO SOMETHING ABOUT HIS DICK.
BOY CAN'T WASH THE SMELL OF HIS DEAD MOTHER OFF IT.
TSCH.
MEANWHILE, THE BODY OF A YOUNG WOMAN HAS BEEN PULLED OUT OF A CANAL NOT FAR FROM HERE.
LIKE I SAID, GREEK STREET IS A DANGEROUS PLACE...

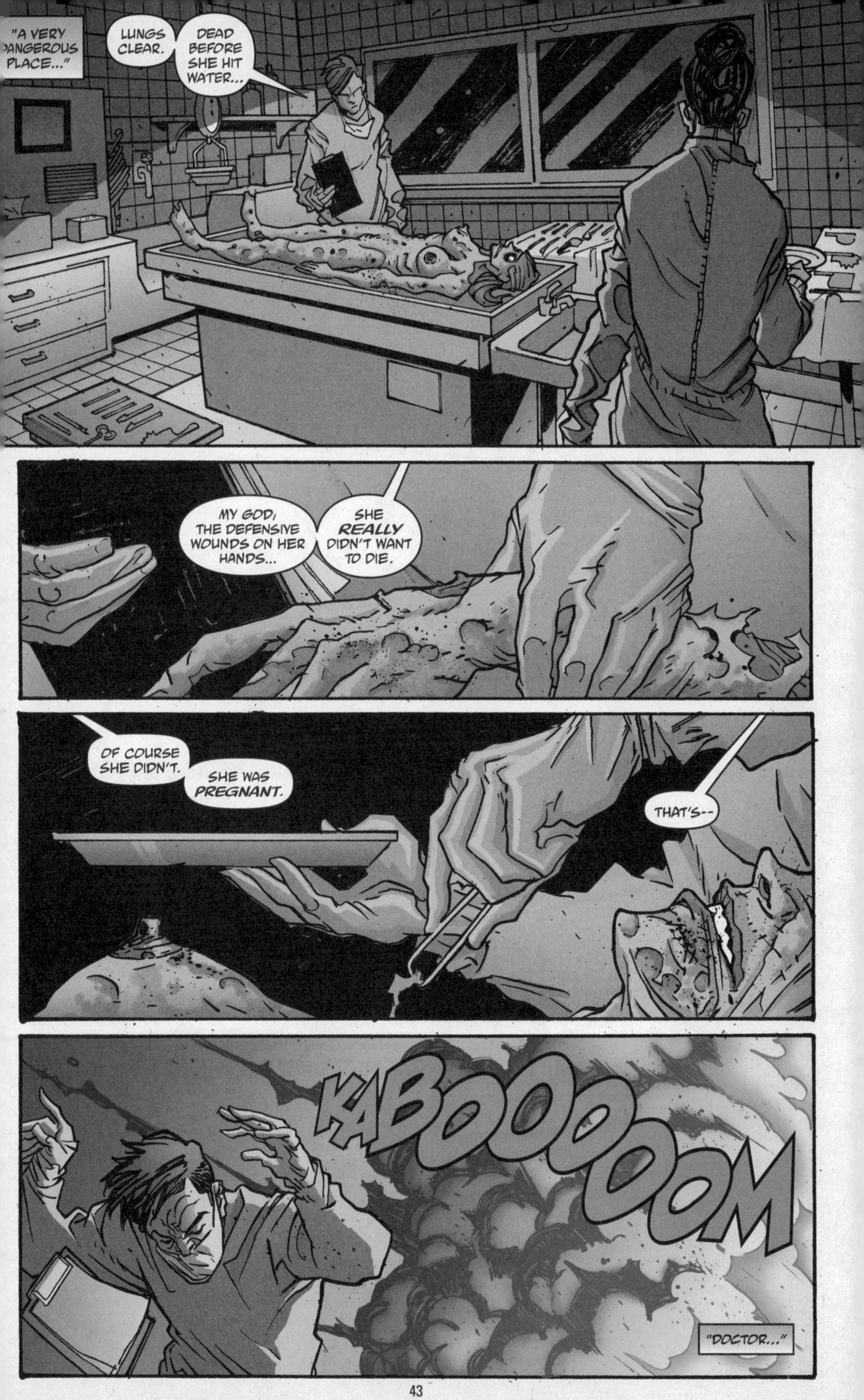
"A VERY DANGEROUS PLACE..."
LUNGS CLEAR.
DEAD BEFORE SHE HIT WATER...
MY GOD, THE DEFENSIVE WOUNDS ON HER HANDS...
SHE *REALLY* DIDN'T WANT TO DIE.
OF COURSE SHE DIDN'T.
SHE WAS *PREGNANT*.
THAT'S--
KABOOOOOOM
"DOCTOR..."

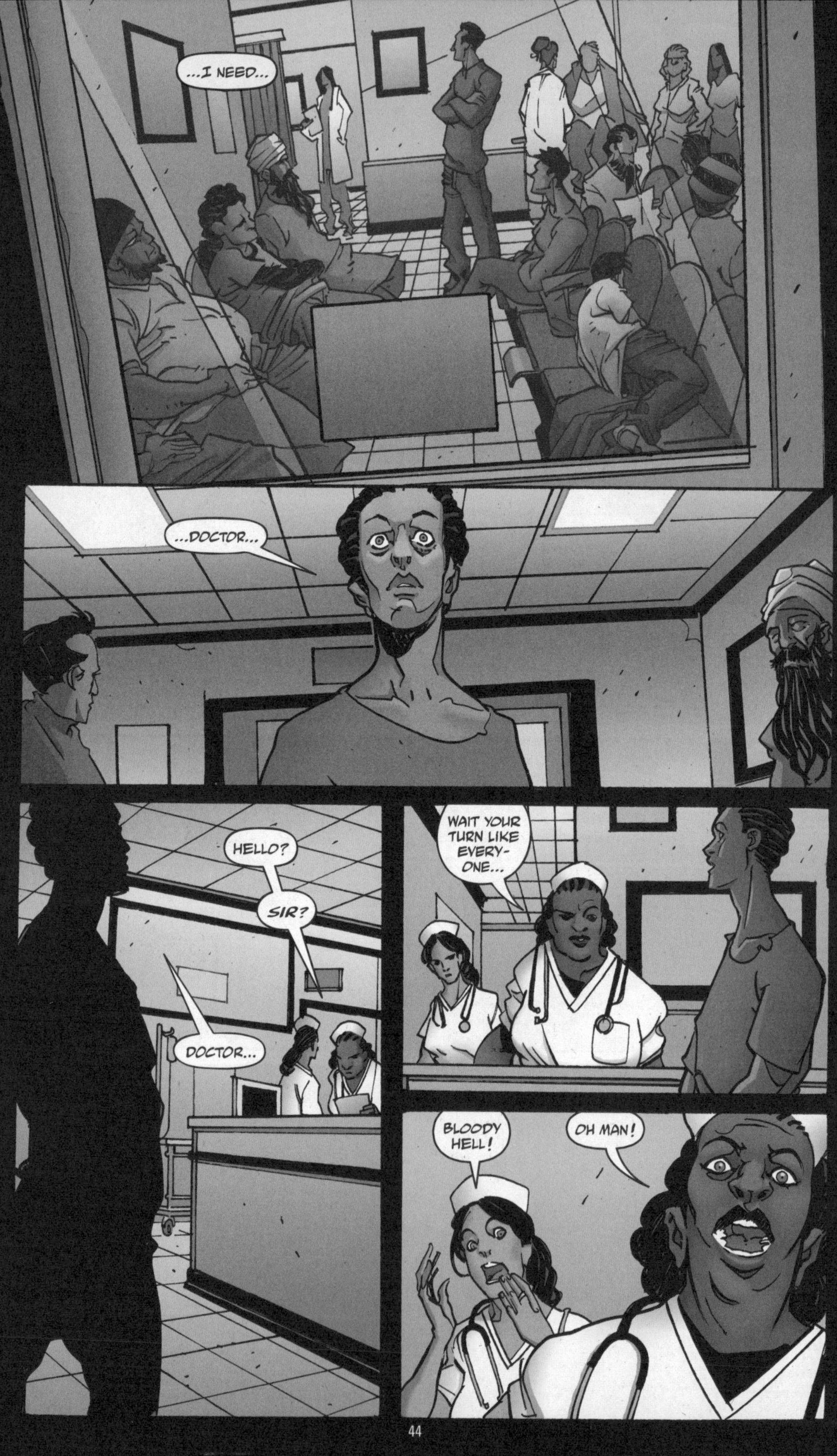
...I NEED...
...DOCTOR...
HELLO?
SIR?
DOCTOR...
WAIT YOUR TURN LIKE EVERY-ONE...
BLOODY HELL!
OH MAN!

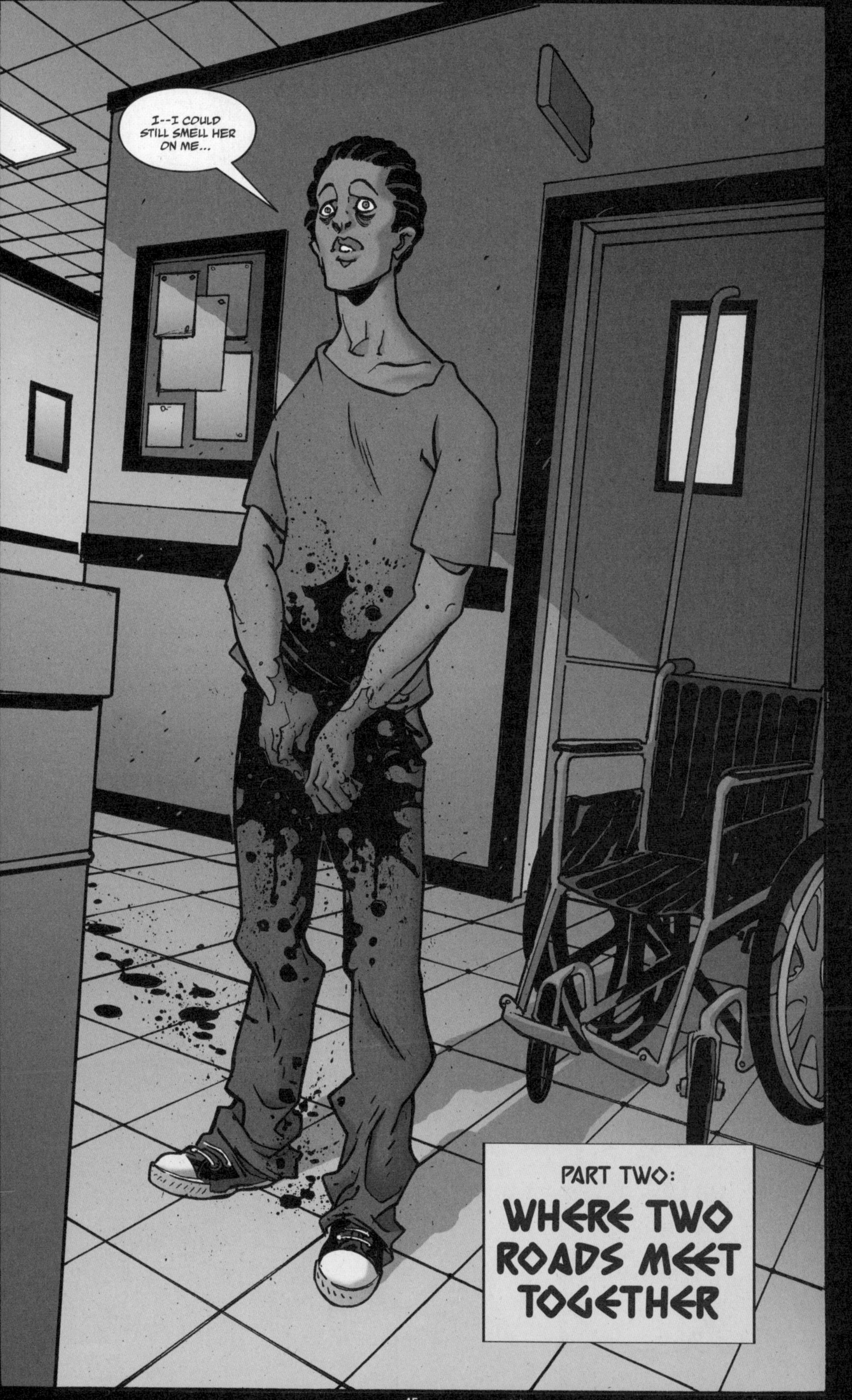

I--I COULD STILL SMELL HER ON ME...
PART TWO:
WHERE TWO ROADS MEET TOGETHER

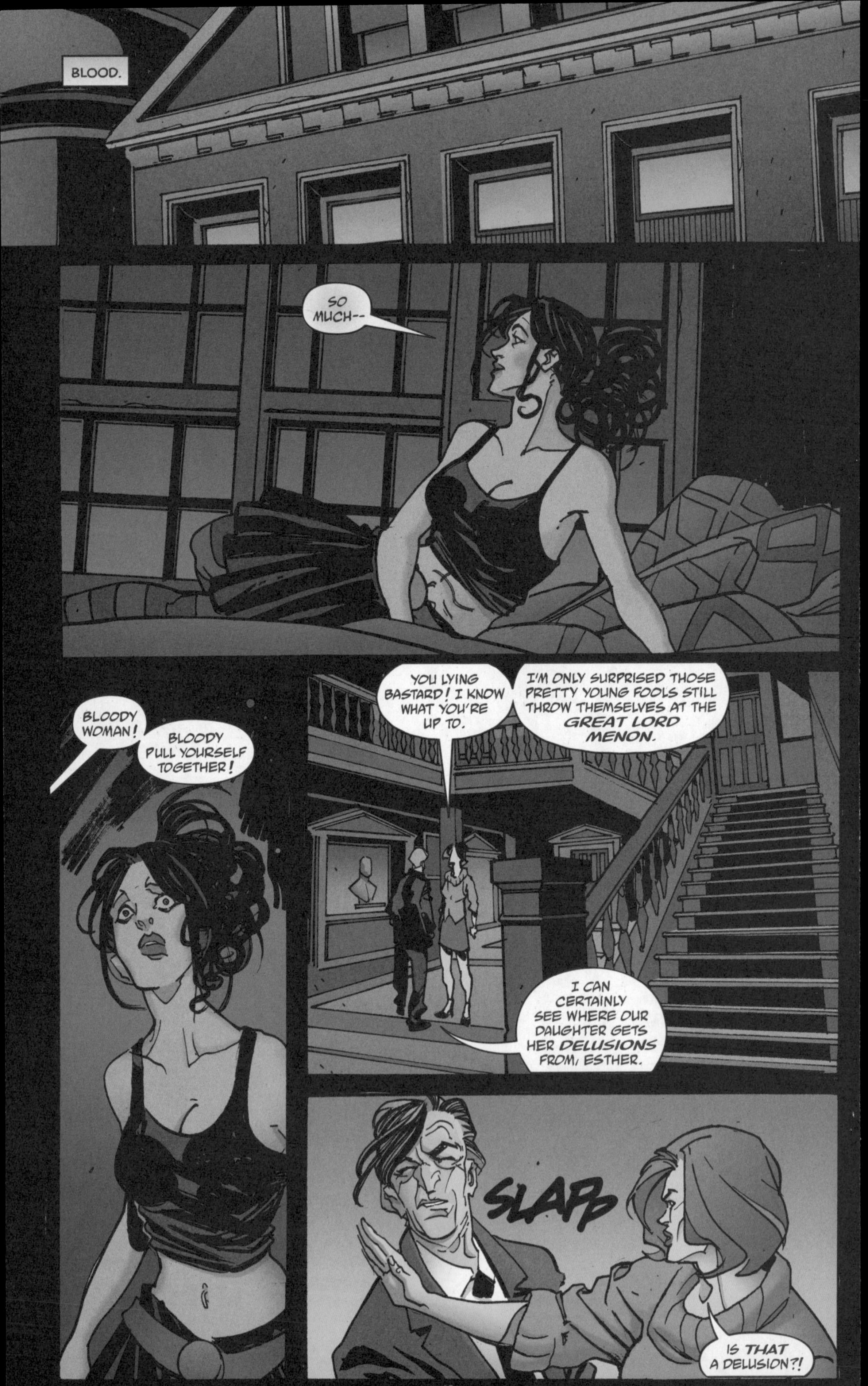
BLOOD.
SO MUCH--
BLOODY WOMAN!
BLOODY PULL YOURSELF TOGETHER!
YOU LYING BASTARD! I KNOW WHAT YOU'RE UP TO.
I'M ONLY SURPRISED THOSE PRETTY YOUNG FOOLS STILL THROW THEMSELVES AT THE GREAT LORD MENON.
I CAN CERTAINLY SEE WHERE OUR DAUGHTER GETS HER DELUSIONS FROM, ESTHER.
SLAPP
IS THAT A DELUSION?!

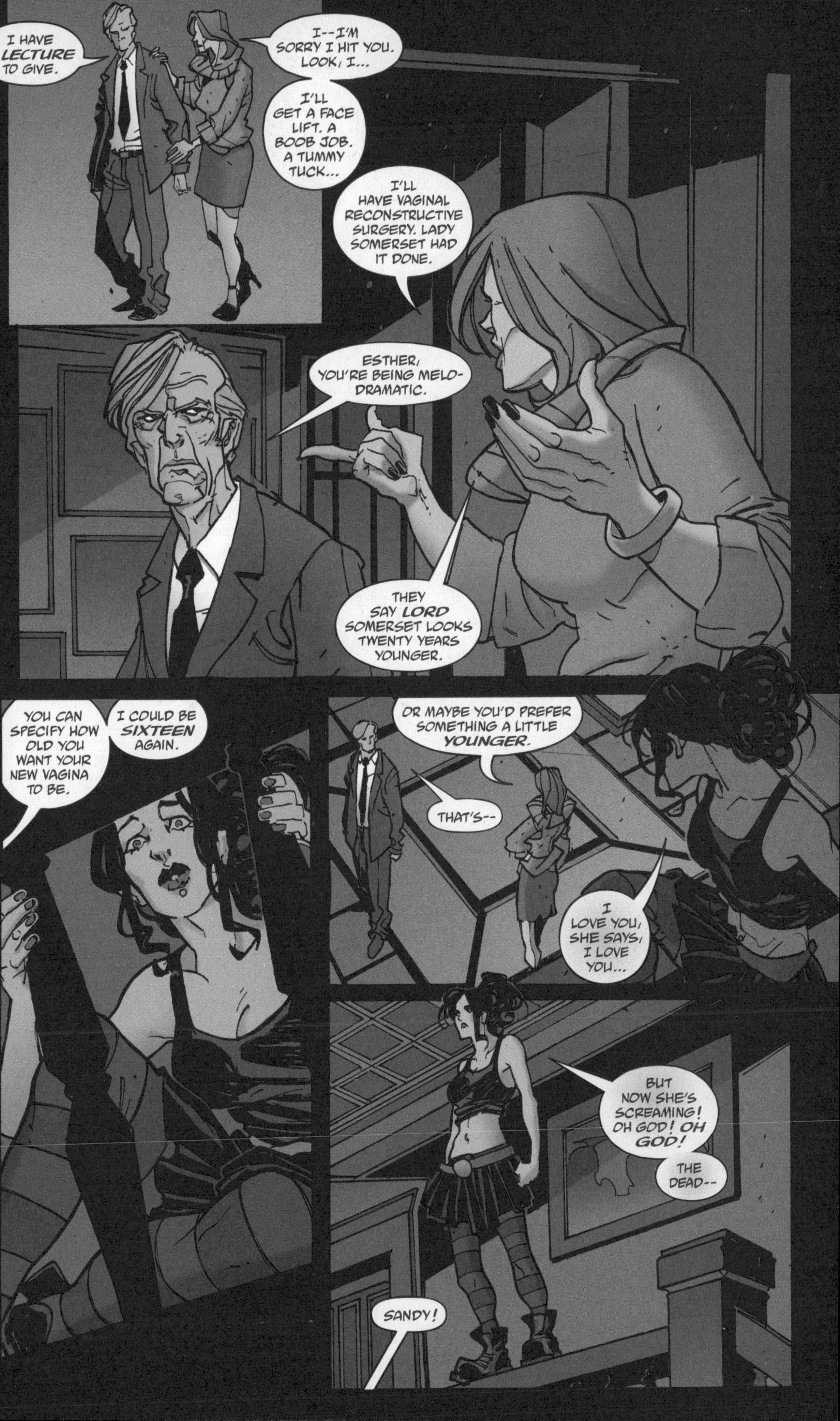
I HAVE A LECTURE TO GIVE.
I--I'M SORRY I HIT YOU. LOOK, I...
I'LL GET A FACE LIFT. A BOOB JOB. A TUMMY TUCK...
I'LL HAVE VAGINAL RECONSTRUCTIVE SURGERY. LADY SOMERSET HAD IT DONE.
ESTHER, YOU'RE BEING MELO-DRAMATIC.
THEY SAY LORD SOMERSET LOOKS TWENTY YEARS YOUNGER.
YOU CAN SPECIFY HOW OLD YOU WANT YOUR NEW VAGINA TO BE.
I COULD BE SIXTEEN AGAIN.
OR MAYBE YOU'D PREFER SOMETHING A LITTLE YOUNGER.
THAT'S--
I LOVE YOU, SHE SAYS, I LOVE YOU...
BUT NOW SHE'S SCREAMING! OH GOD! OH GOD!
THE DEAD--
SANDY!

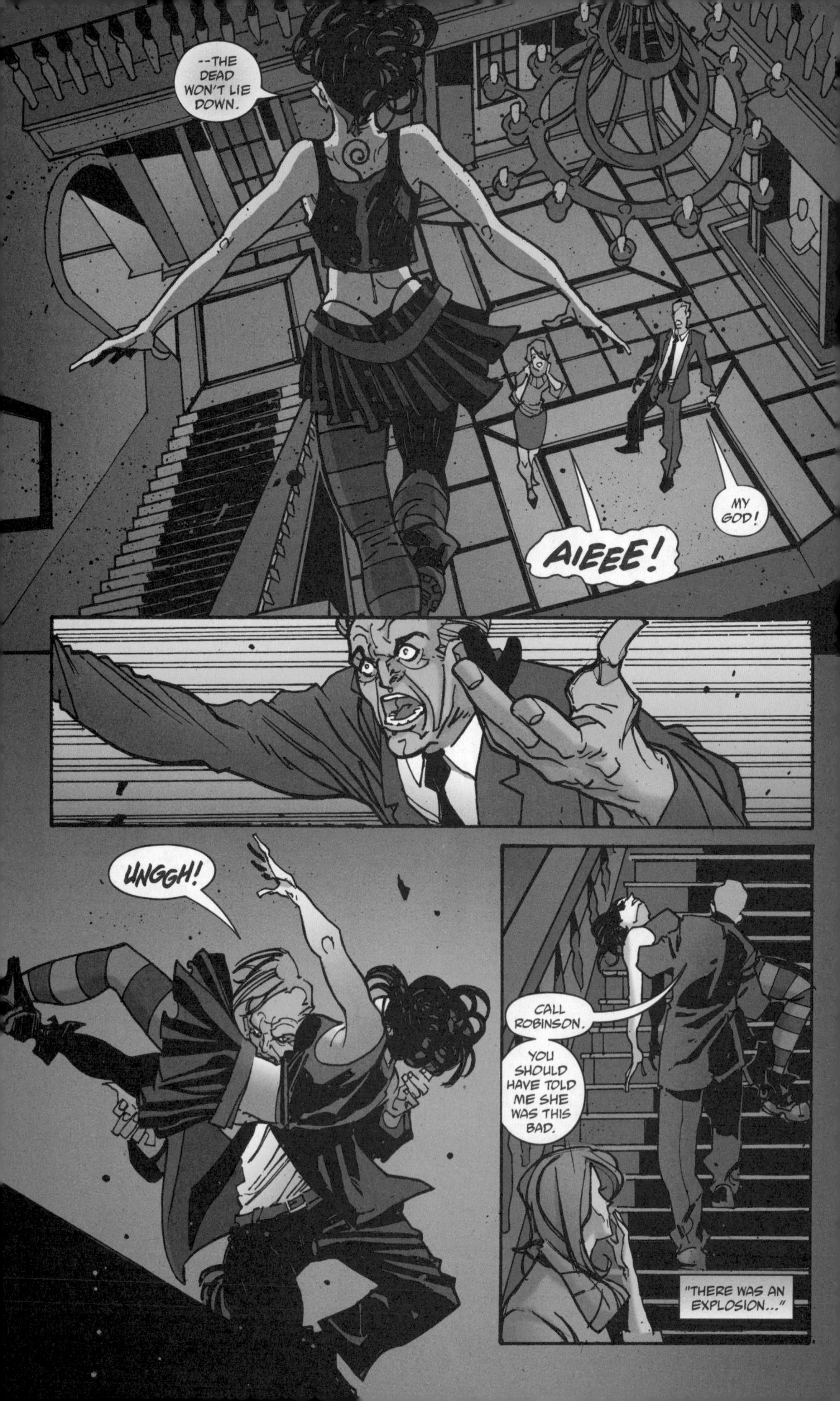
--THE DEAD WON'T LIE DOWN.
AIEEE!
MY GOD!
UNGGH!
CALL ROBINSON.
YOU SHOULD HAVE TOLD ME SHE WAS THIS BAD.
"THERE WAS AN EXPLOSION..."

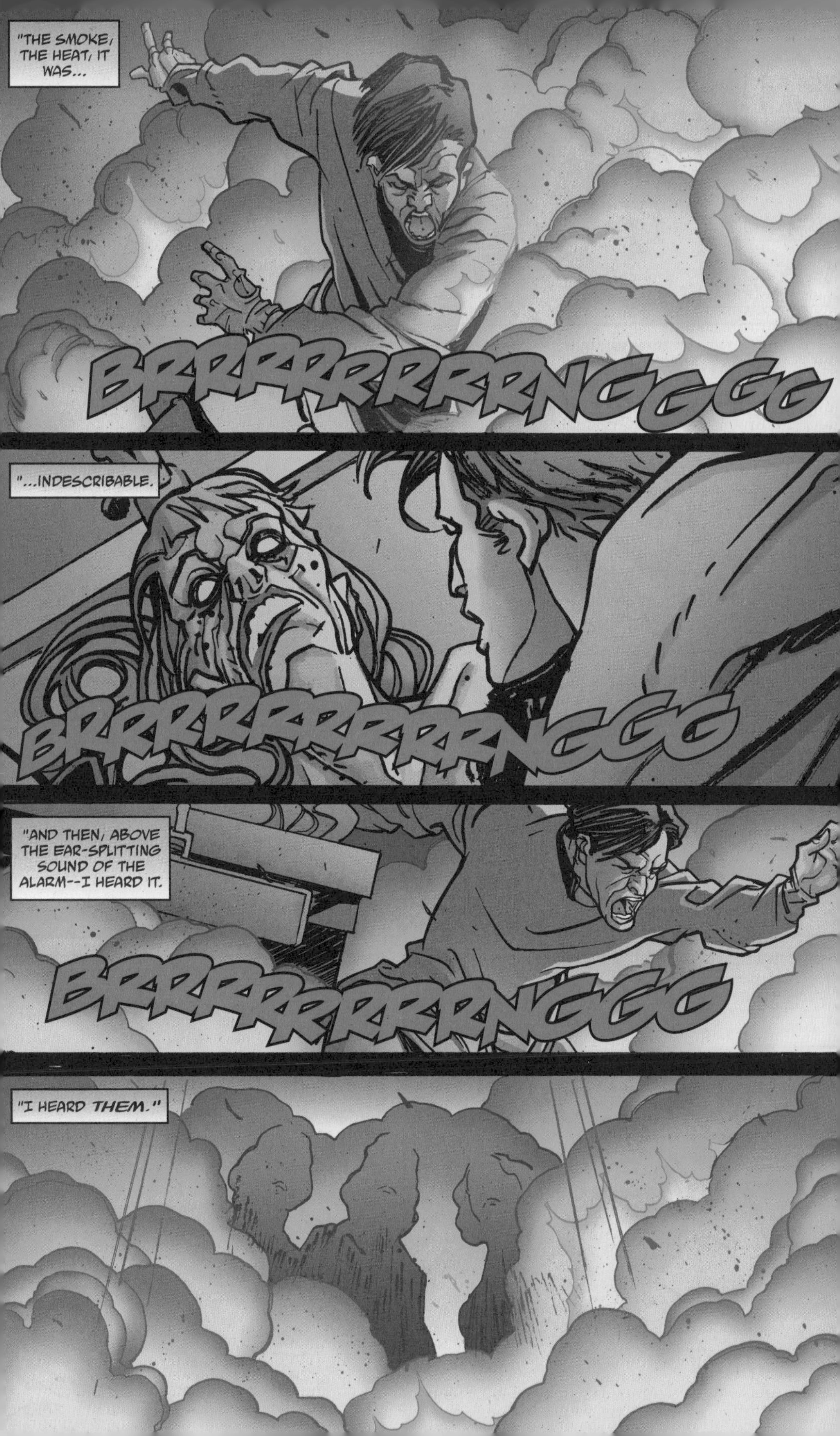
"THE SMOKE, THE HEAT, IT WAS...
BRRRRRRRRRNGGGG
"...INDESCRIBABLE.
BRRRRRRRRRNGGG
"AND THEN, ABOVE THE EAR-SPLITTING SOUND OF THE ALARM--I HEARD IT.
BRRRRRRRRRNGGG
"I HEARD THEM."

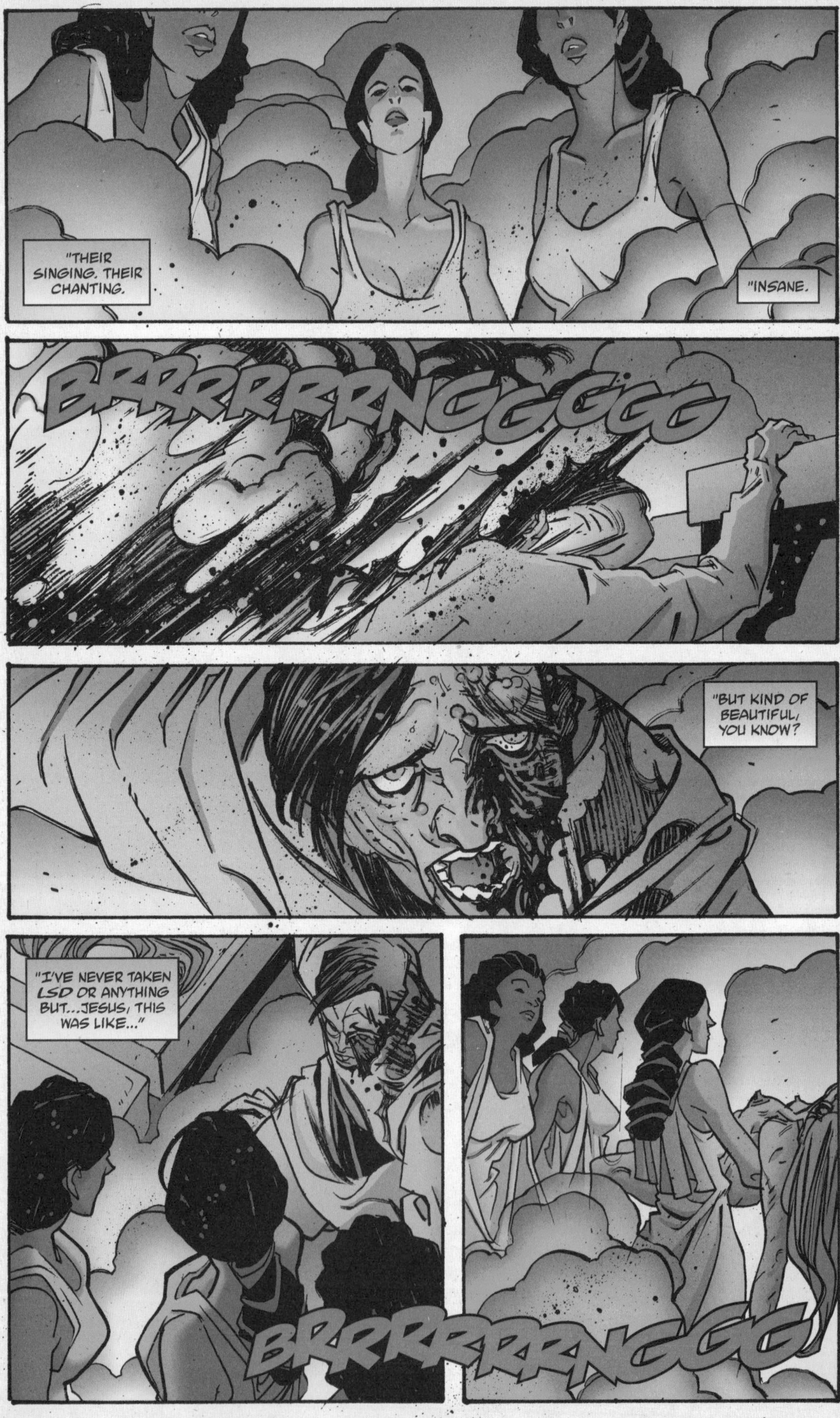
"THEIR SINGING. THEIR CHANTING.
"INSANE.
BRRRRRRNGGGGG
"BUT KIND OF BEAUTIFUL, YOU KNOW?
"I'VE NEVER TAKEN LSD OR ANYTHING BUT...JESUS, THIS WAS LIKE..."
BRRRRRRNGGG

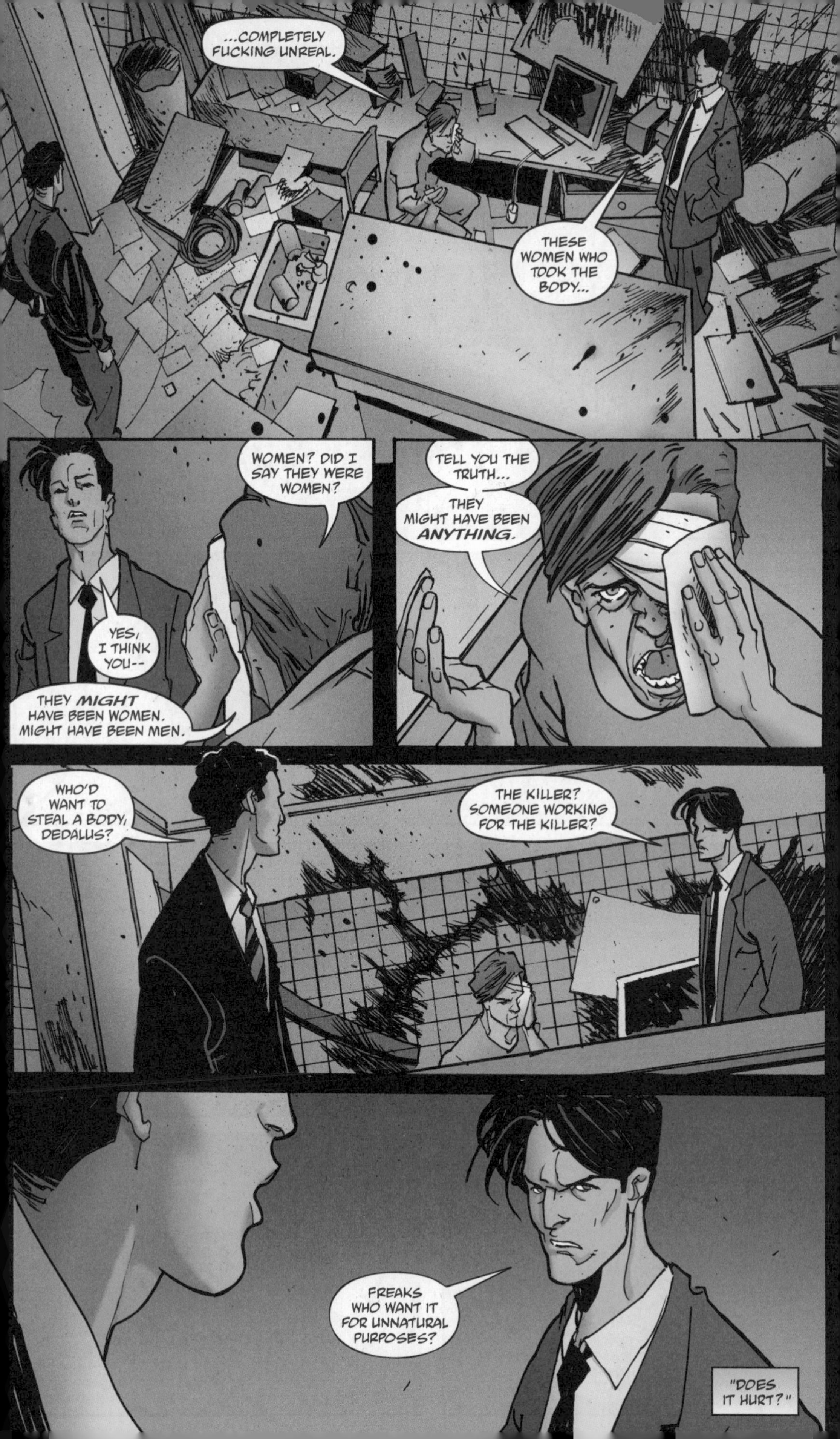

...COMPLETELY FUCKING UNREAL.
THESE WOMEN WHO TOOK THE BODY...
WOMEN? DID I SAY THEY WERE WOMEN?
YES, I THINK YOU--
THEY MIGHT HAVE BEEN WOMEN. MIGHT HAVE BEEN MEN.
TELL YOU THE TRUTH...
THEY MIGHT HAVE BEEN ANYTHING.
WHO'D WANT TO STEAL A BODY, DEDALUS?
THE KILLER? SOMEONE WORKING FOR THE KILLER?
FREAKS WHO WANT IT FOR UNNATURAL PURPOSES?
"DOES IT HURT?"

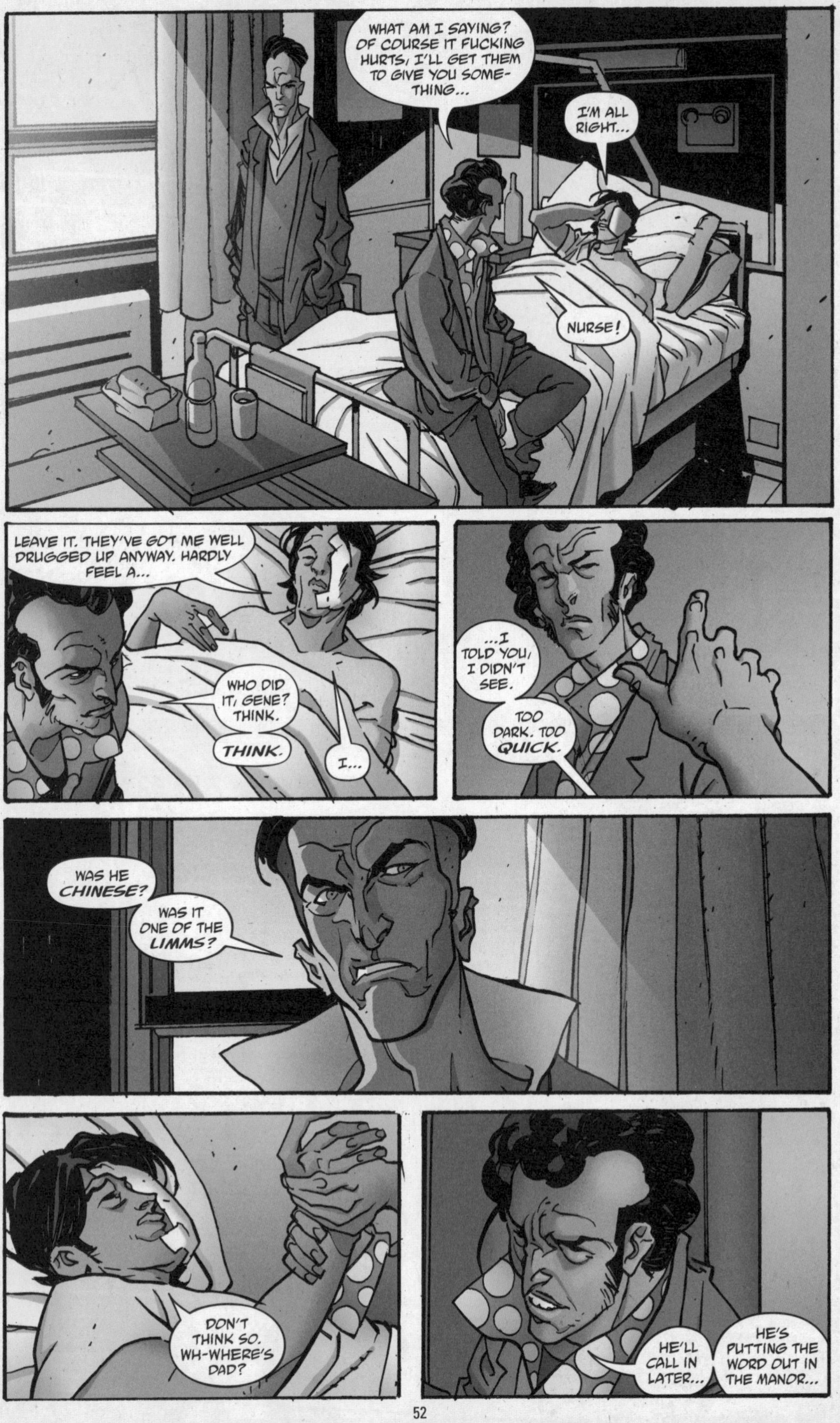
WHAT AM I SAYING? OF COURSE IT FUCKING HURTS, I'LL GET THEM TO GIVE YOU SOME-THING...
I'M ALL RIGHT...
NURSE!
LEAVE IT. THEY'VE GOT ME WELL DRUGGED UP ANYWAY. HARDLY FEEL A...
WHO DID IT, GENE? THINK.
THINK.
I...
...I TOLD YOU, I DIDN'T SEE.
TOO DARK. TOO QUICK.
WAS HE CHINESE?
WAS IT ONE OF THE LIMMS?
DON'T THINK SO. WH-WHERE'S DAD?
HE'S PUTTING THE WORD OUT IN THE MANOR...
HE'LL CALL IN LATER...

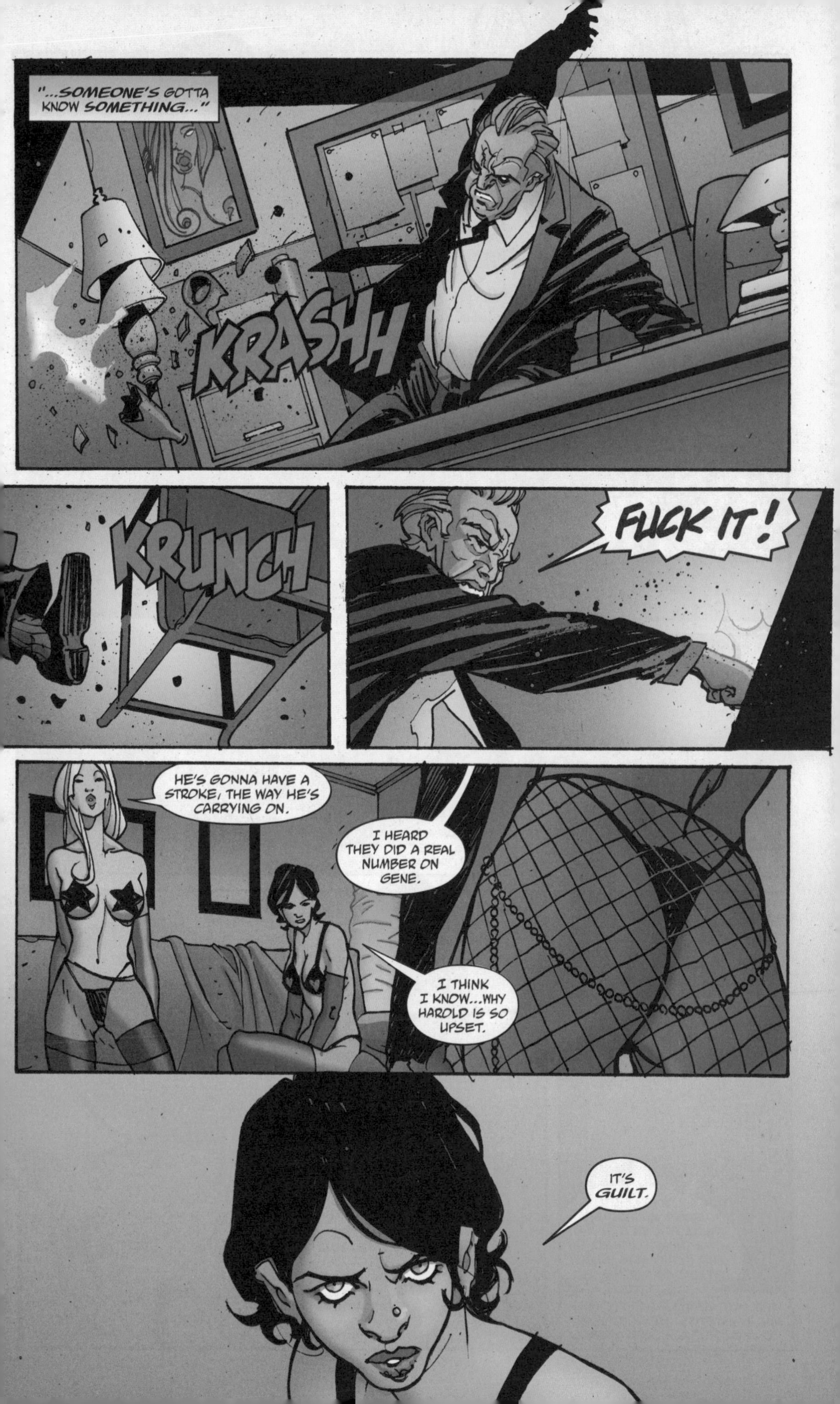
"...SOMEONE'S GOTTA KNOW SOMETHING..."
KRASHH
KRUNCH
FUCK IT!
HE'S GONNA HAVE A STROKE, THE WAY HE'S CARRYING ON.
I HEARD THEY DID A REAL NUMBER ON GENE.
I THINK I KNOW...WHY HAROLD IS SO UPSET.
IT'S GUILT.

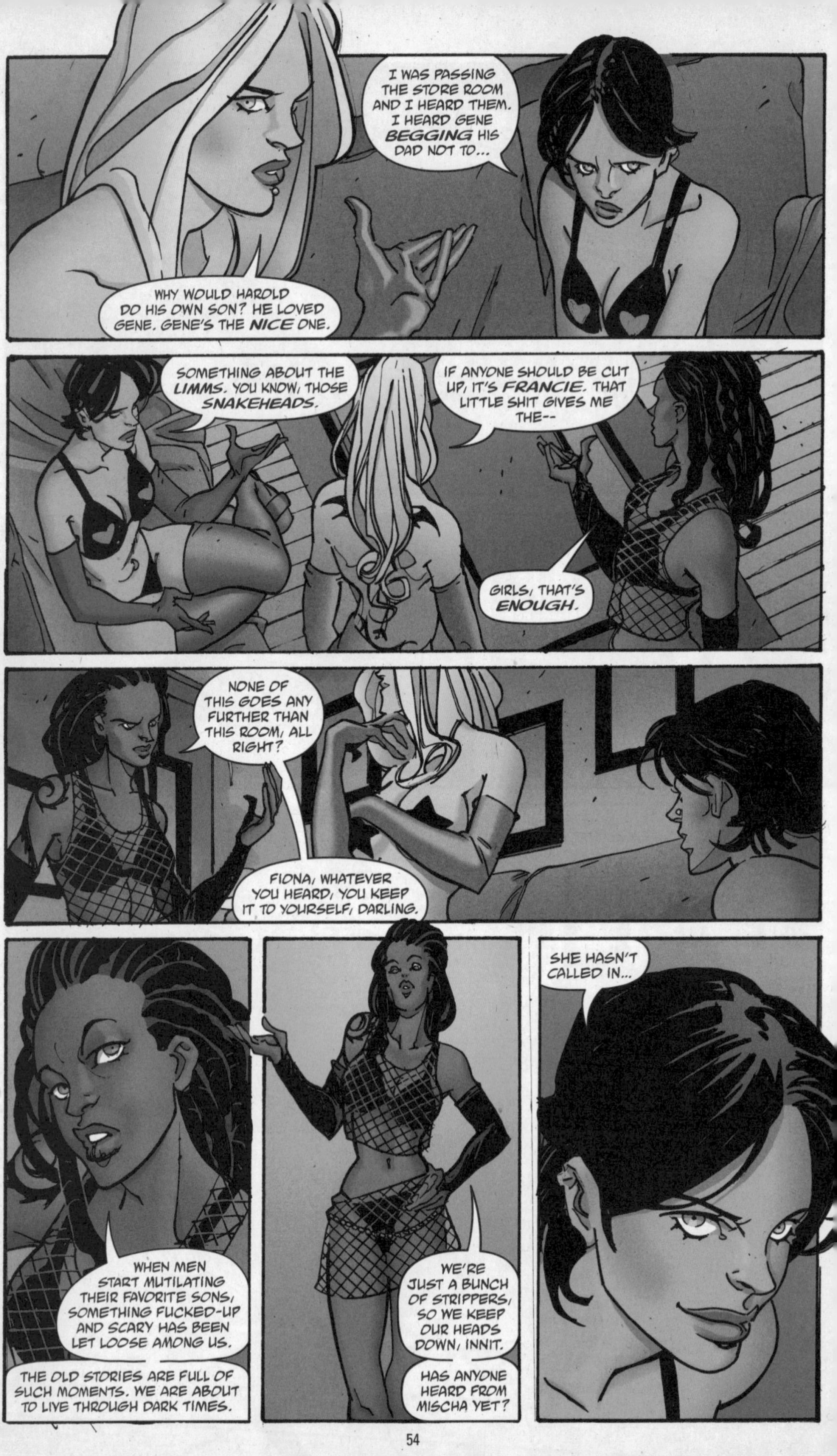
I WAS PASSING THE STORE ROOM AND I HEARD THEM. I HEARD GENE BEGGING HIS DAD NOT TO...
WHY WOULD HAROLD DO HIS OWN SON? HE LOVED GENE. GENE'S THE NICE ONE.
SOMETHING ABOUT THE LIMMS. YOU KNOW, THOSE SNAKEHEADS.
IF ANYONE SHOULD BE CUT UP, IT'S FRANCIE. THAT LITTLE SHIT GIVES ME THE--
GIRLS, THAT'S ENOUGH.
NONE OF THIS GOES ANY FURTHER THAN THIS ROOM, ALL RIGHT?
FIONA, WHATEVER YOU HEARD, YOU KEEP IT TO YOURSELF, DARLING.
WHEN MEN START MUTILATING THEIR FAVORITE SONS, SOMETHING FUCKED-UP AND SCARY HAS BEEN LET LOOSE AMONG US.
THE OLD STORIES ARE FULL OF SUCH MOMENTS. WE ARE ABOUT TO LIVE THROUGH DARK TIMES.
WE'RE JUST A BUNCH OF STRIPPERS, SO WE KEEP OUR HEADS DOWN, INNIT.
HAS ANYONE HEARD FROM MISCHA YET?
SHE HASN'T CALLED IN...

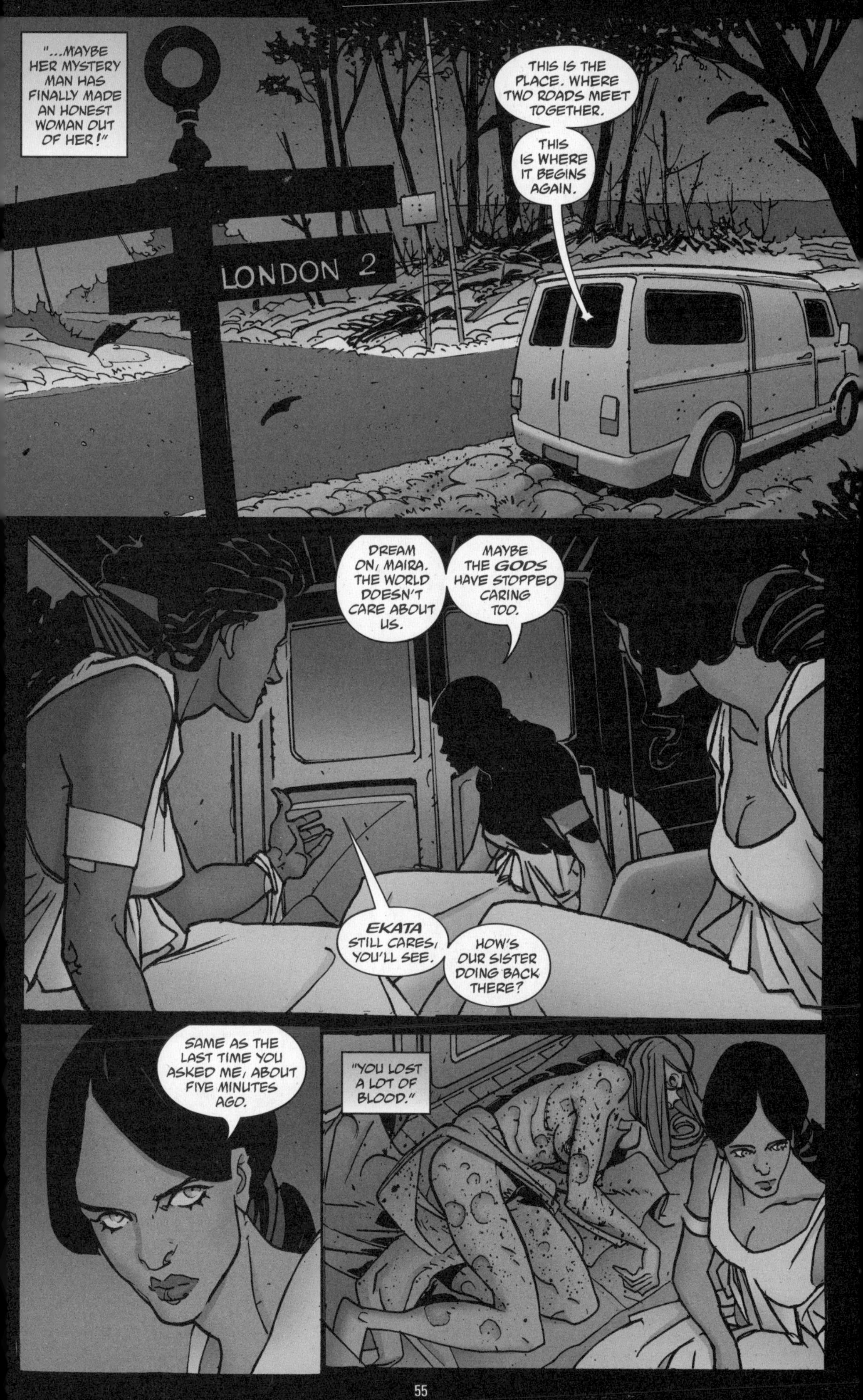
"...MAYBE HER MYSTERY MAN HAS FINALLY MADE AN HONEST WOMAN OUT OF HER!"
LONDON 2
THIS IS THE PLACE. WHERE TWO ROADS MEET TOGETHER.
THIS IS WHERE IT BEGINS AGAIN.
DREAM ON, MAIRA. THE WORLD DOESN'T CARE ABOUT US.
MAYBE THE GODS HAVE STOPPED CARING TOO.
EKATA STILL CARES, YOU'LL SEE.
HOW'S OUR SISTER DOING BACK THERE?
SAME AS THE LAST TIME YOU ASKED ME, ABOUT FIVE MINUTES AGO.
"YOU LOST A LOT OF BLOOD."

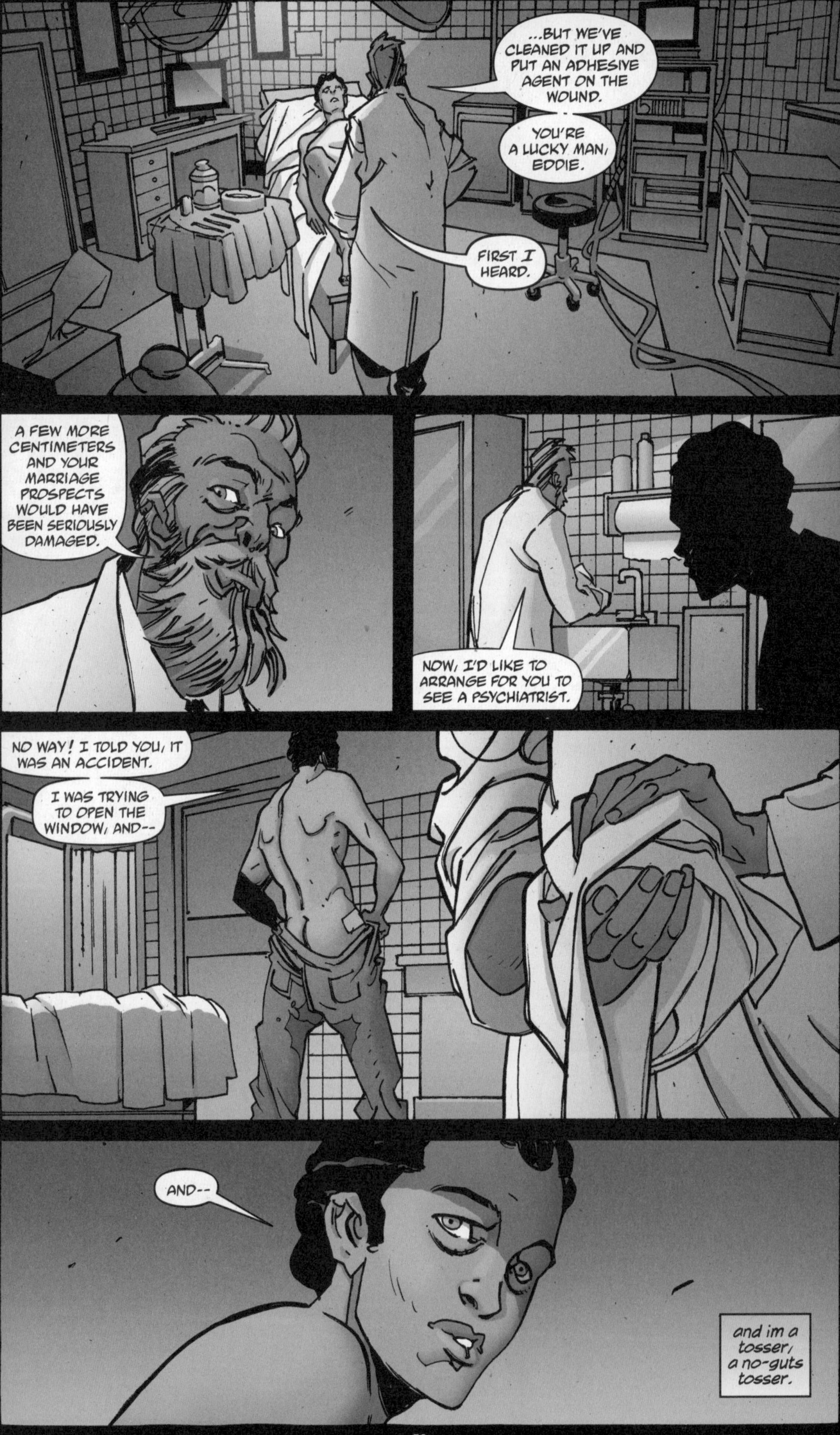
...BUT WE'VE CLEANED IT UP AND PUT AN ADHESIVE AGENT ON THE WOUND.
YOU'RE A LUCKY MAN, EDDIE.
FIRST I HEARD.
A FEW MORE CENTIMETERS AND YOUR MARRIAGE PROSPECTS WOULD HAVE BEEN SERIOUSLY DAMAGED.
NOW, I'D LIKE TO ARRANGE FOR YOU TO SEE A PSYCHIATRIST.
NO WAY! I TOLD YOU, IT WAS AN ACCIDENT.
I WAS TRYING TO OPEN THE WINDOW, AND--
AND--
and im a tosser, a no-guts tosser.

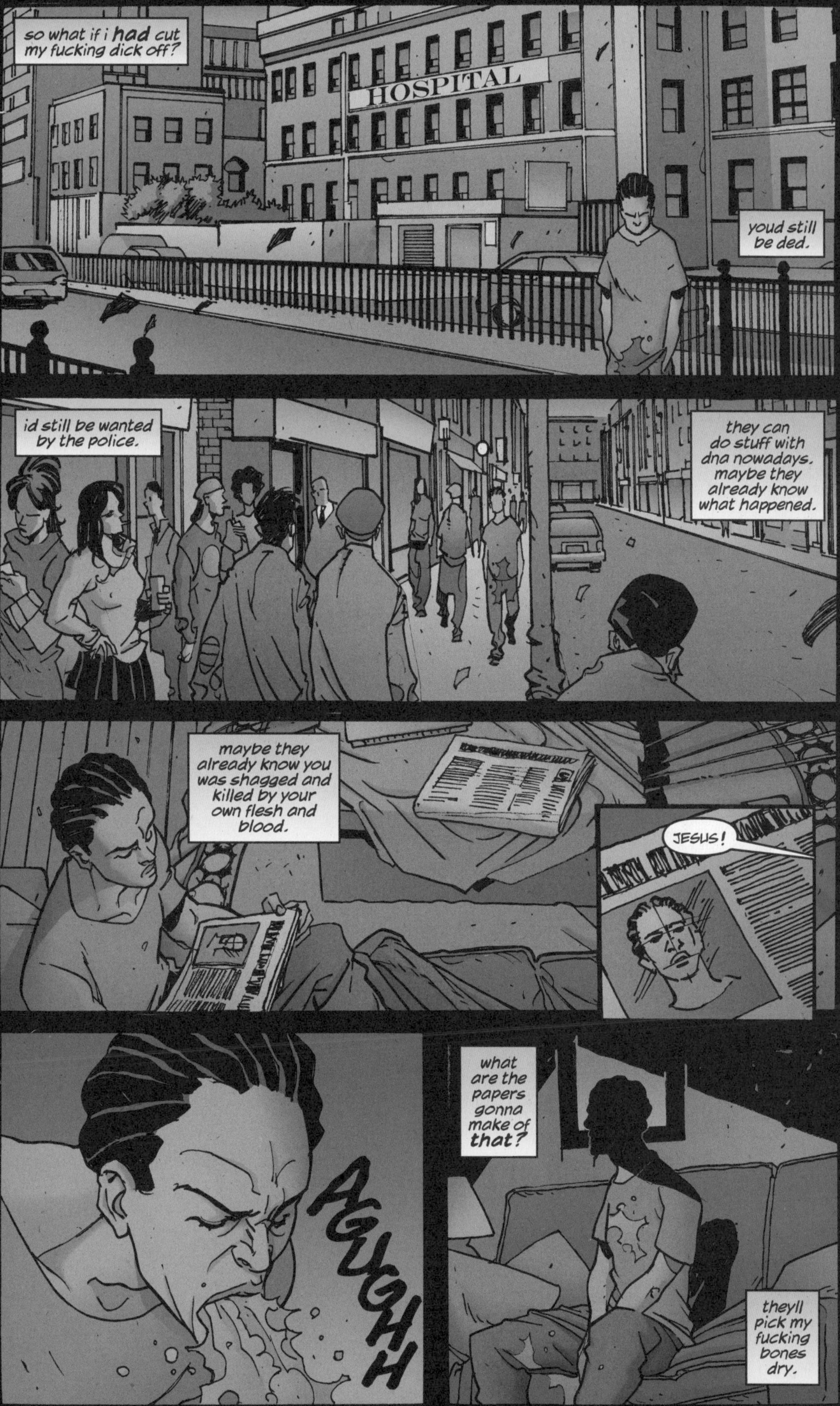
so what if i had cut my fucking dick off?
HOSPITAL
youd still be ded.
id still be wanted by the police.
they can do stuff with dna nowadays. maybe they already know what happened.
maybe they already know you was shagged and killed by your own flesh and blood.
JESUS!
AUGGHH
what are the papers gonna make of that?
theyll pick my fucking bones dry.

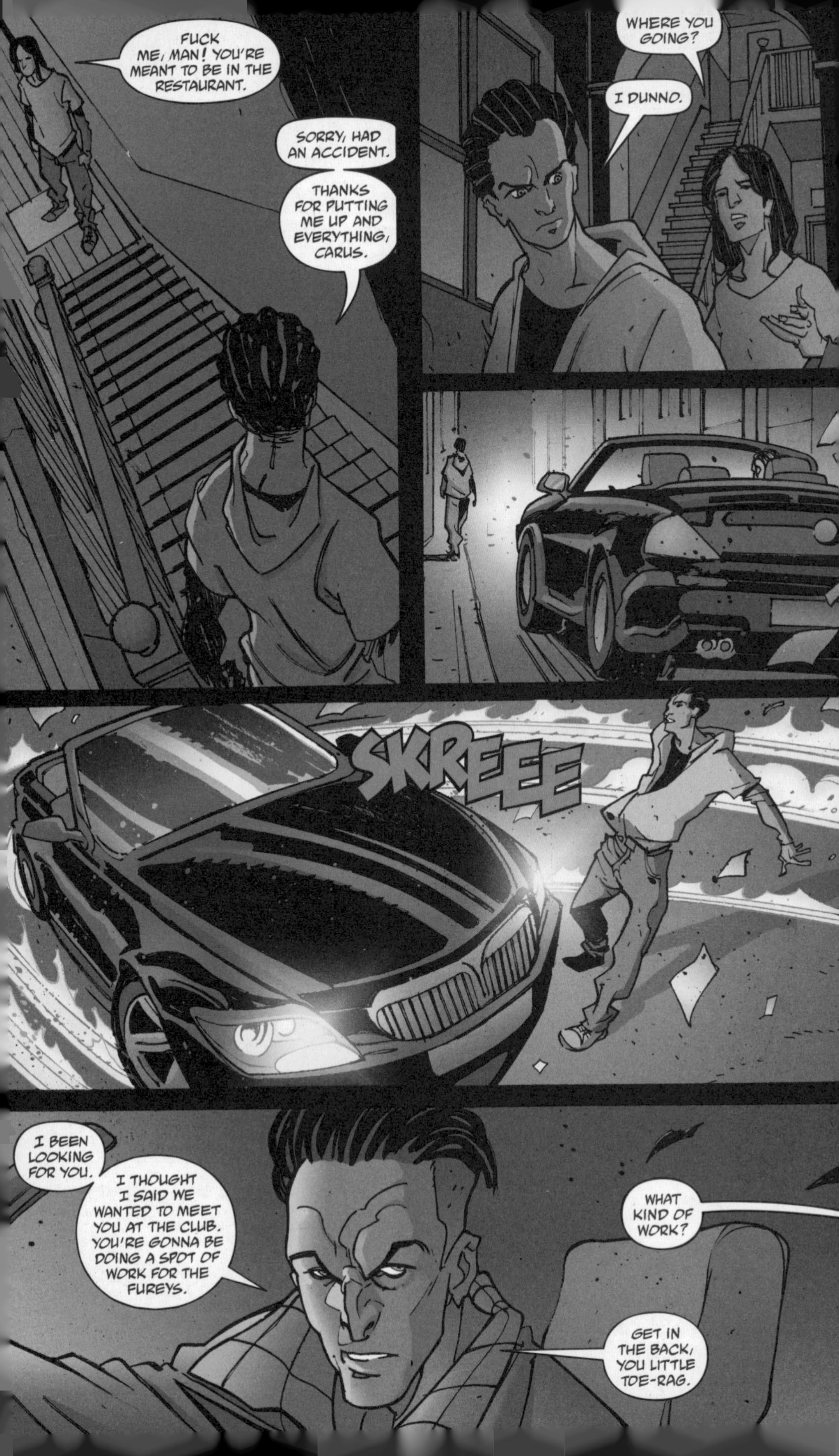
FUCK ME, MAN! YOU'RE MEANT TO BE IN THE RESTAURANT.
SORRY, HAD AN ACCIDENT.
THANKS FOR PUTTING ME UP AND EVERYTHING, CARUS.
WHERE YOU GOING?
I DUNNO.
SKREEE
I BEEN LOOKING FOR YOU.
I THOUGHT I SAID WE WANTED TO MEET YOU AT THE CLUB. YOU'RE GONNA BE DOING A SPOT OF WORK FOR THE FUREYS.
WHAT KIND OF WORK?
GET IN THE BACK, YOU LITTLE TOE-RAG.

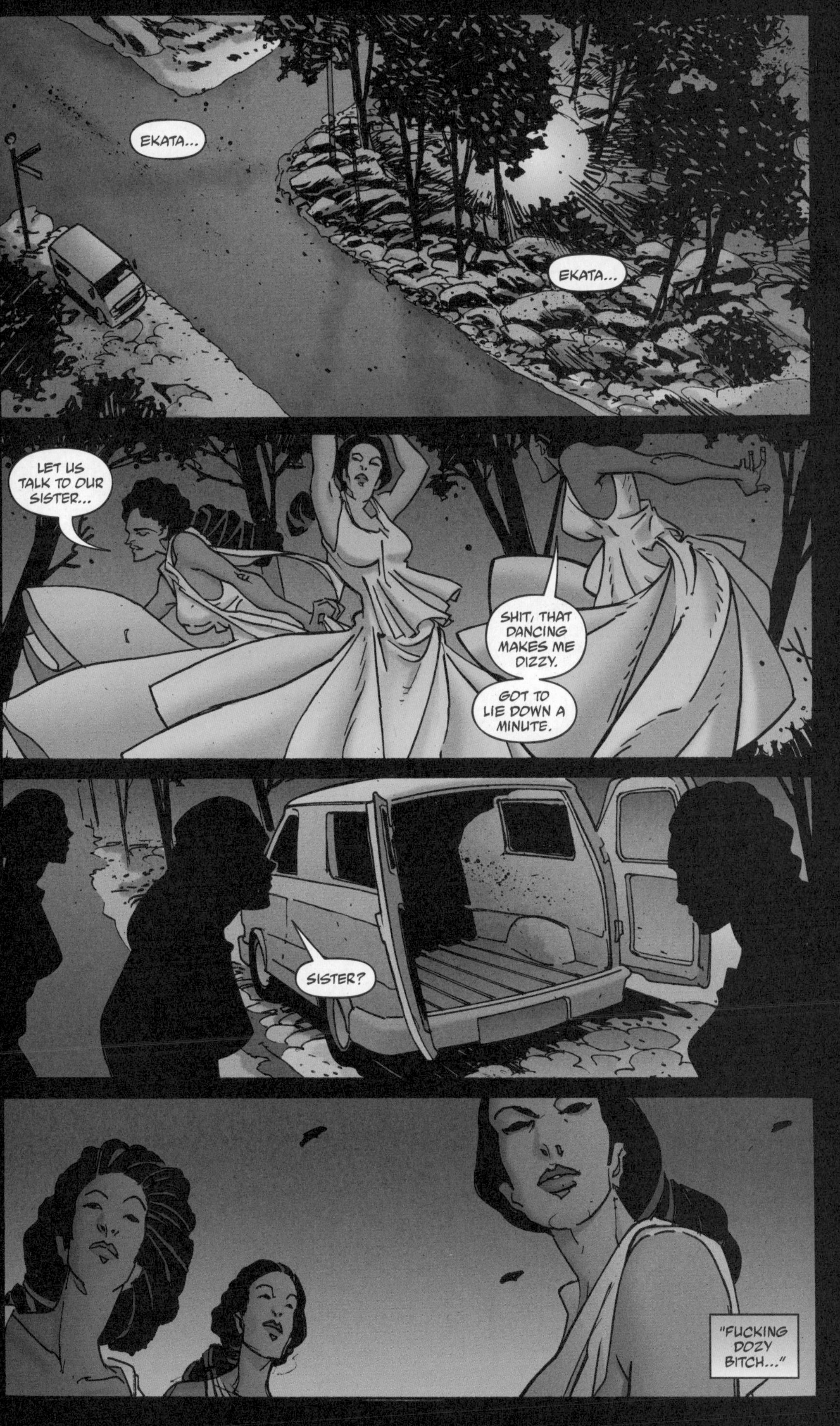
EKATA...
EKATA...
LET US TALK TO OUR SISTER...
SHIT, THAT DANCING MAKES ME DIZZY.
GOT TO LIE DOWN A MINUTE.
SISTER?
"FUCKING DOZY BITCH..."

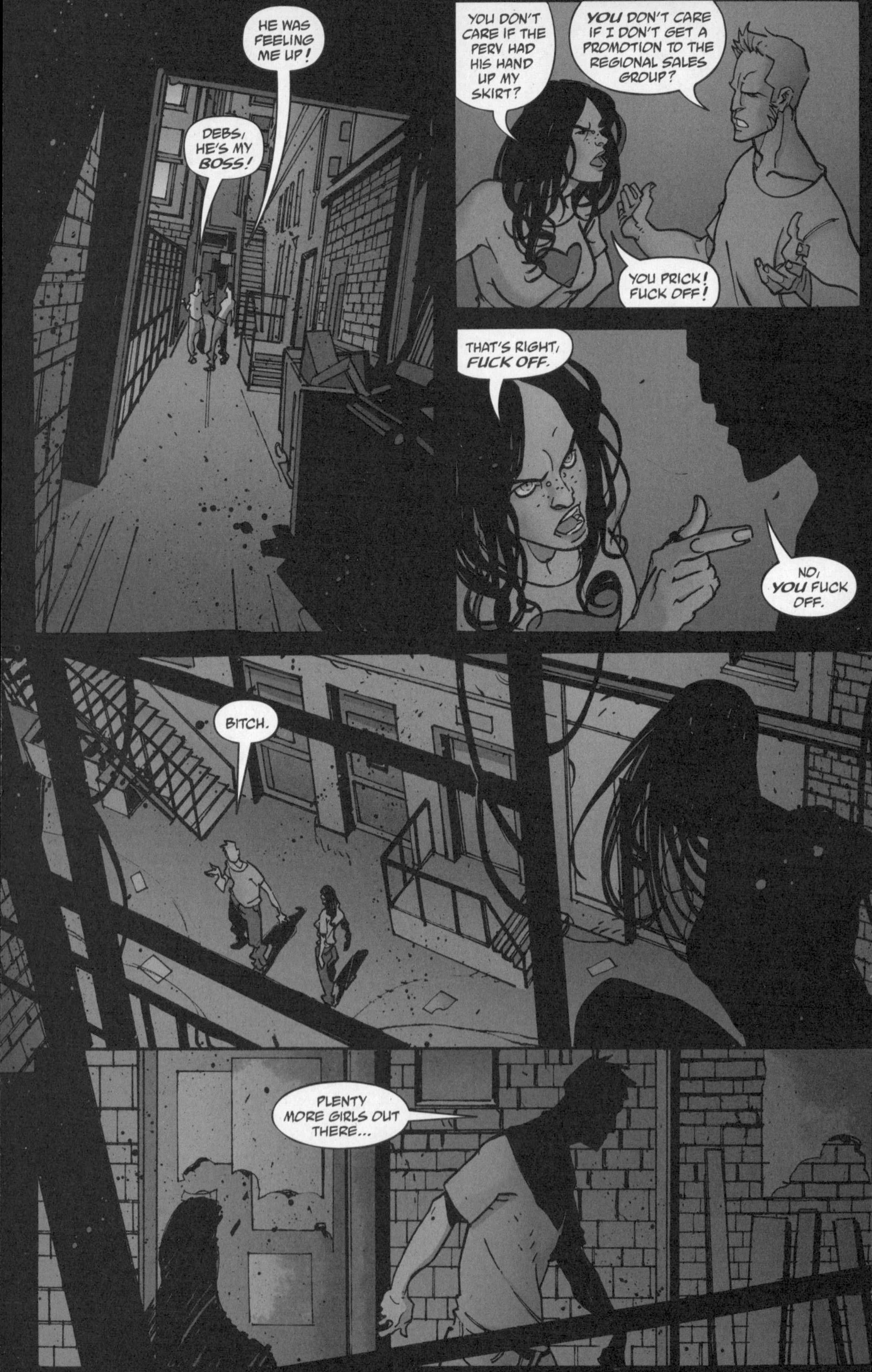

HE WAS FEELING ME UP!
DEBS, HE'S MY BOSS!
YOU DON'T CARE IF THE PERV HAD HIS HAND UP MY SKIRT?
YOU DON'T CARE IF I DON'T GET A PROMOTION TO THE REGIONAL SALES GROUP?
YOU PRICK! FUCK OFF!
THAT'S RIGHT, FUCK OFF.
NO, YOU FUCK OFF.
BITCH.
PLENTY MORE GIRLS OUT THERE...

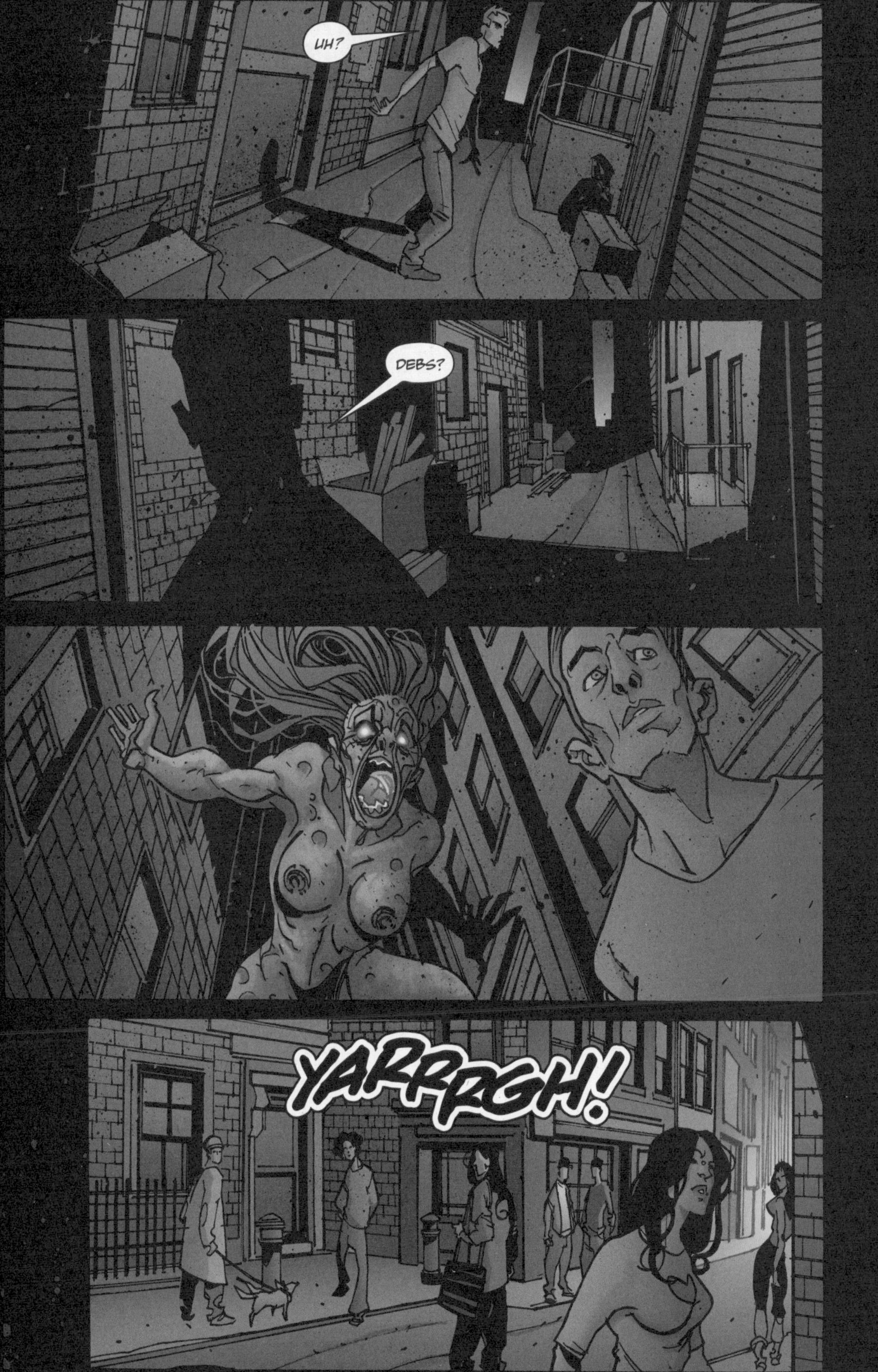
UH?
DEBS?
YARRRGH!

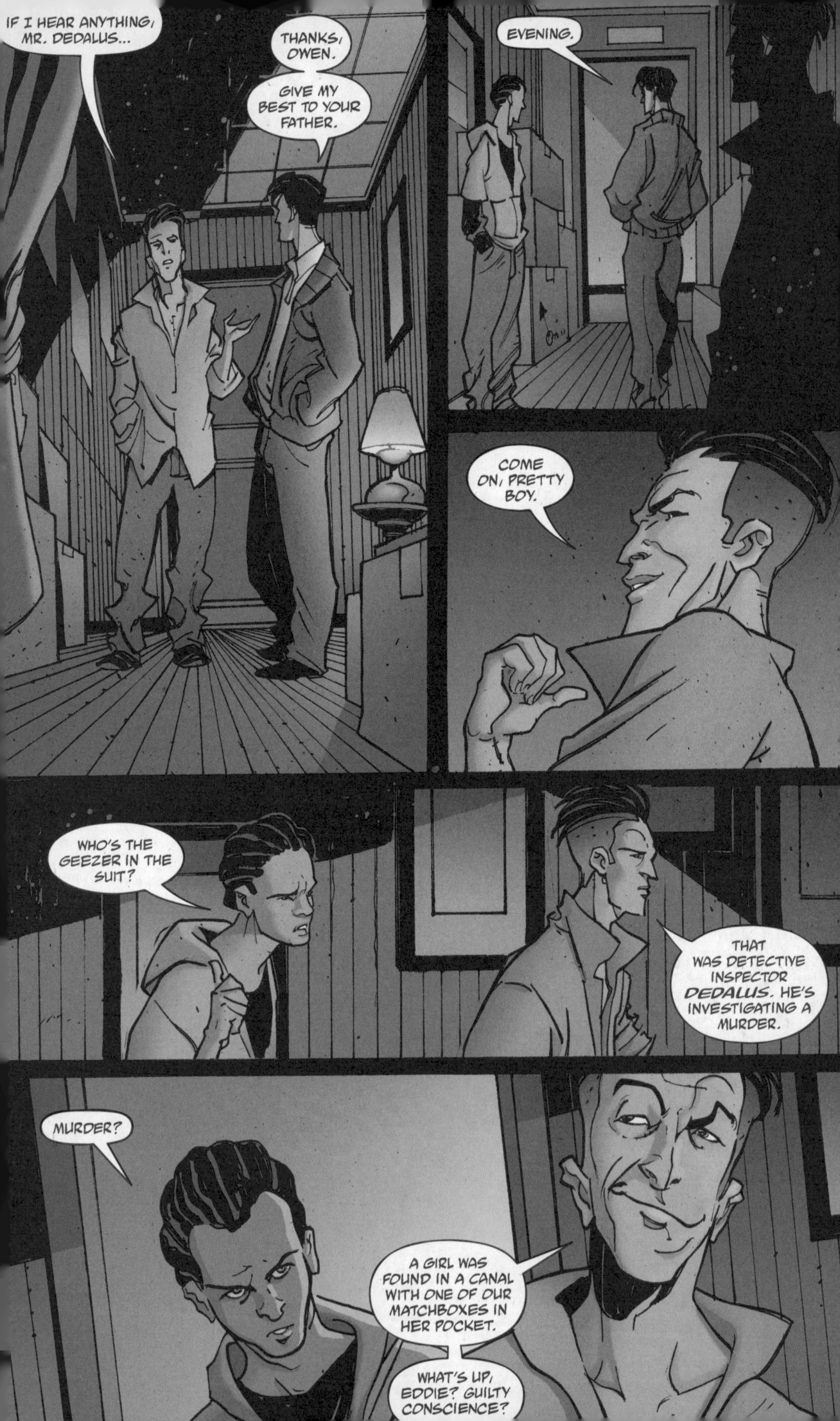
IF I HEAR ANYTHING, MR. DEDALUS...
THANKS, OWEN.
GIVE MY BEST TO YOUR FATHER.
EVENING.
COME ON, PRETTY BOY.
WHO'S THE GEEZER IN THE SUIT?
THAT WAS DETECTIVE INSPECTOR DEDALUS. HE'S INVESTIGATING A MURDER.
MURDER?
A GIRL WAS FOUND IN A CANAL WITH ONE OF OUR MATCHBOXES IN HER POCKET.
WHAT'S UP, EDDIE? GUILTY CONSCIENCE?

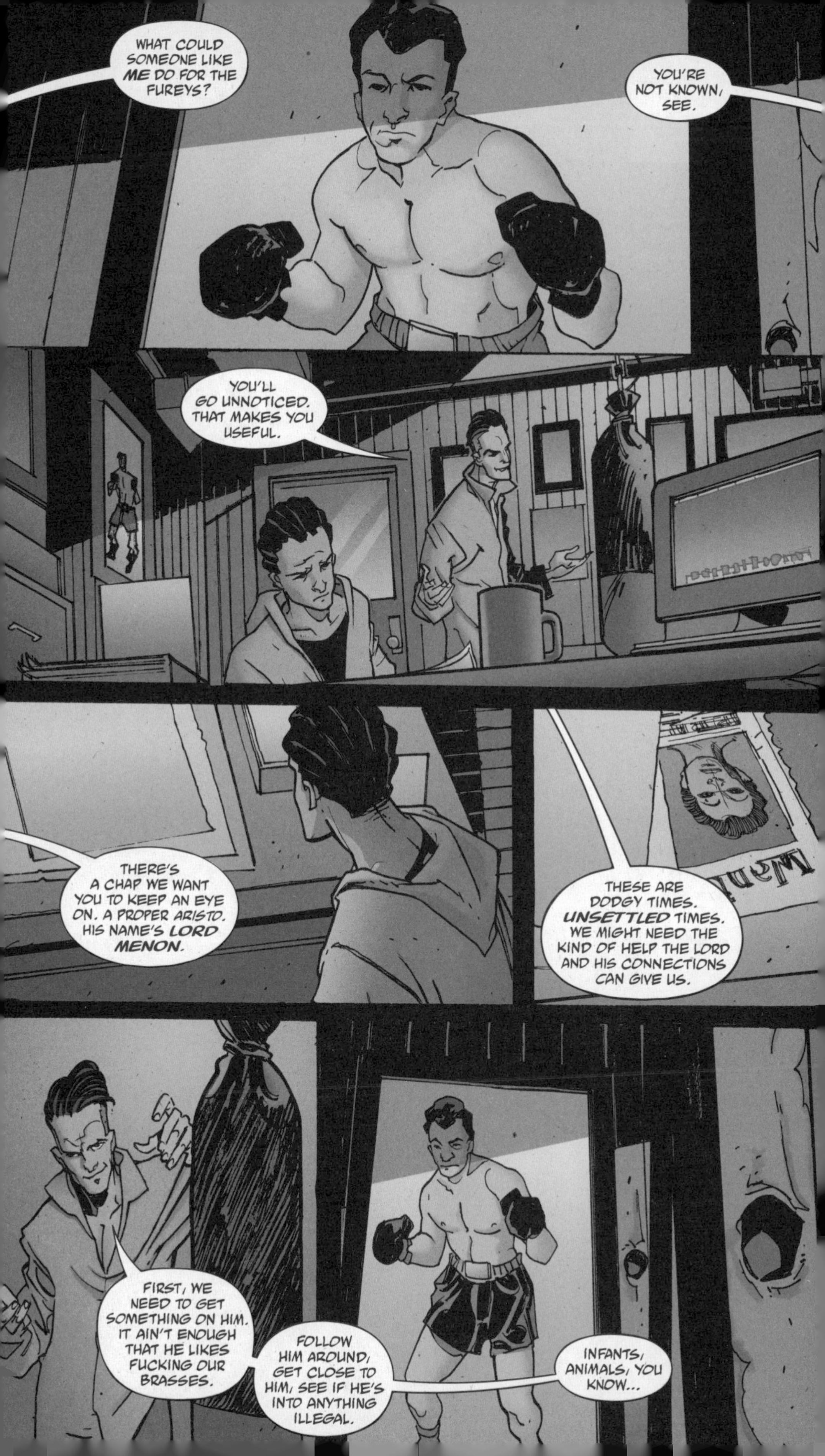

WHAT COULD SOMEONE LIKE ME DO FOR THE FUREYS?
YOU'RE NOT KNOWN, SEE.
YOU'LL GO UNNOTICED. THAT MAKES YOU USEFUL.
THERE'S A CHAP WE WANT YOU TO KEEP AN EYE ON. A PROPER ARISTO. HIS NAME'S LORD MENON.
THESE ARE DODGY TIMES. UNSETTLED TIMES. WE MIGHT NEED THE KIND OF HELP THE LORD AND HIS CONNECTIONS CAN GIVE US.
FIRST, WE NEED TO GET SOMETHING ON HIM. IT AIN'T ENOUGH THAT HE LIKES FUCKING OUR BRASSES.
FOLLOW HIM AROUND, GET CLOSE TO HIM, SEE IF HE'S INTO ANYTHING ILLEGAL.
INFANTS, ANIMALS, YOU KNOW...

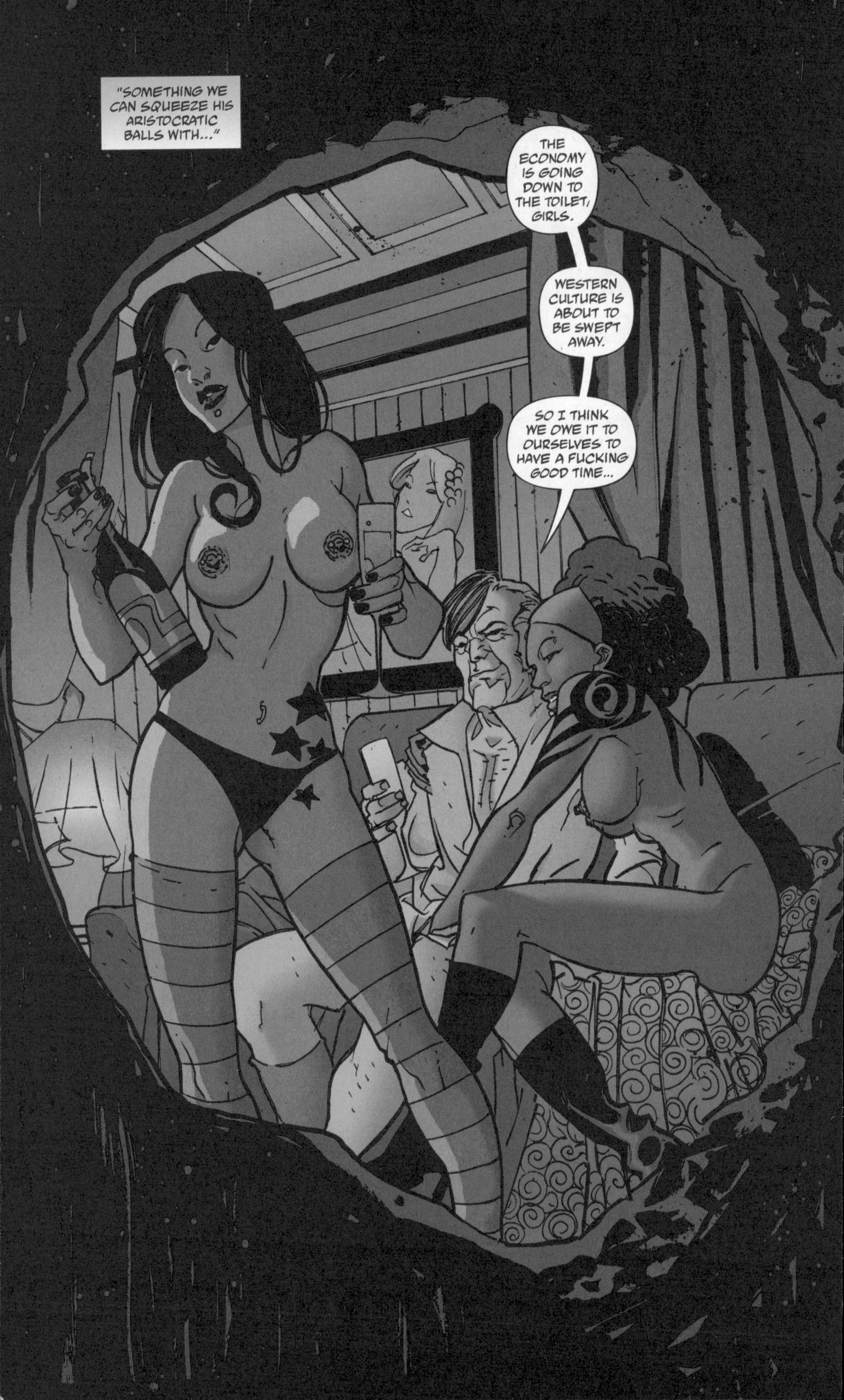
"SOMETHING WE CAN SQUEEZE HIS ARISTOCRATIC BALLS WITH..."
THE ECONOMY IS GOING DOWN TO THE TOILET, GIRLS.
WESTERN CULTURE IS ABOUT TO BE SWEPT AWAY.
SO I THINK WE OWE IT TO OURSELVES TO HAVE A FUCKING GOOD TIME...

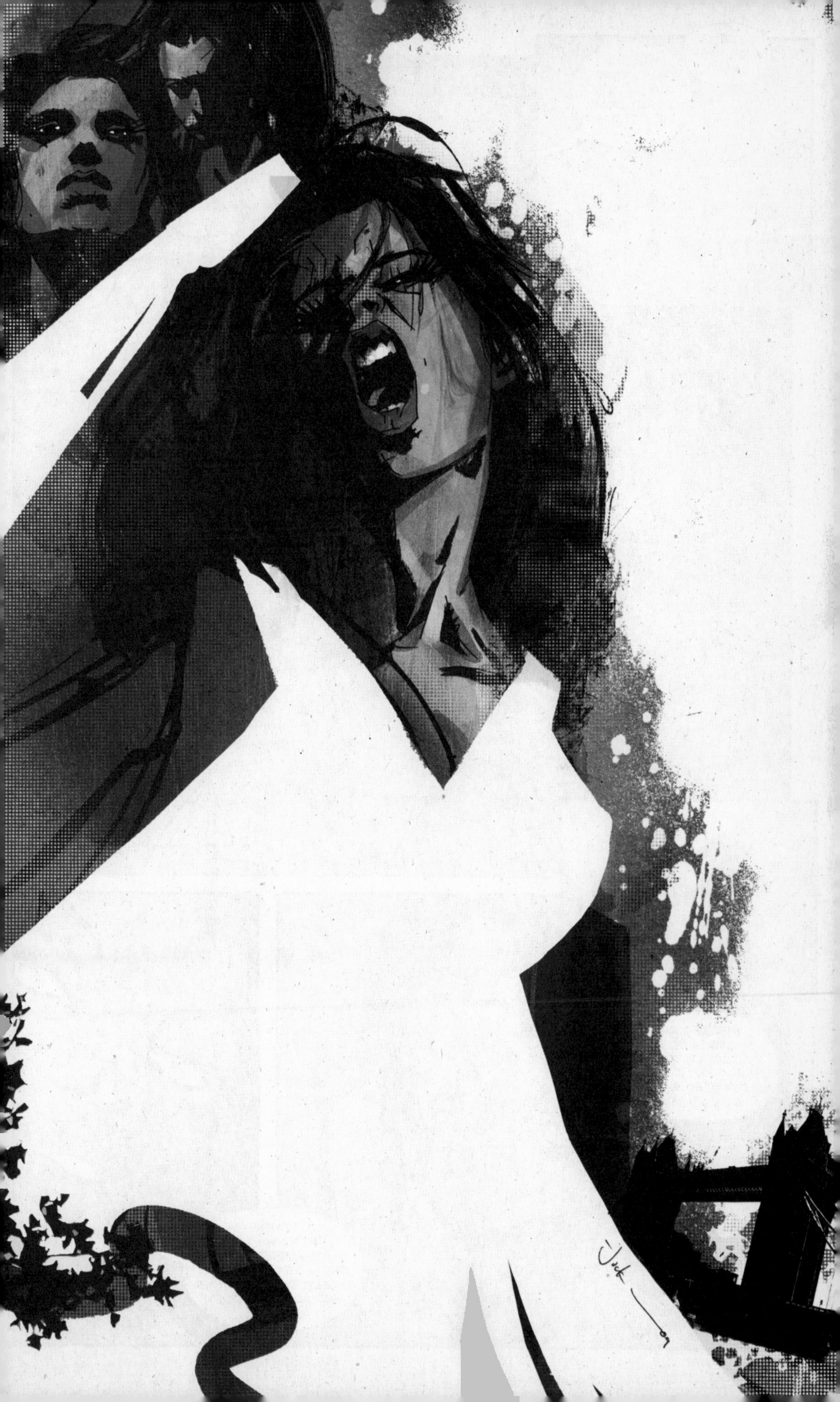

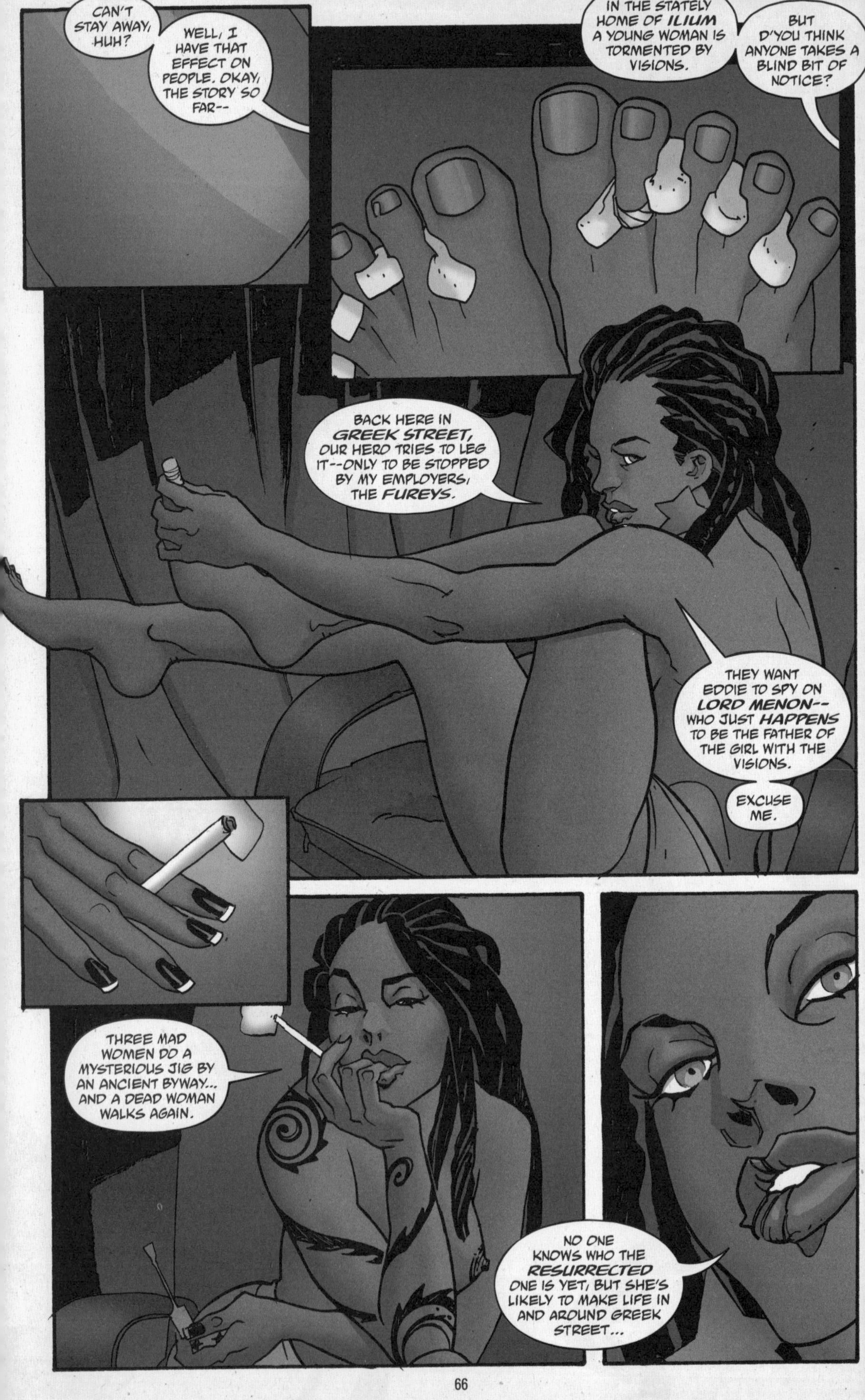

CAN'T STAY AWAY, HUH?
WELL, I HAVE THAT EFFECT ON PEOPLE. OKAY, THE STORY SO FAR--
IN THE STATELY HOME OF ILIUM A YOUNG WOMAN IS TORMENTED BY VISIONS.
BUT D'YOU THINK ANYONE TAKES A BLIND BIT OF NOTICE?
BACK HERE IN GREEK STREET, OUR HERO TRIES TO LEG IT--ONLY TO BE STOPPED BY MY EMPLOYERS, THE FUREYS.
THEY WANT EDDIE TO SPY ON LORD MENON--WHO JUST HAPPENS TO BE THE FATHER OF THE GIRL WITH THE VISIONS.
EXCUSE ME.
THREE MAD WOMEN DO A MYSTERIOUS JIG BY AN ANCIENT BYWAY... AND A DEAD WOMAN WALKS AGAIN.
NO ONE KNOWS WHO THE RESURRECTED ONE IS YET, BUT SHE'S LIKELY TO MAKE LIFE IN AND AROUND GREEK STREET...

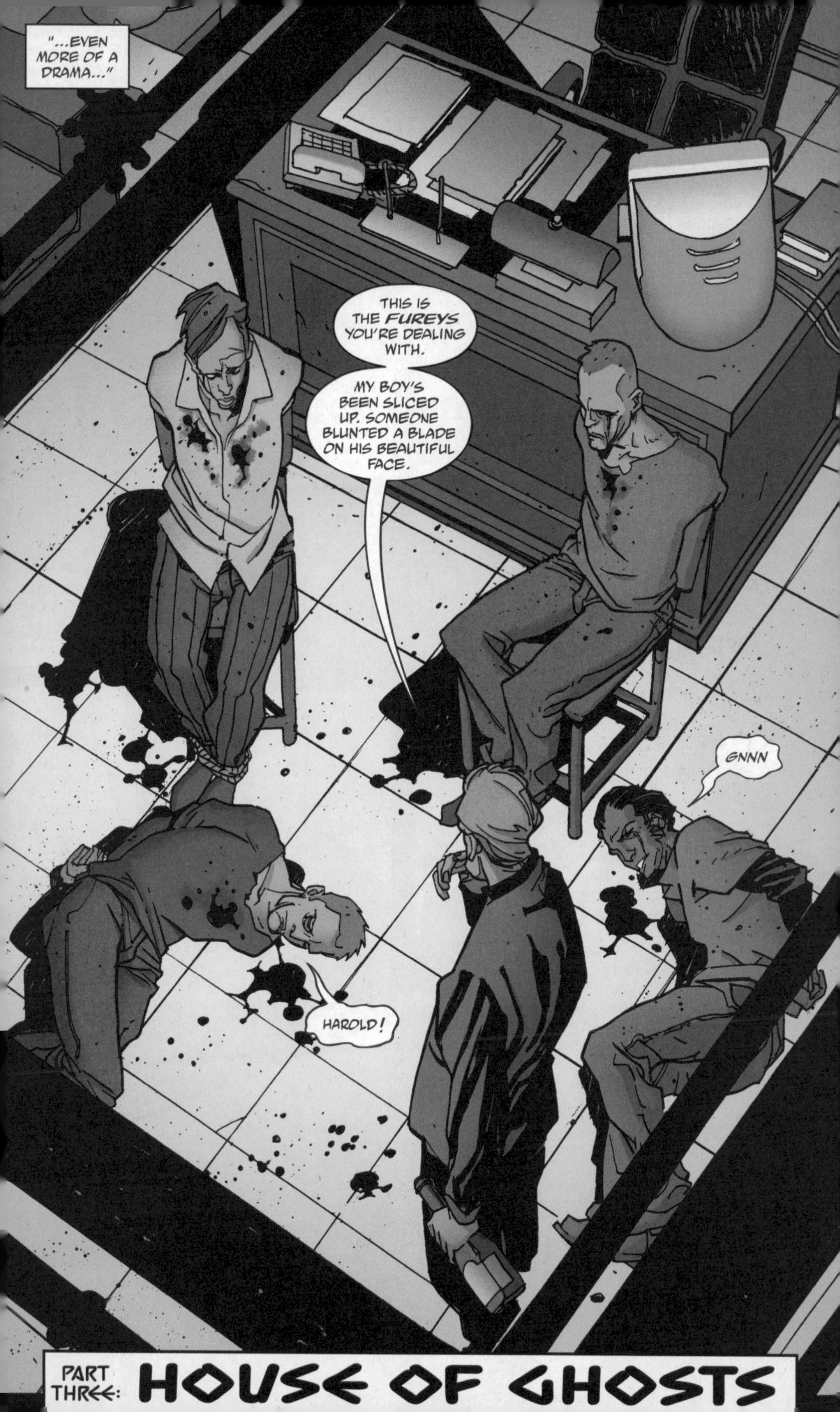
"...EVEN MORE OF A DRAMA..."
THIS IS THE FUREYS YOU'RE DEALING WITH.
MY BOY'S BEEN SLICED UP. SOMEONE BLUNTED A BLADE ON HIS BEAUTIFUL FACE.
GNNN
HAROLD!
PART THREE: HOUSE OF GHOSTS

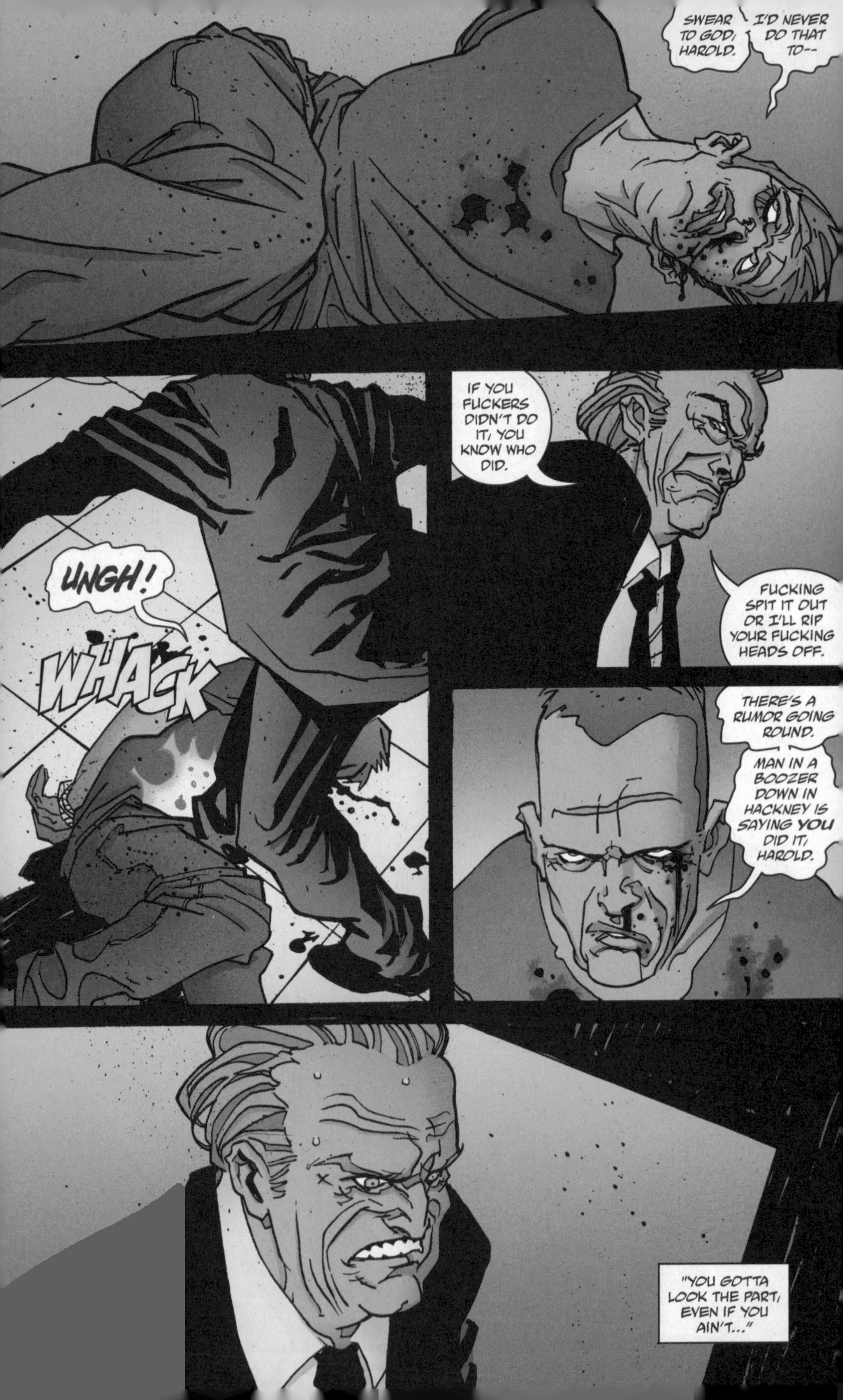

SWEAR TO GOD, HAROLD.
I'D NEVER DO THAT TO--
IF YOU FUCKERS DIDN'T DO IT, YOU KNOW WHO DID.
UNGH!
WHACK
FUCKING SPIT IT OUT OR I'LL RIP YOUR FUCKING HEADS OFF.
THERE'S A RUMOR GOING ROUND.
MAN IN A BOOZER DOWN IN HACKNEY IS SAYING YOU DID IT, HAROLD.
"YOU GOTTA LOOK THE PART, EVEN IF YOU AIN'T..."

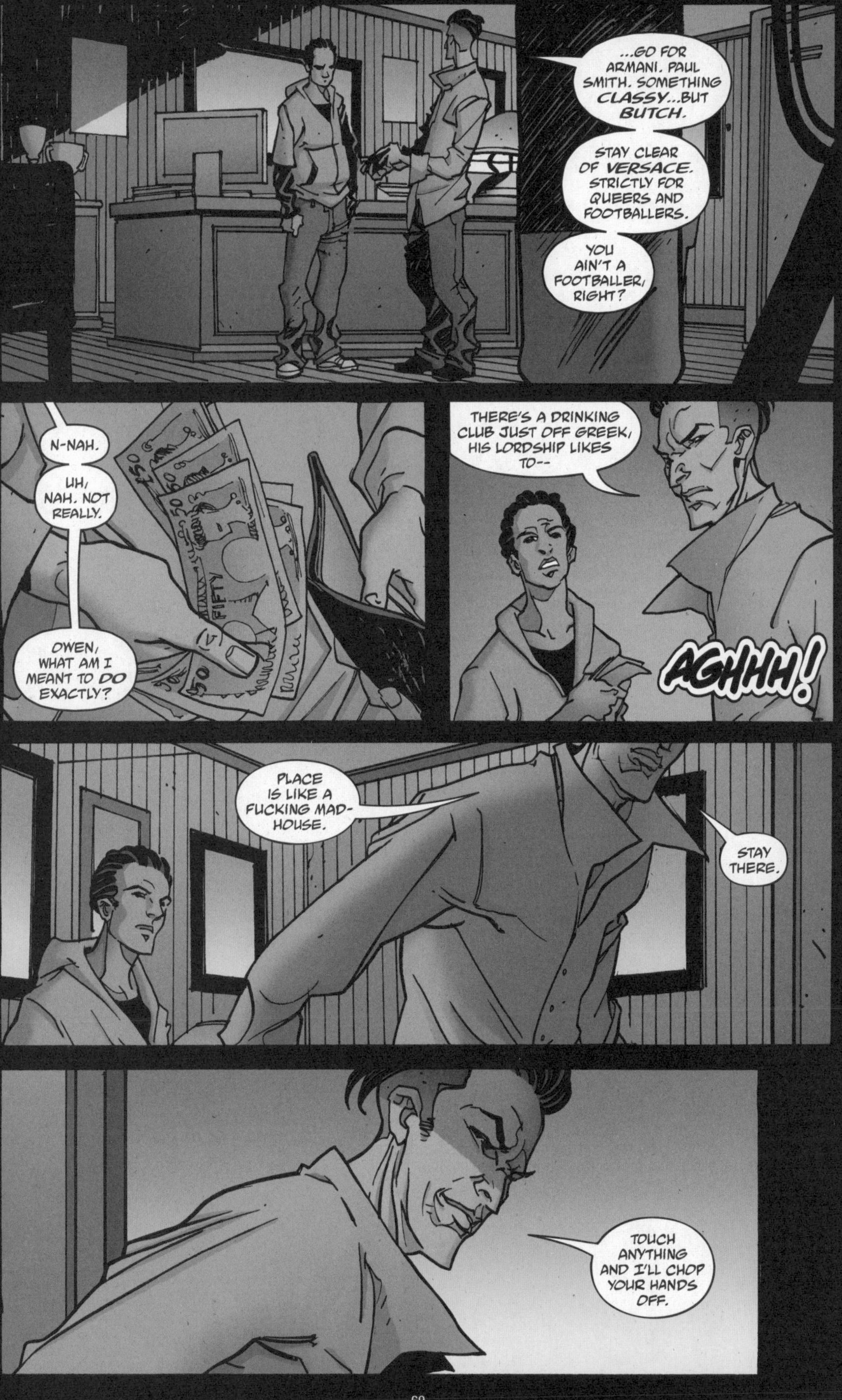
...GO FOR ARMANI. PAUL SMITH. SOMETHING CLASSY...BUT BUTCH.
STAY CLEAR OF VERSACE. STRICTLY FOR QUEERS AND FOOTBALLERS.
YOU AIN'T A FOOTBALLER, RIGHT?
N-NAH.
UH, NAH. NOT REALLY.
OWEN, WHAT AM I MEANT TO DO EXACTLY?
THERE'S A DRINKING CLUB JUST OFF GREEK, HIS LORDSHIP LIKES TO--
AGHHH!
PLACE IS LIKE A FUCKING MAD-HOUSE.
STAY THERE.
TOUCH ANYTHING AND I'LL CHOP YOUR HANDS OFF.

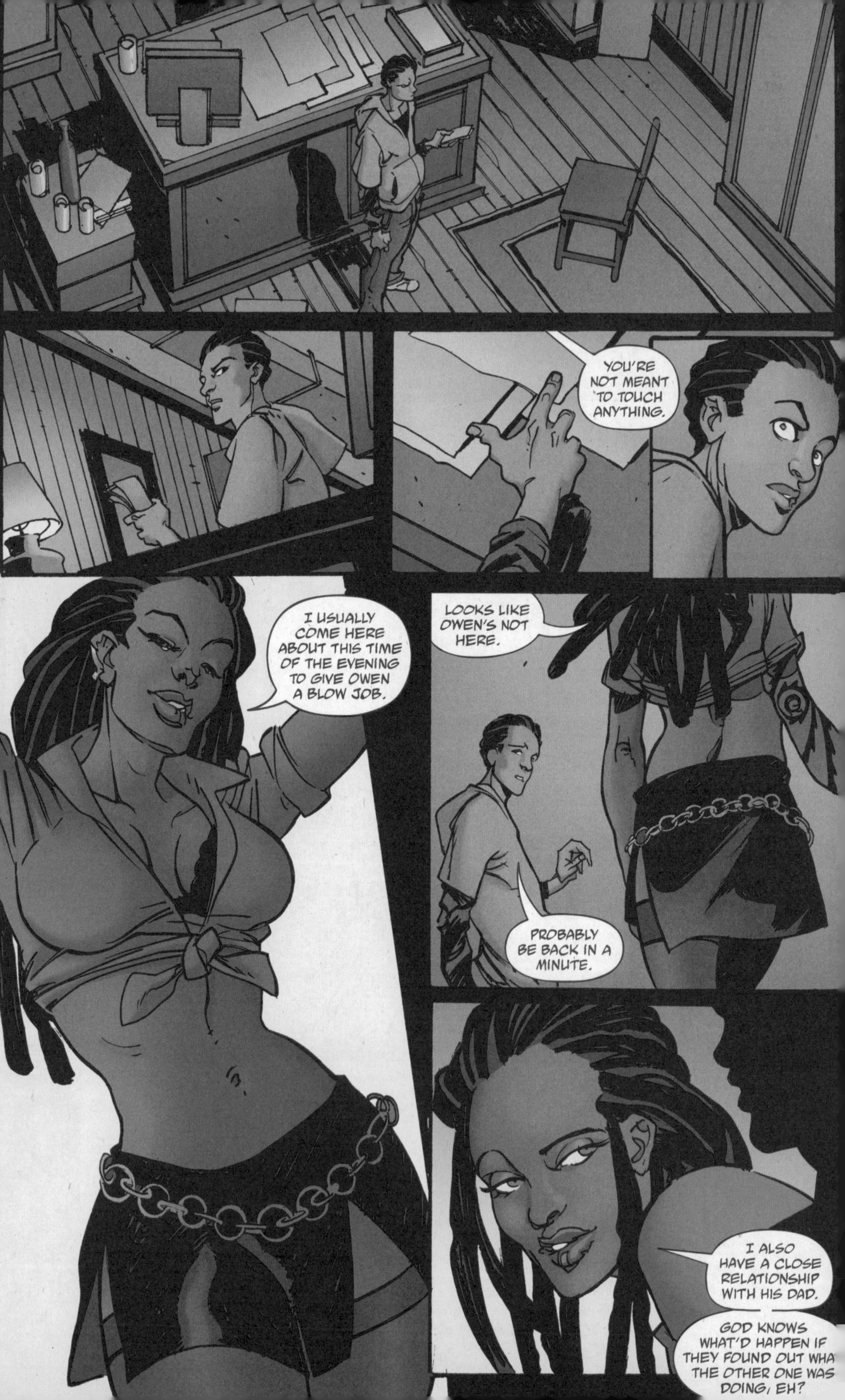

YOU'RE NOT MEANT TO TOUCH ANYTHING.
I USUALLY COME HERE ABOUT THIS TIME OF THE EVENING TO GIVE OWEN A BLOW JOB.
LOOKS LIKE OWEN'S NOT HERE.
PROBABLY BE BACK IN A MINUTE.
I ALSO HAVE A CLOSE RELATIONSHIP WITH HIS DAD.
GOD KNOWS WHAT'D HAPPEN IF THEY FOUND OUT WHA THE OTHER ONE WAS DOING, EH?

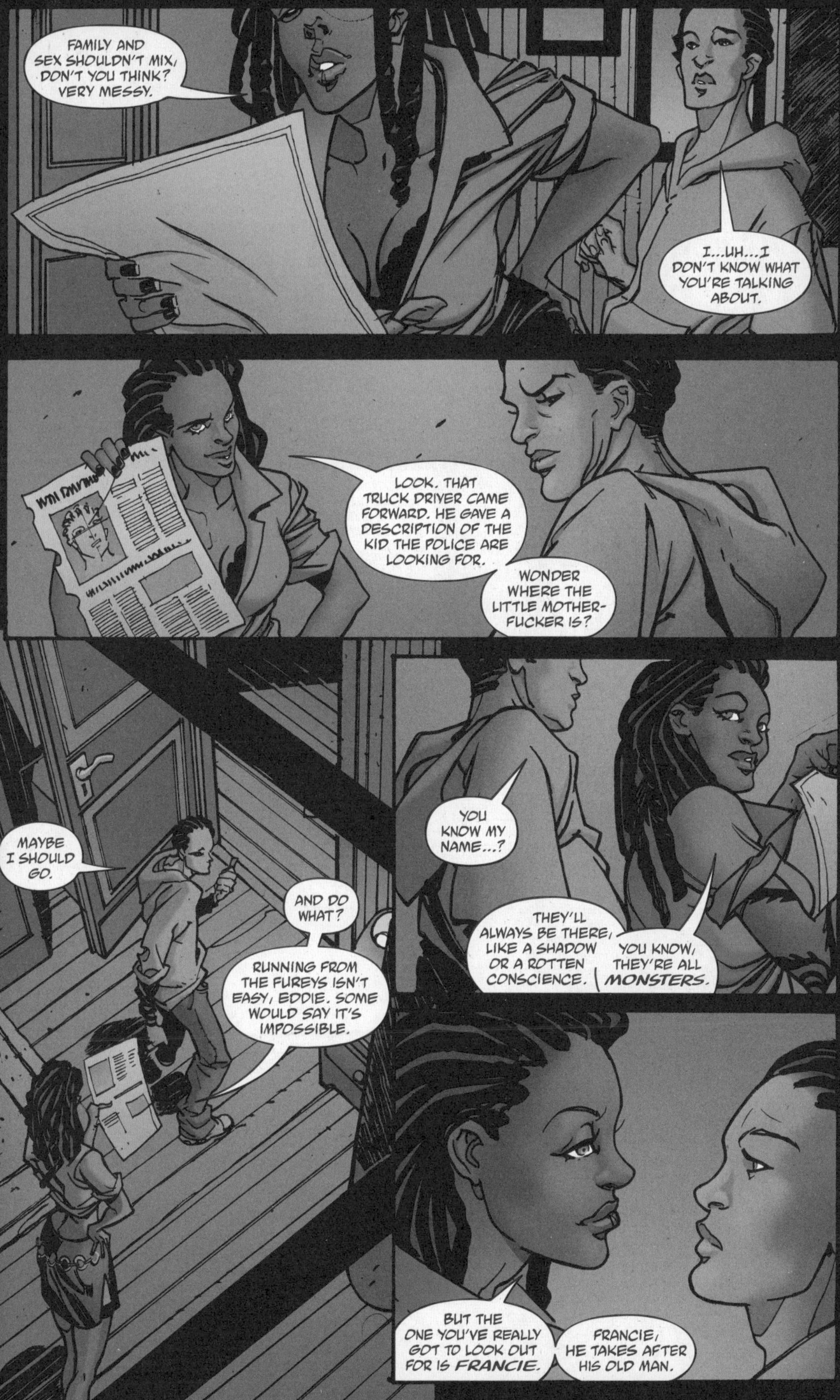

FAMILY AND SEX SHOULDN'T MIX, DON'T YOU THINK? VERY MESSY.
I...UH...I DON'T KNOW WHAT YOU'RE TALKING ABOUT.
LOOK. THAT TRUCK DRIVER CAME FORWARD. HE GAVE A DESCRIPTION OF THE KID THE POLICE ARE LOOKING FOR.
WONDER WHERE THE LITTLE MOTHER-FUCKER IS?
MAYBE I SHOULD GO.
AND DO WHAT?
RUNNING FROM THE FUREYS ISN'T EASY, EDDIE. SOME WOULD SAY IT'S IMPOSSIBLE.
YOU KNOW MY NAME...?
YOU KNOW, THEY'RE ALL *MONSTERS*.
THEY'LL ALWAYS BE THERE, LIKE A SHADOW OR A ROTTEN CONSCIENCE.
BUT THE ONE YOU'VE REALLY GOT TO LOOK OUT FOR IS *FRANCIE*.
FRANCIE, HE TAKES AFTER HIS OLD MAN.

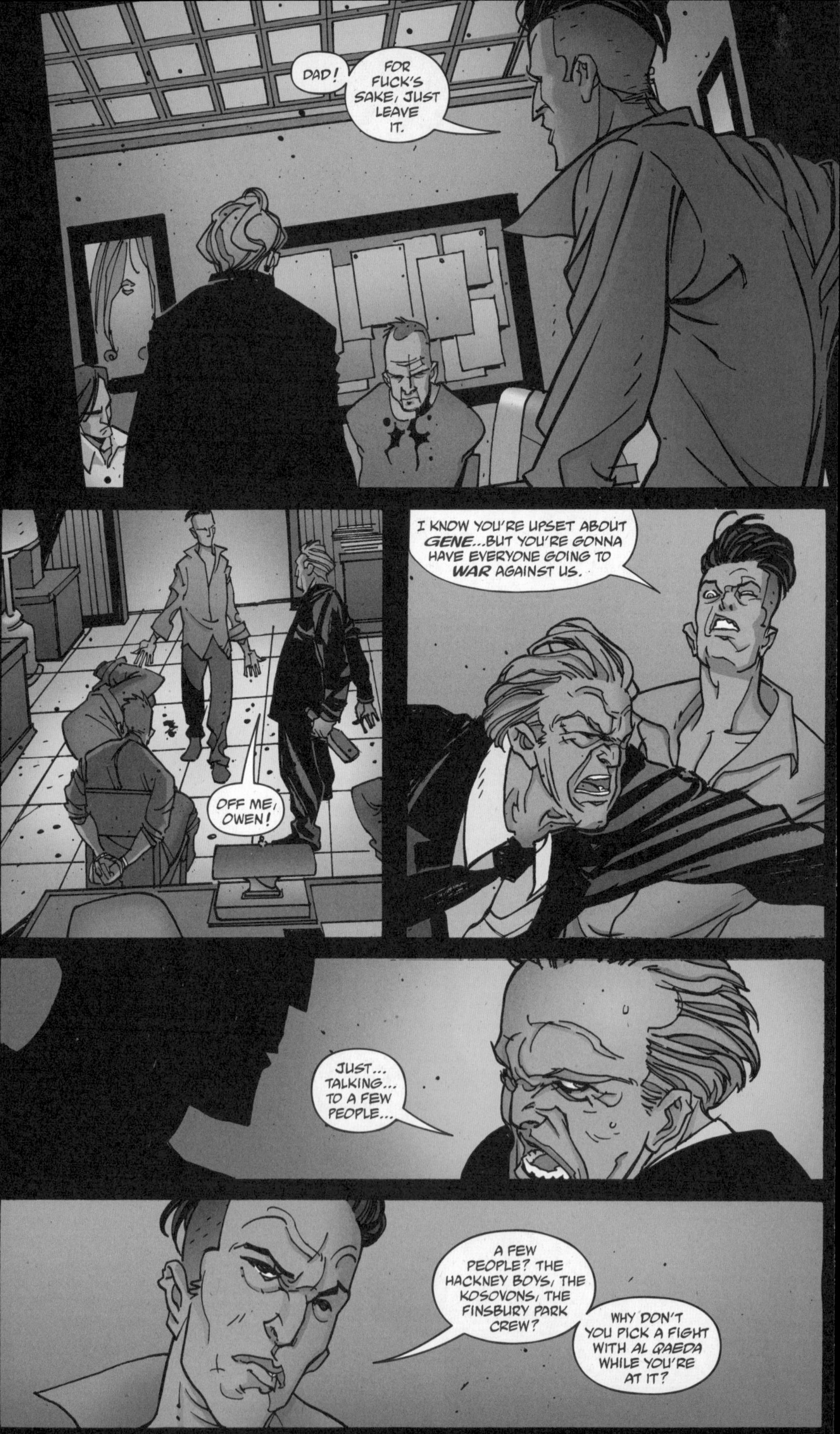
DAD!
FOR FUCK'S SAKE, JUST LEAVE IT.
OFF ME, OWEN!
I KNOW YOU'RE UPSET ABOUT GENE...BUT YOU'RE GONNA HAVE EVERYONE GOING TO WAR AGAINST US.
JUST... TALKING... TO A FEW PEOPLE...
A FEW PEOPLE? THE HACKNEY BOYS, THE KOSOVONS, THE FINSBURY PARK CREW?
WHY DON'T YOU PICK A FIGHT WITH AL QAEDA WHILE YOU'RE AT IT?

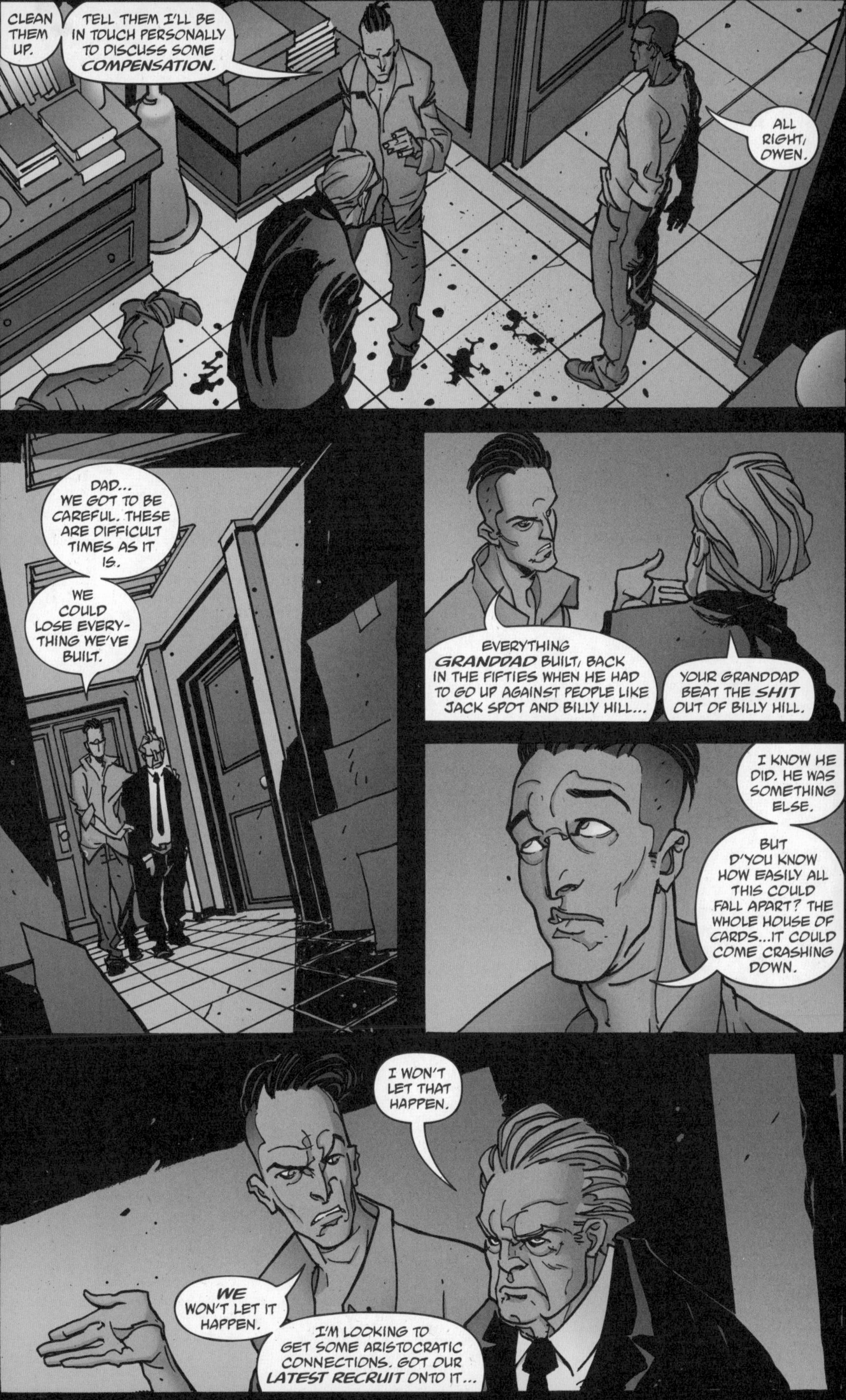
CLEAN THEM UP.
TELL THEM I'LL BE IN TOUCH PERSONALLY TO DISCUSS SOME COMPENSATION.
ALL RIGHT, OWEN.
DAD... WE GOT TO BE CAREFUL. THESE ARE DIFFICULT TIMES AS IT IS.
WE COULD LOSE EVERY-THING WE'VE BUILT.
EVERYTHING GRANDDAD BUILT, BACK IN THE FIFTIES WHEN HE HAD TO GO UP AGAINST PEOPLE LIKE JACK SPOT AND BILLY HILL...
YOUR GRANDDAD BEAT THE SHIT OUT OF BILLY HILL.
I KNOW HE DID. HE WAS SOMETHING ELSE.
BUT D'YOU KNOW HOW EASILY ALL THIS COULD FALL APART? THE WHOLE HOUSE OF CARDS...IT COULD COME CRASHING DOWN.
I WON'T LET THAT HAPPEN.
WE WON'T LET IT HAPPEN.
I'M LOOKING TO GET SOME ARISTOCRATIC CONNECTIONS. GOT OUR LATEST RECRUIT ONTO IT...

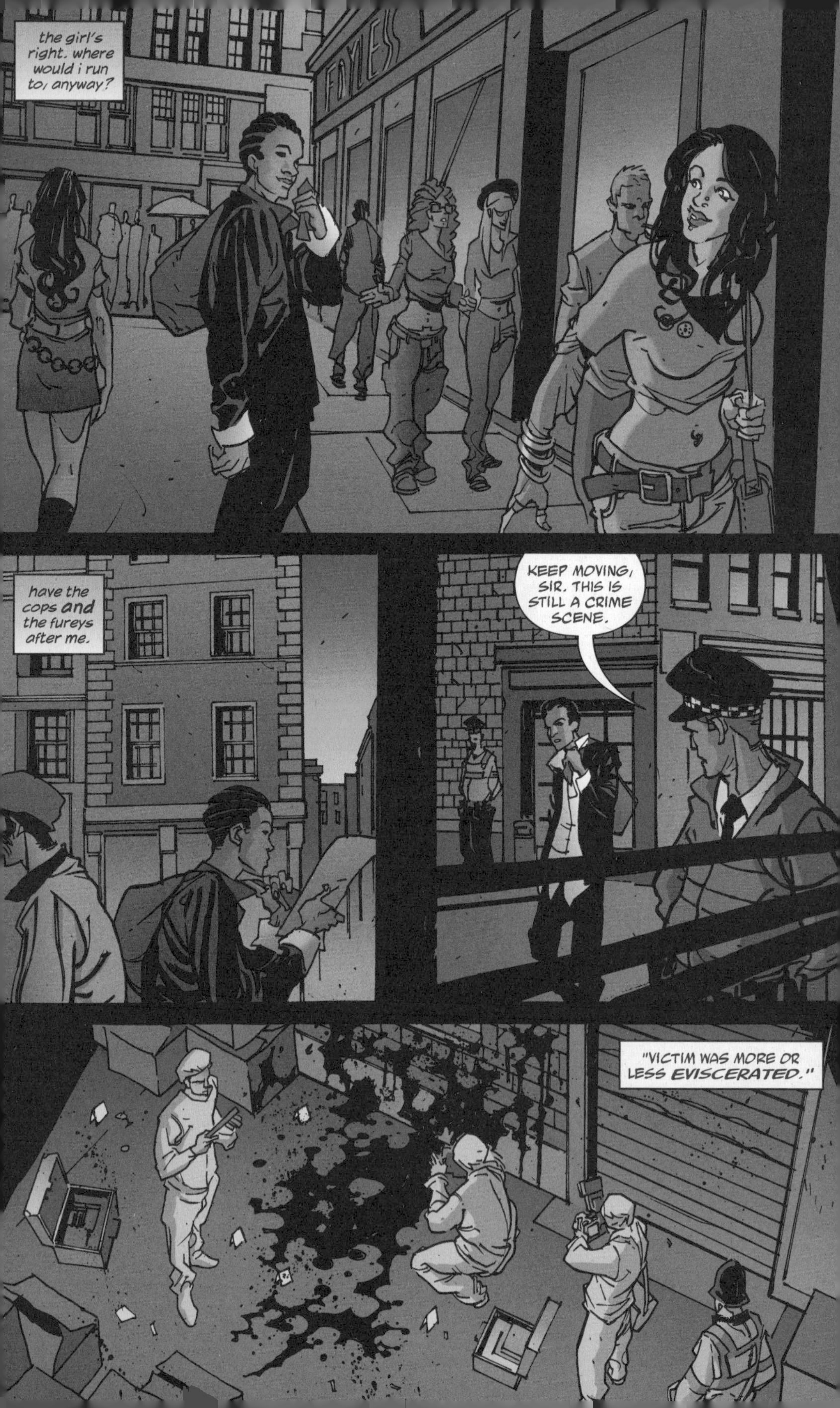

the girl's right. where would i run to, anyway?
FOYLES
have the cops and the fureys after me.
KEEP MOVING, SIR. THIS IS STILL A CRIME SCENE.
"VICTIM WAS MORE OR LESS EVISCERATED."

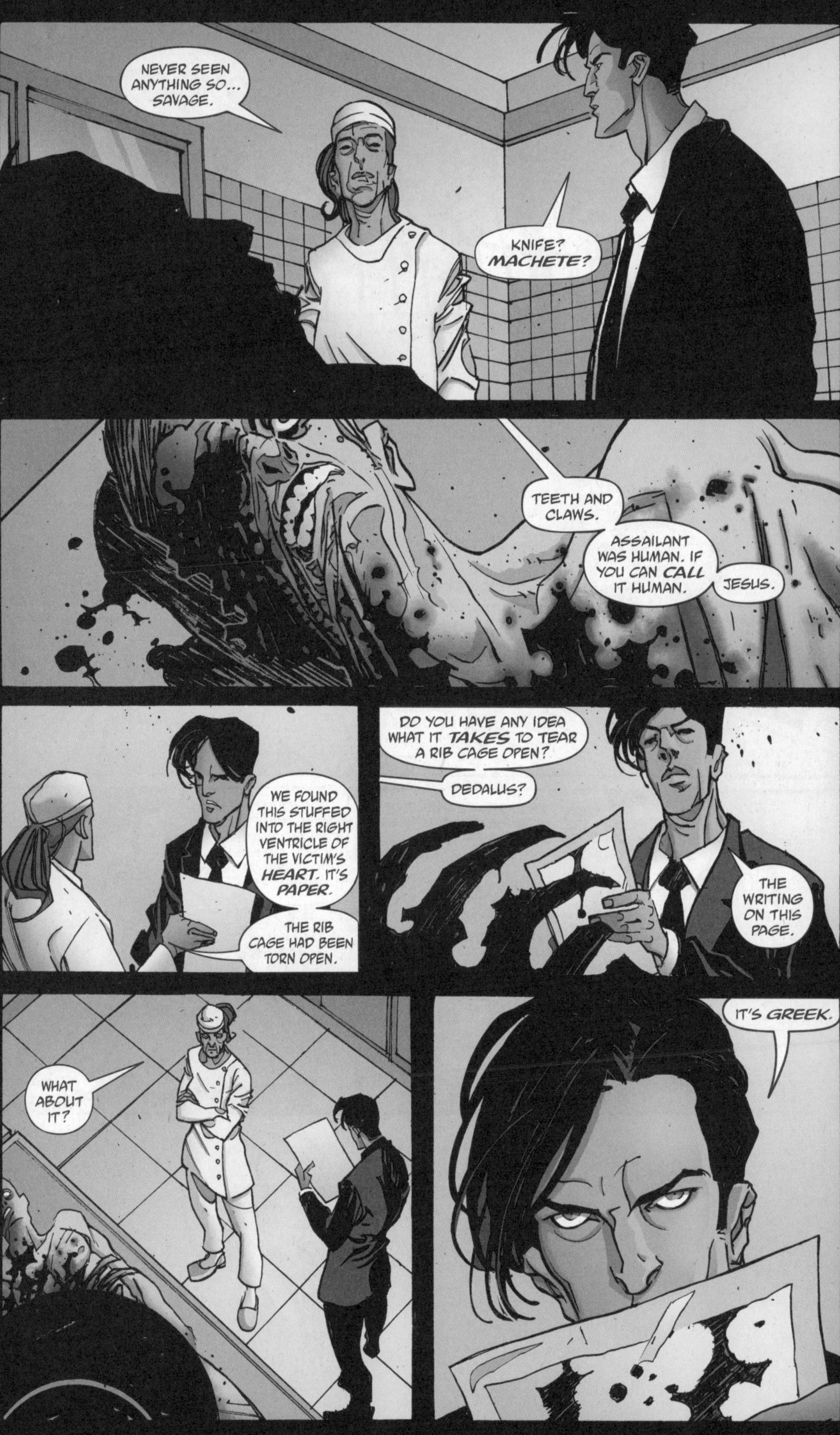
NEVER SEEN ANYTHING SO... SAVAGE.
KNIFE? MACHETE?
TEETH AND CLAWS.
ASSAILANT WAS HUMAN. IF YOU CAN CALL IT HUMAN.
JESUS.
WE FOUND THIS STUFFED INTO THE RIGHT VENTRICLE OF THE VICTIM'S HEART. IT'S PAPER.
THE RIB CAGE HAD BEEN TORN OPEN.
DO YOU HAVE ANY IDEA WHAT IT TAKES TO TEAR A RIB CAGE OPEN?
DEDALUS?
THE WRITING ON THIS PAGE.
WHAT ABOUT IT?
IT'S GREEK.

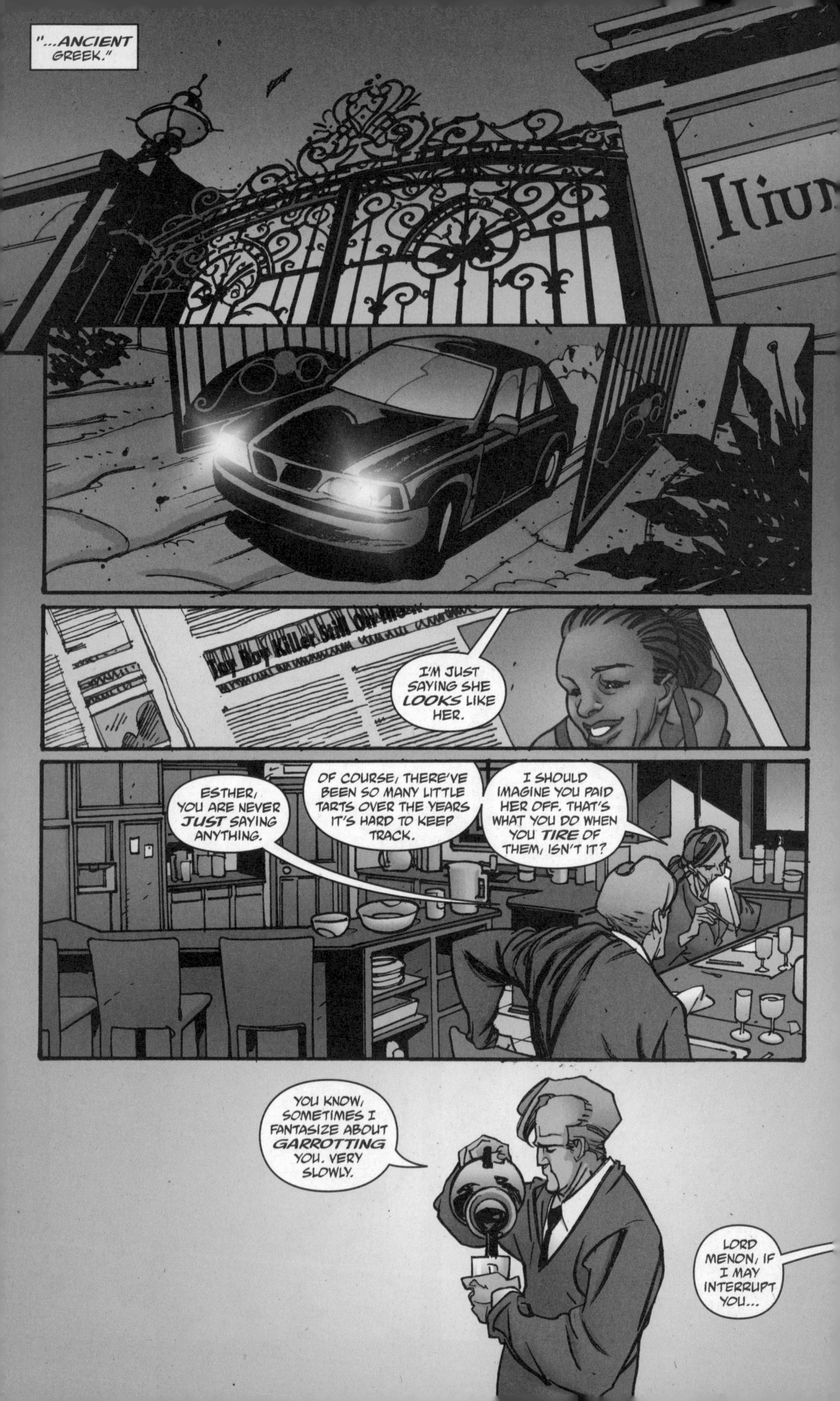
"...ANCIENT GREEK."
I'M JUST SAYING SHE LOOKS LIKE HER.
ESTHER, YOU ARE NEVER JUST SAYING ANYTHING.
OF COURSE, THERE'VE BEEN SO MANY LITTLE TARTS OVER THE YEARS IT'S HARD TO KEEP TRACK.
I SHOULD IMAGINE YOU PAID HER OFF. THAT'S WHAT YOU DO WHEN YOU TIRE OF THEM, ISN'T IT?
YOU KNOW, SOMETIMES I FANTASIZE ABOUT GARROTTING YOU. VERY SLOWLY.
LORD MENON, IF I MAY INTERRUPT YOU...

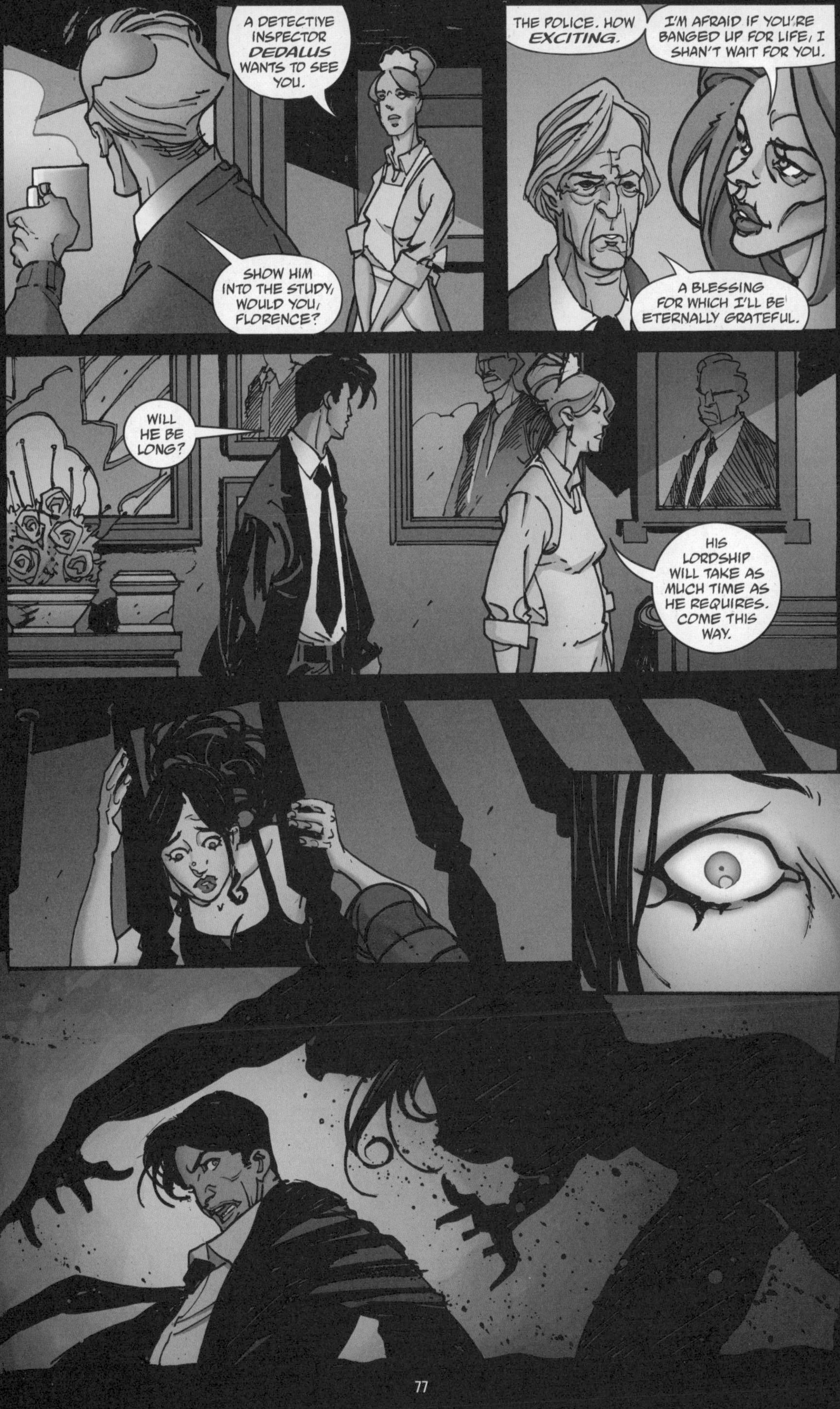
A DETECTIVE INSPECTOR DEDALUS WANTS TO SEE YOU.
SHOW HIM INTO THE STUDY, WOULD YOU, FLORENCE?
THE POLICE. HOW EXCITING.
I'M AFRAID IF YOU'RE BANGED UP FOR LIFE, I SHAN'T WAIT FOR YOU.
A BLESSING FOR WHICH I'LL BE ETERNALLY GRATEFUL.
WILL HE BE LONG?
HIS LORDSHIP WILL TAKE AS MUCH TIME AS HE REQUIRES. COME THIS WAY.

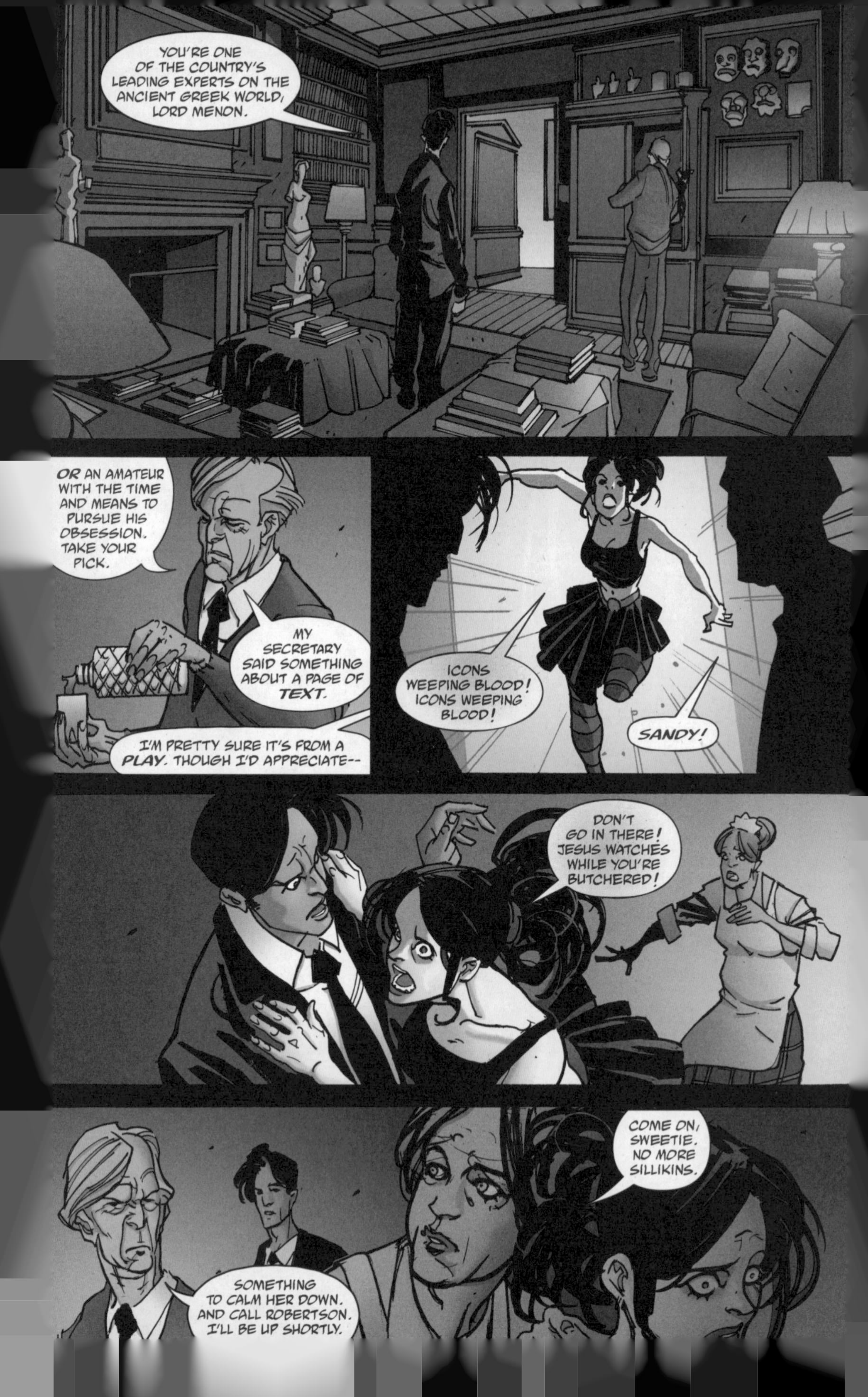
YOU'RE ONE OF THE COUNTRY'S LEADING EXPERTS ON THE ANCIENT GREEK WORLD, LORD MENON.
OR AN AMATEUR WITH THE TIME AND MEANS TO PURSUE HIS OBSESSION. TAKE YOUR PICK.
MY SECRETARY SAID SOMETHING ABOUT A PAGE OF TEXT.
I'M PRETTY SURE IT'S FROM A PLAY. THOUGH I'D APPRECIATE--
ICONS WEEPING BLOOD! ICONS WEEPING BLOOD!
SANDY!
DON'T GO IN THERE! JESUS WATCHES WHILE YOU'RE BUTCHERED!
COME ON, SWEETIE. NO MORE SILLIKINS.
SOMETHING TO CALM HER DOWN. AND CALL ROBERTSON. I'LL BE UP SHORTLY.

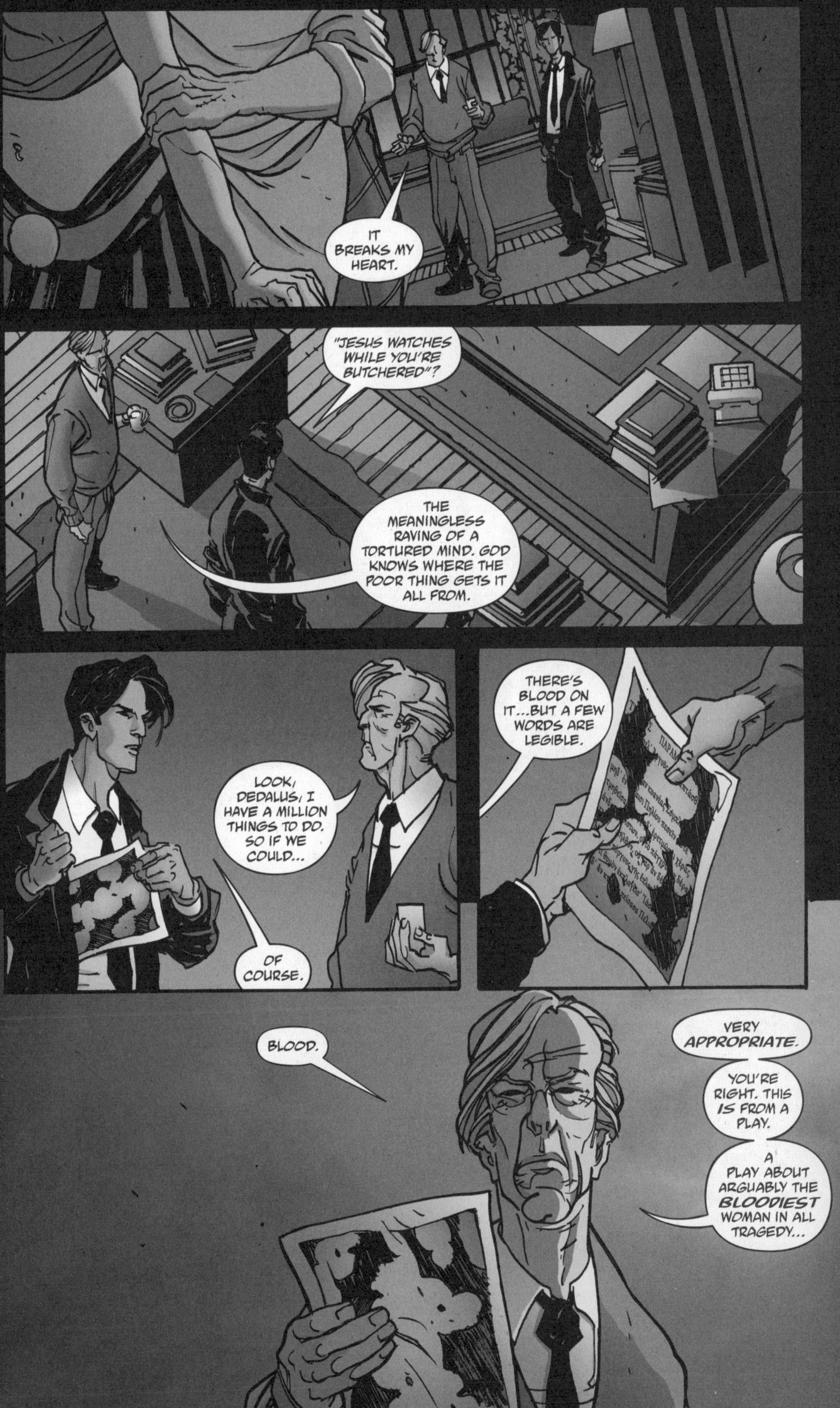

IT BREAKS MY HEART.
"JESUS WATCHES WHILE YOU'RE BUTCHERED"?
THE MEANINGLESS RAVING OF A TORTURED MIND. GOD KNOWS WHERE THE POOR THING GETS IT ALL FROM.
LOOK, DEDALUS, I HAVE A MILLION THINGS TO DO. SO IF WE COULD...
OF COURSE.
THERE'S BLOOD ON IT...BUT A FEW WORDS ARE LEGIBLE.
BLOOD.
VERY *APPROPRIATE.*
YOU'RE RIGHT. THIS *IS* FROM A PLAY.
A PLAY ABOUT ARGUABLY THE *BLOODIEST* WOMAN IN ALL TRAGEDY...

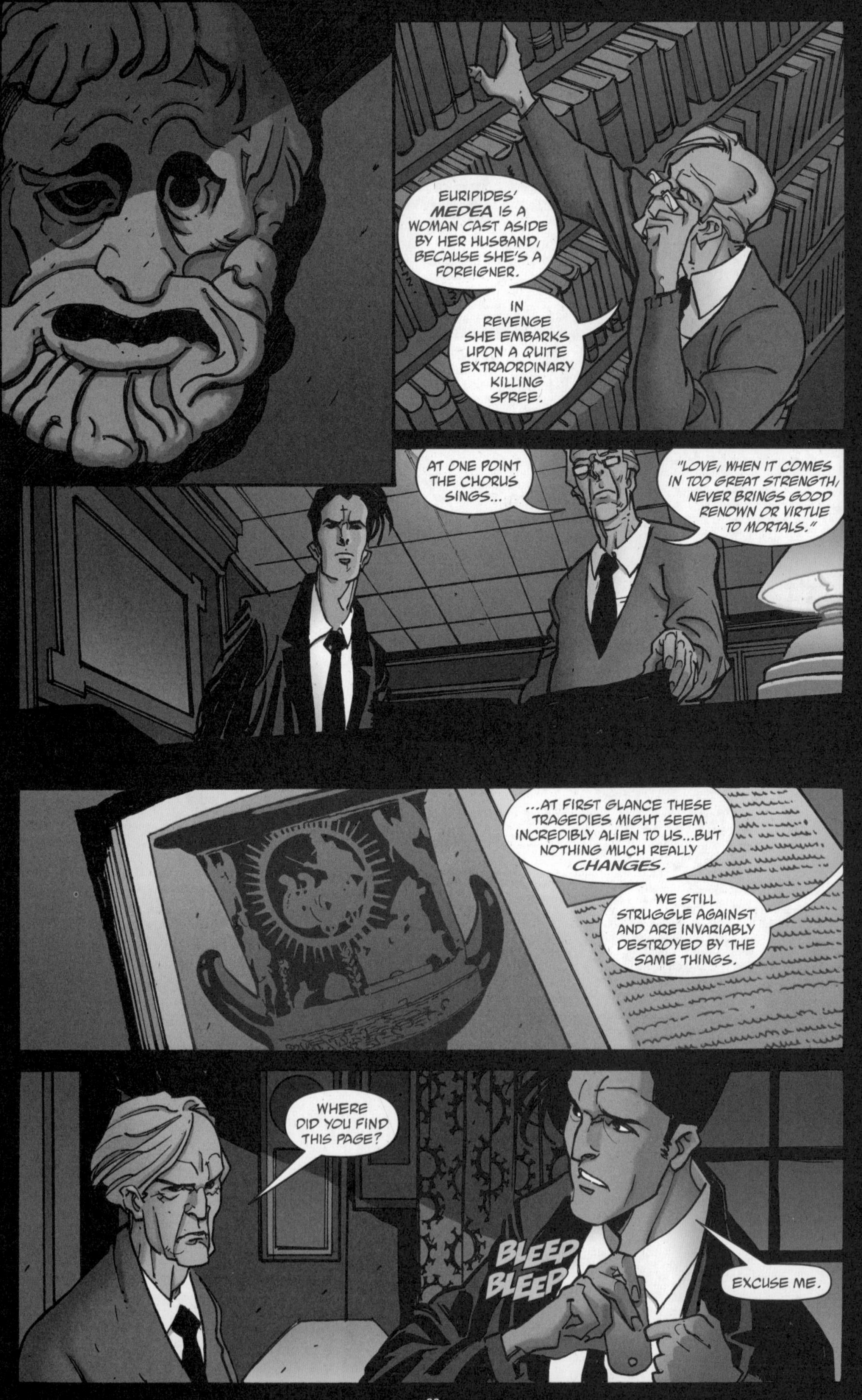
EURIPIDES' MEDEA IS A WOMAN CAST ASIDE BY HER HUSBAND, BECAUSE SHE'S A FOREIGNER.
IN REVENGE SHE EMBARKS UPON A QUITE EXTRAORDINARY KILLING SPREE.
AT ONE POINT THE CHORUS SINGS...
"LOVE, WHEN IT COMES IN TOO GREAT STRENGTH, NEVER BRINGS GOOD RENOWN OR VIRTUE TO MORTALS."
...AT FIRST GLANCE THESE TRAGEDIES MIGHT SEEM INCREDIBLY ALIEN TO US...BUT NOTHING MUCH REALLY CHANGES.
WE STILL STRUGGLE AGAINST AND ARE INVARIABLY DESTROYED BY THE SAME THINGS.
WHERE DID YOU FIND THIS PAGE?
BLEEP BLEEP
EXCUSE ME.

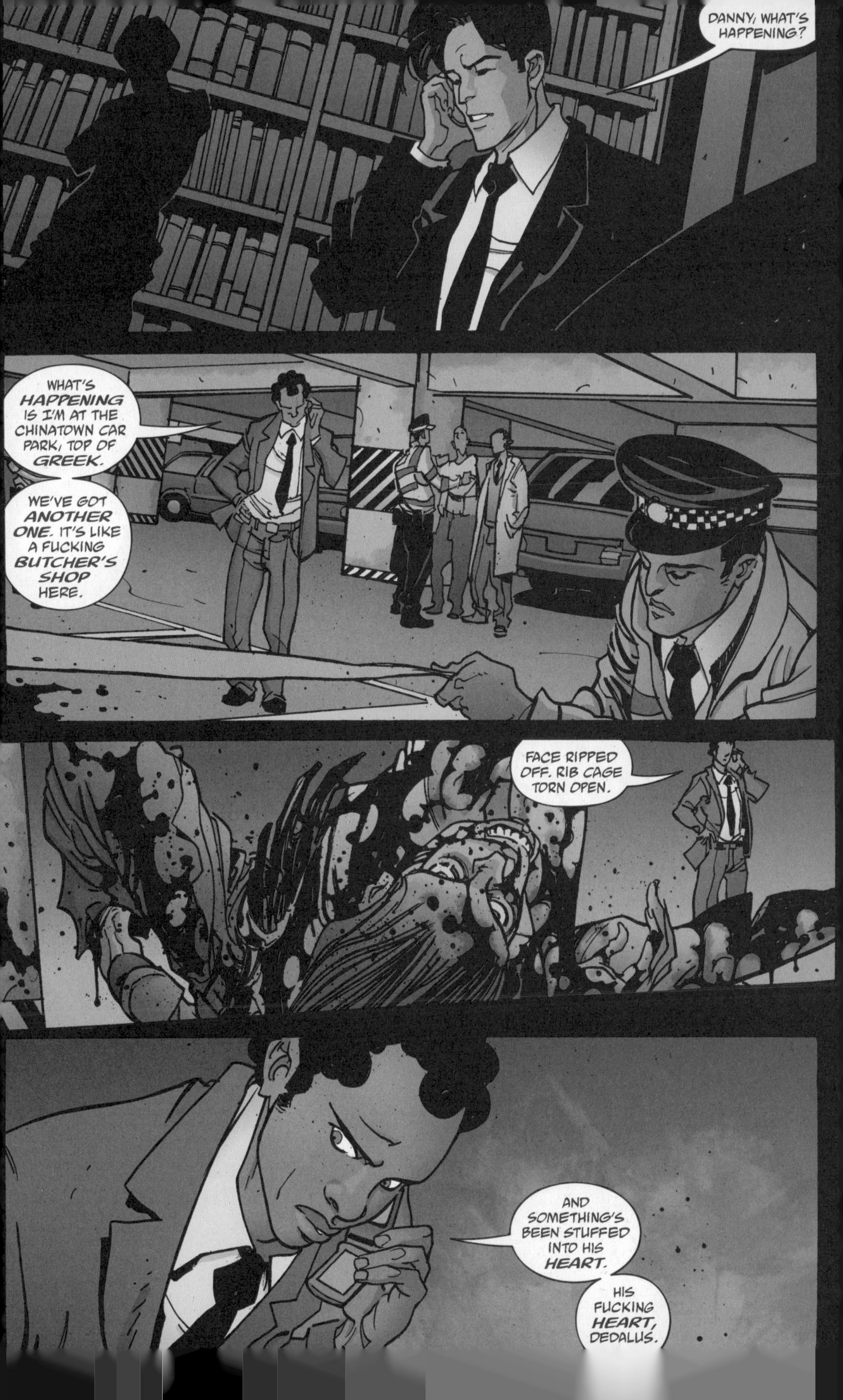
DANNY, WHAT'S HAPPENING?
WHAT'S HAPPENING IS I'M AT THE CHINATOWN CAR PARK, TOP OF GREEK.
WE'VE GOT ANOTHER ONE. IT'S LIKE A FUCKING BUTCHER'S SHOP HERE.
FACE RIPPED OFF. RIB CAGE TORN OPEN.
AND SOMETHING'S BEEN STUFFED INTO HIS HEART.
HIS FUCKING HEART, DEDALUS.

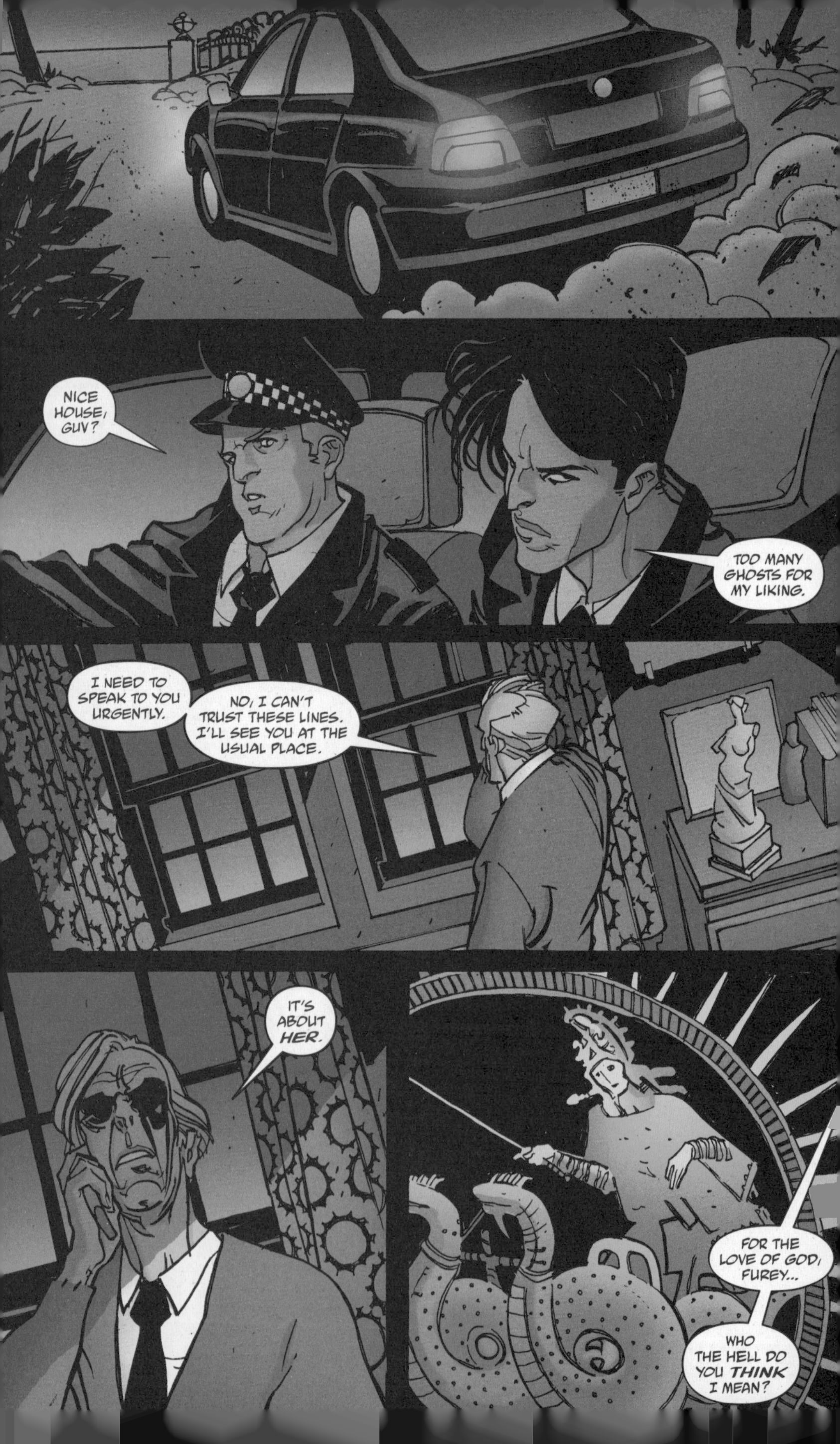

NICE HOUSE, GUV?
TOO MANY GHOSTS FOR MY LIKING.
I NEED TO SPEAK TO YOU URGENTLY.
NO, I CAN'T TRUST THESE LINES. I'LL SEE YOU AT THE USUAL PLACE.
IT'S ABOUT HER.
FOR THE LOVE OF GOD, FUREY...
WHO THE HELL DO YOU THINK I MEAN?

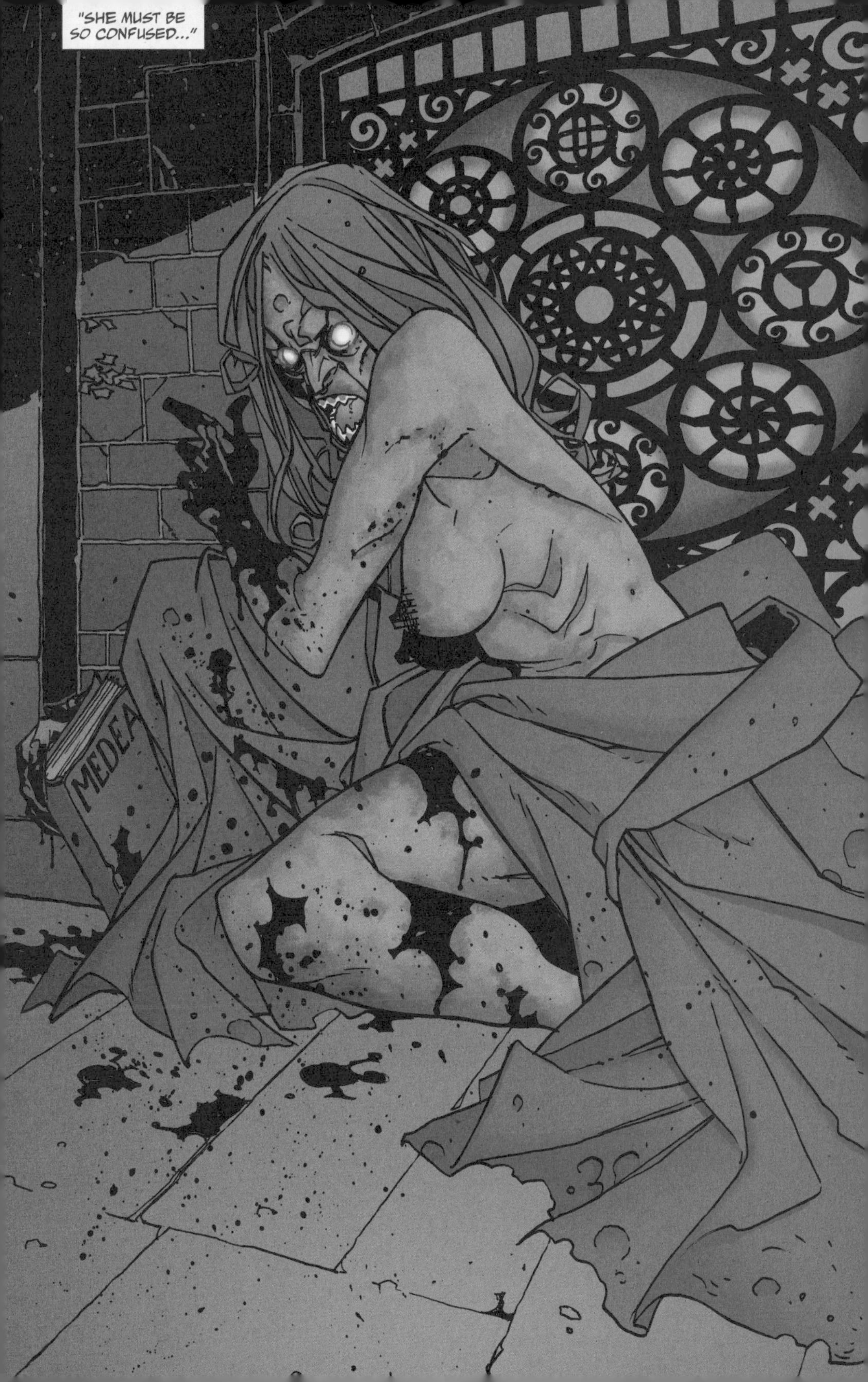
"SHE MUST BE SO CONFUSED..."
MEDEA

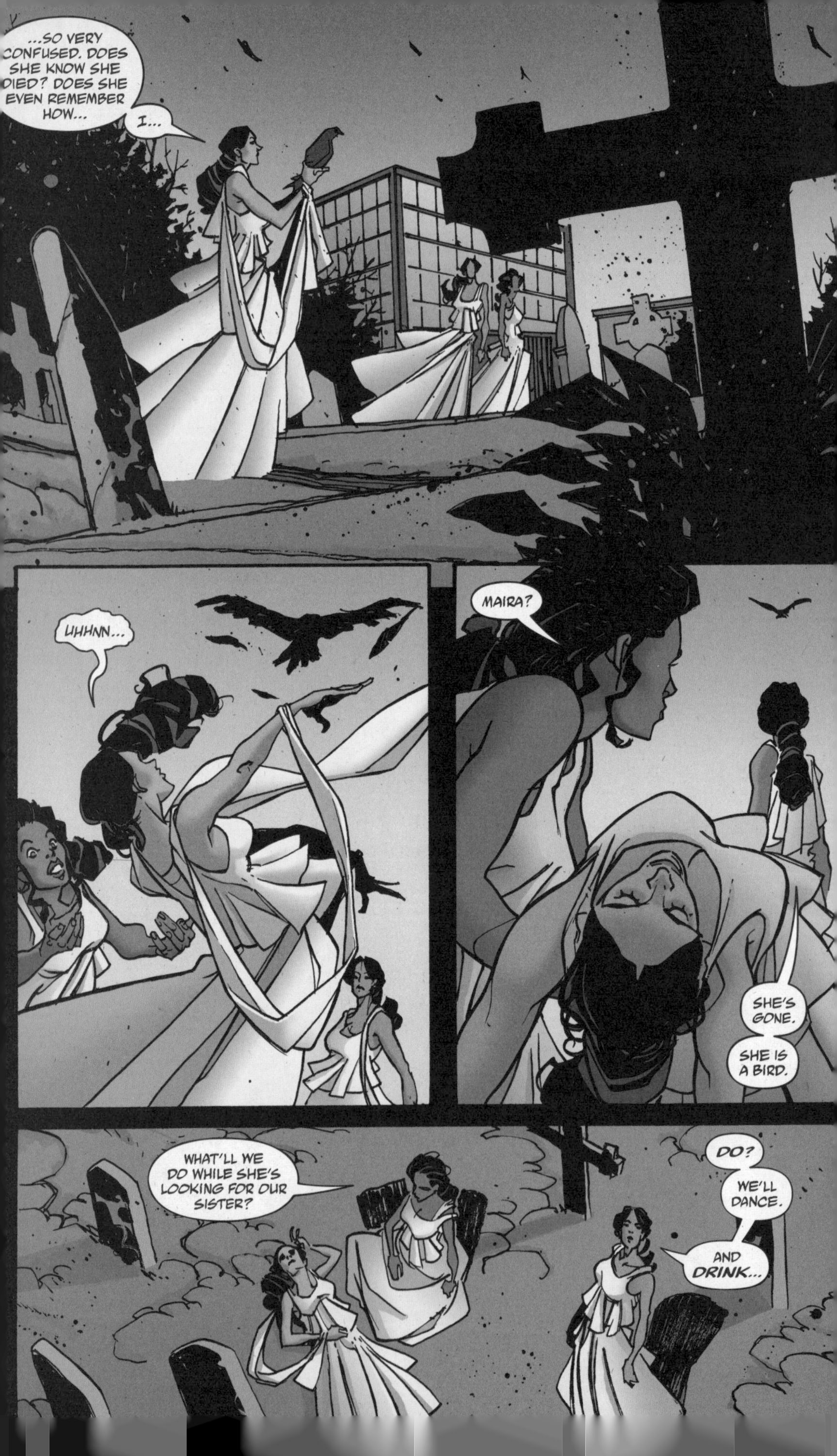
...SO VERY CONFUSED. DOES SHE KNOW SHE DIED? DOES SHE EVEN REMEMBER HOW...
I...
UHHNN...
MAIRA?
SHE'S GONE.
SHE IS A BIRD.
WHAT'LL WE DO WHILE SHE'S LOOKING FOR OUR SISTER?
DO?
WE'LL DANCE.
AND DRINK...

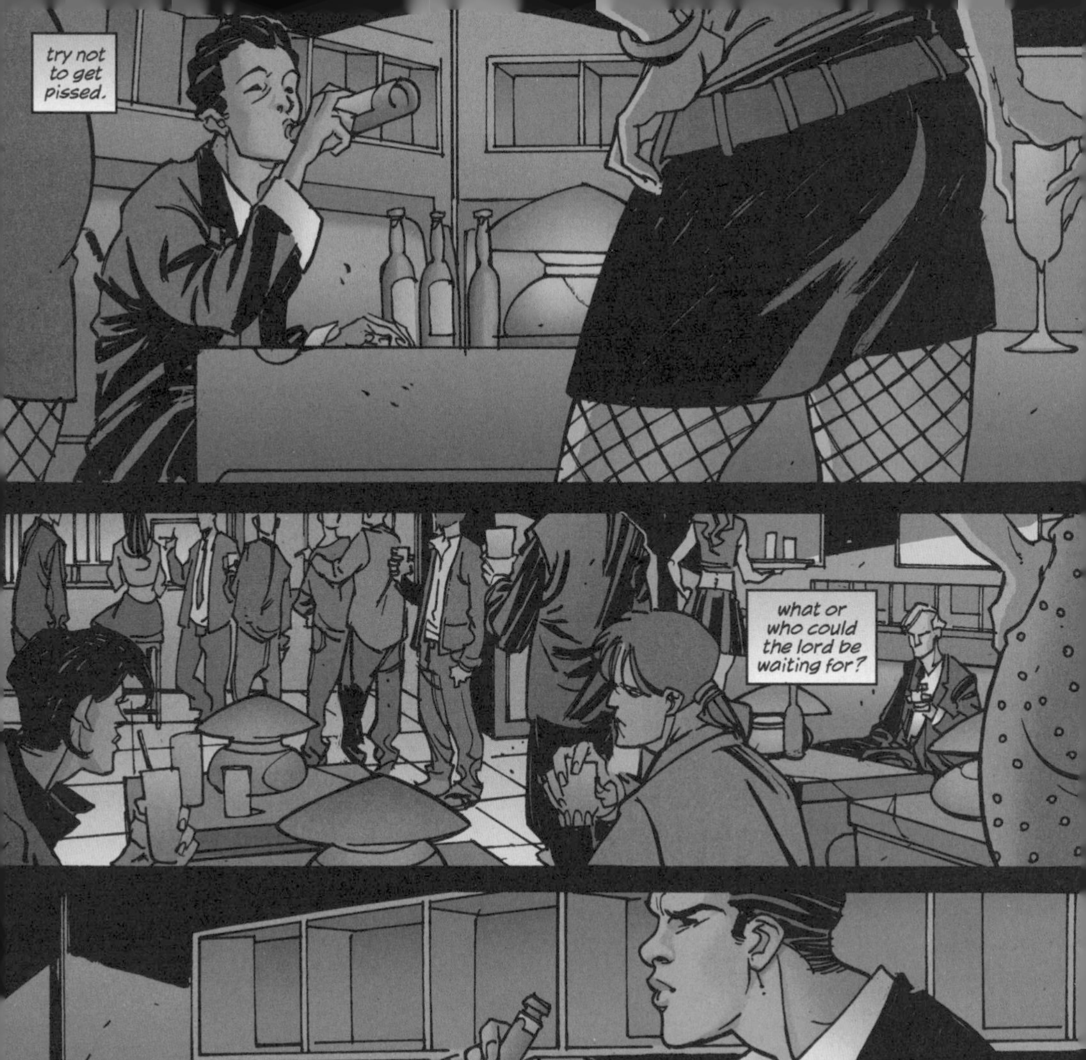
try not to get pissed.
what or who could the lord be waiting for?
the one you've really got to look out for
francie furey.

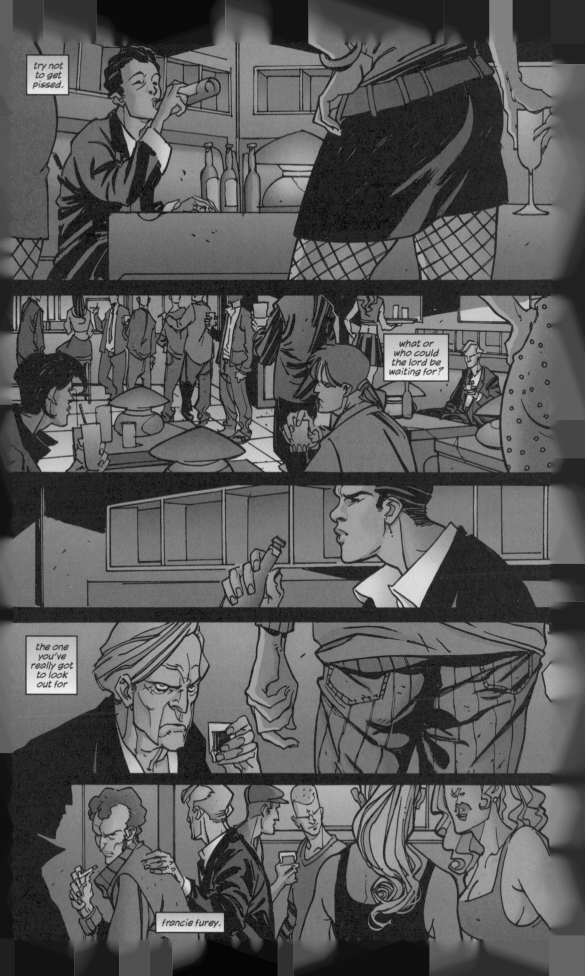

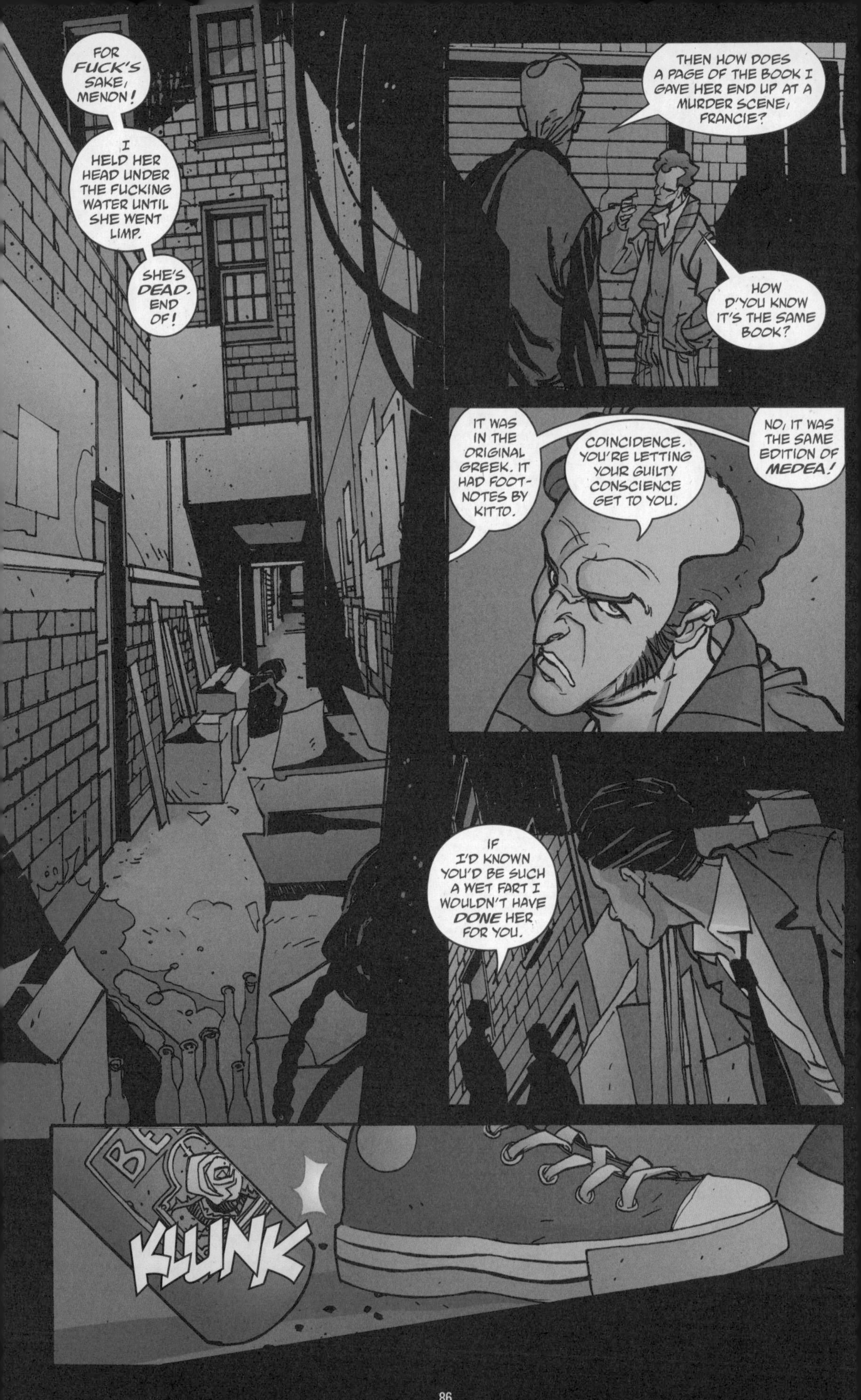

FOR FUCK'S SAKE, MENON!
I HELD HER HEAD UNDER THE FUCKING WATER UNTIL SHE WENT LIMP.
SHE'S DEAD. END OF!
THEN HOW DOES A PAGE OF THE BOOK I GAVE HER END UP AT A MURDER SCENE, FRANCIE?
HOW D'YOU KNOW IT'S THE SAME BOOK?
NO, IT WAS THE SAME EDITION OF MEDEA!
IT WAS IN THE ORIGINAL GREEK. IT HAD FOOT-NOTES BY KITTO.
COINCIDENCE. YOU'RE LETTING YOUR GUILTY CONSCIENCE GET TO YOU.
IF I'D KNOWN YOU'D BE SUCH A WET FART I WOULDN'T HAVE DONE HER FOR YOU.
KLUNK

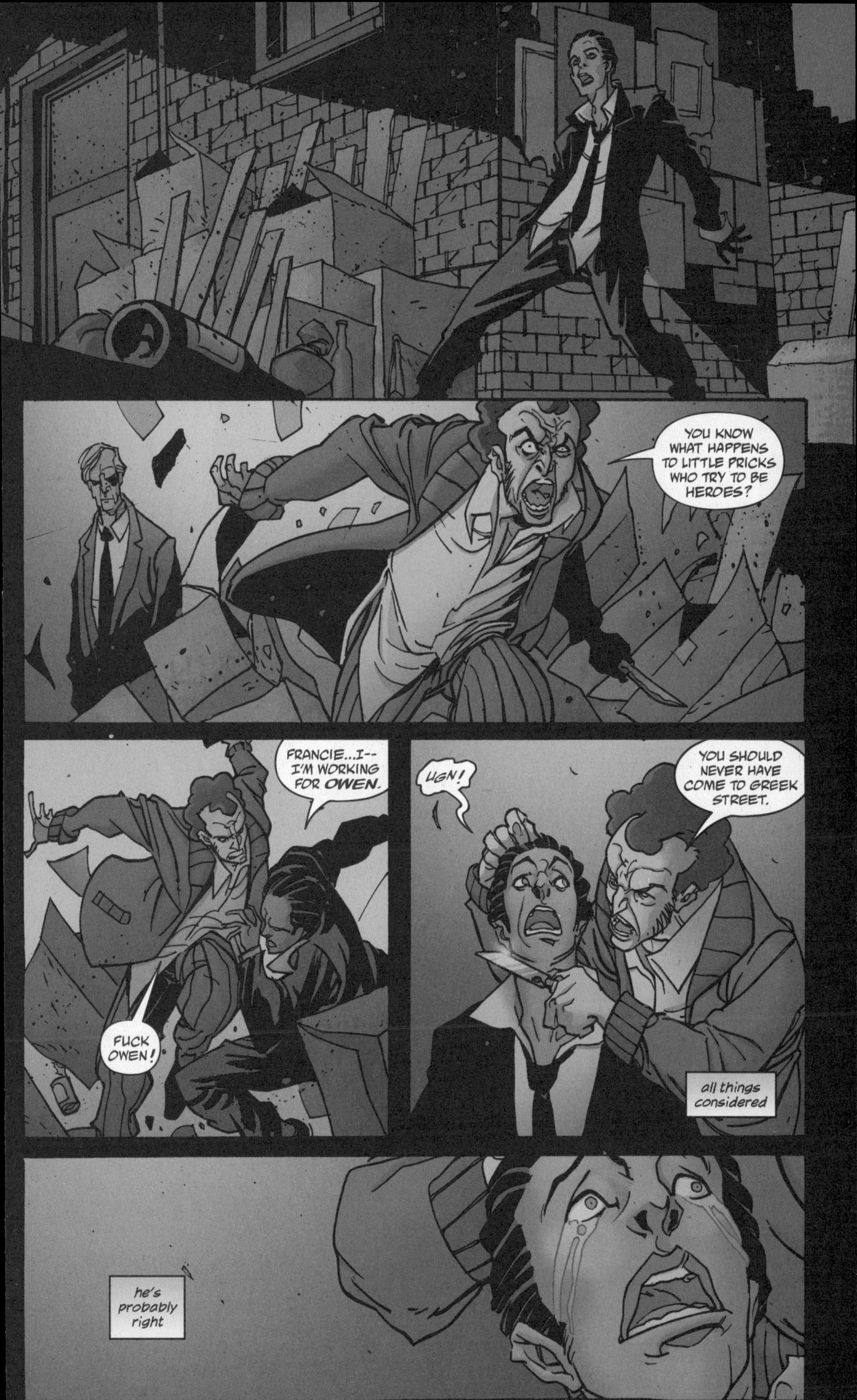

YOU KNOW WHAT HAPPENS TO LITTLE PRICKS WHO TRY TO BE HEROES?
FRANCIE...I-- I'M WORKING FOR OWEN.
FUCK OWEN!
UGN!
YOU SHOULD NEVER HAVE COME TO GREEK STREET.
all things considered
he's probably right

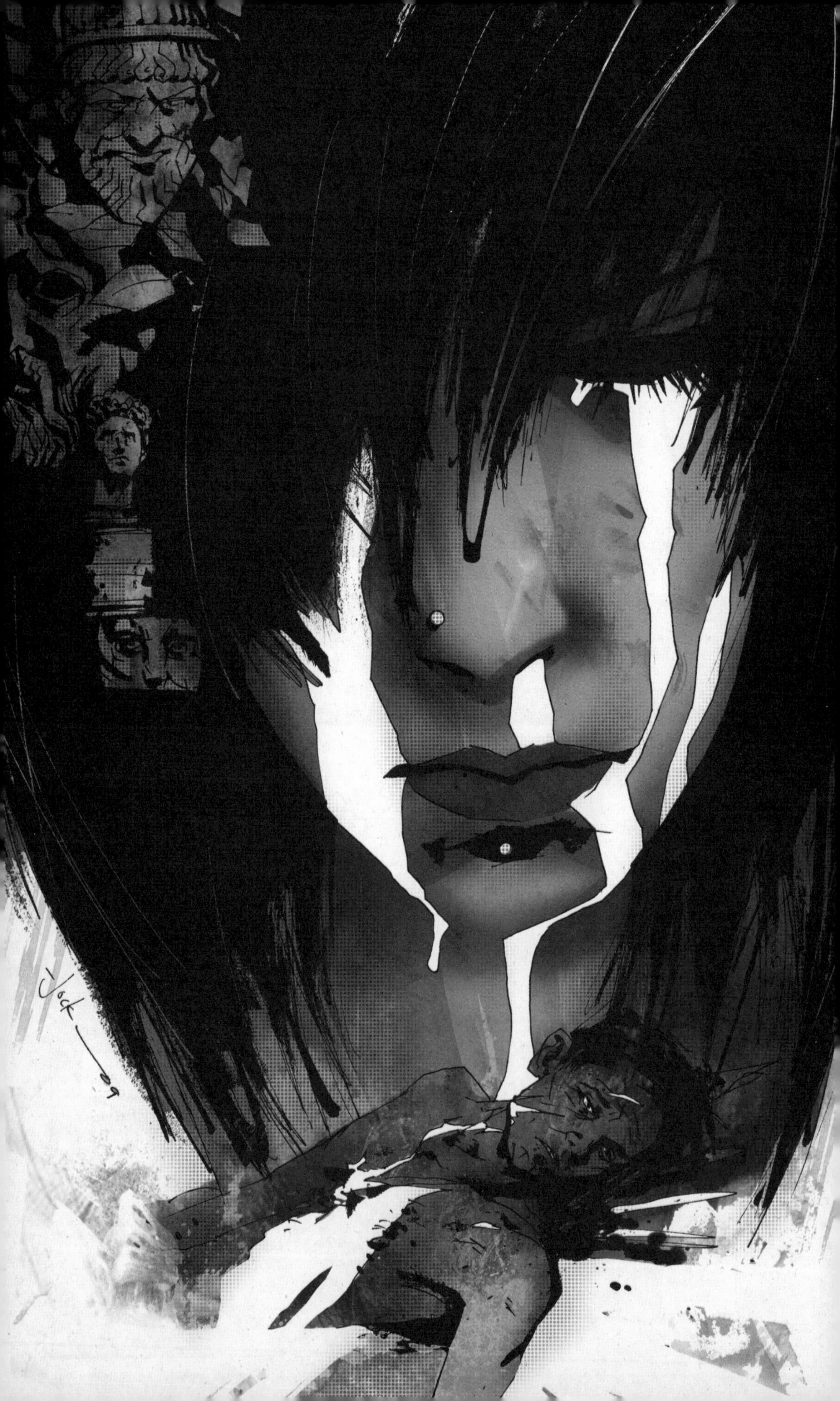
Jock 09

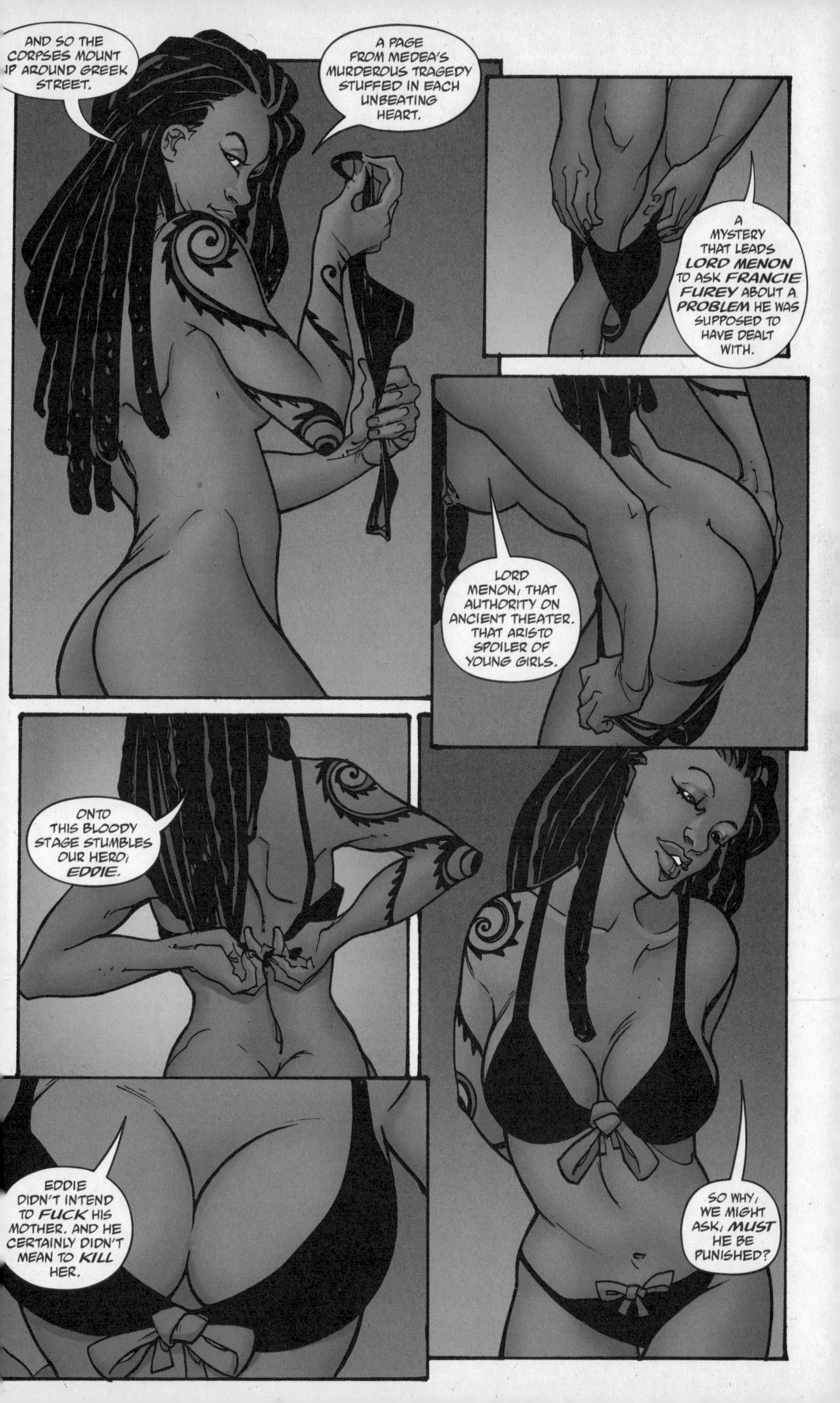

AND SO THE CORPSES MOUNT UP AROUND GREEK STREET.
A PAGE FROM MEDEA'S MURDEROUS TRAGEDY STUFFED IN EACH UNBEATING HEART.
A MYSTERY THAT LEADS LORD MENON TO ASK FRANCIE FUREY ABOUT A PROBLEM HE WAS SUPPOSED TO HAVE DEALT WITH.
LORD MENON, THAT AUTHORITY ON ANCIENT THEATER. THAT ARISTO SPOILER OF YOUNG GIRLS.
ONTO THIS BLOODY STAGE STUMBLES OUR HERO, EDDIE.
EDDIE DIDN'T INTEND TO FUCK HIS MOTHER. AND HE CERTAINLY DIDN'T MEAN TO KILL HER.
SO WHY, WE MIGHT ASK, MUST HE BE PUNISHED?

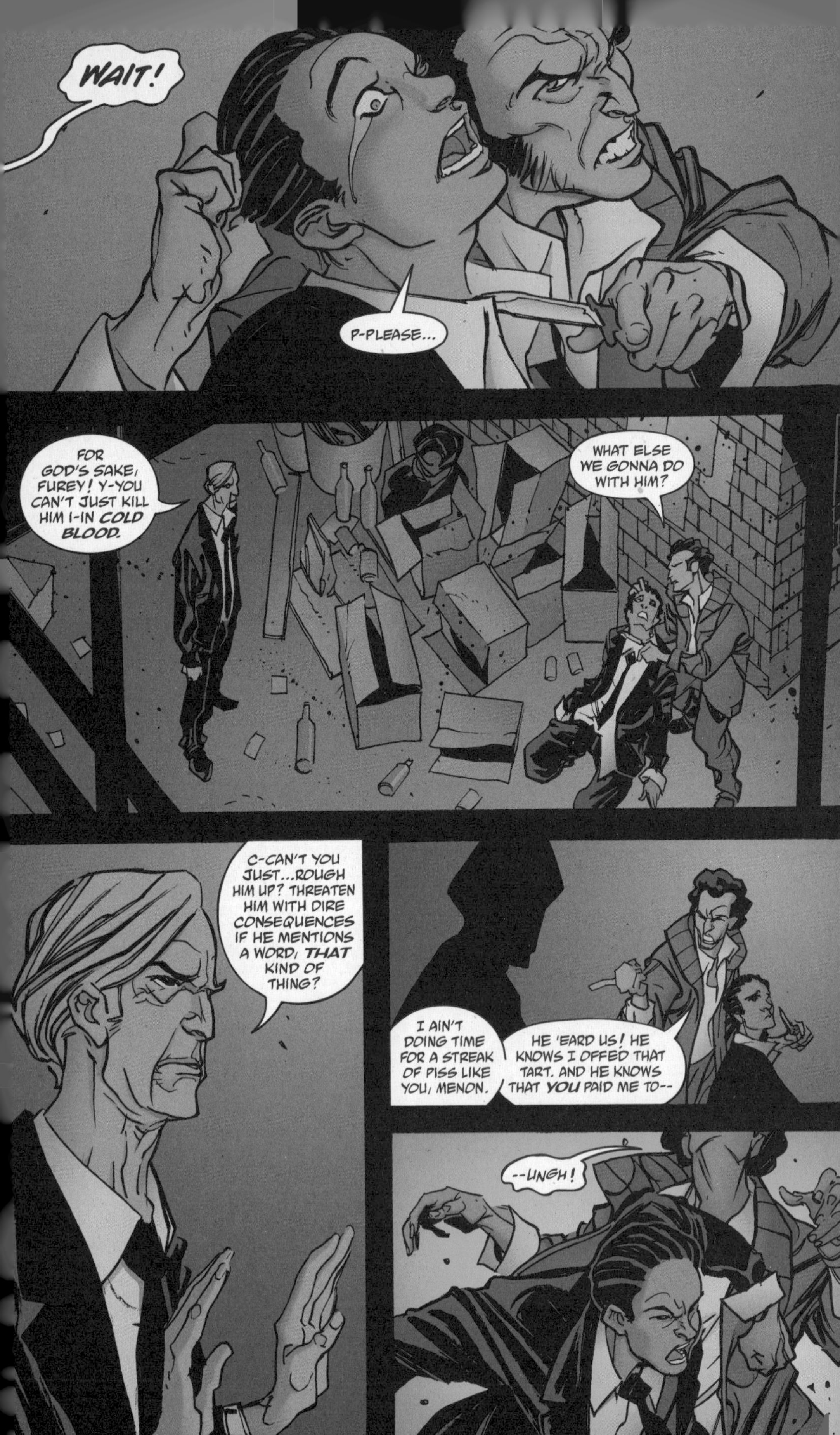
WAIT!
P-PLEASE...
FOR GOD'S SAKE, FUREY! Y-YOU CAN'T JUST KILL HIM I-IN COLD BLOOD.
WHAT ELSE WE GONNA DO WITH HIM?
C-CAN'T YOU JUST...ROUGH HIM UP? THREATEN HIM WITH DIRE CONSEQUENCES IF HE MENTIONS A WORD, THAT KIND OF THING?
I AIN'T DOING TIME FOR A STREAK OF PISS LIKE YOU, MENON.
HE 'EARD US! HE KNOWS I OFFED THAT TART. AND HE KNOWS THAT YOU PAID ME TO--
--UNGH!

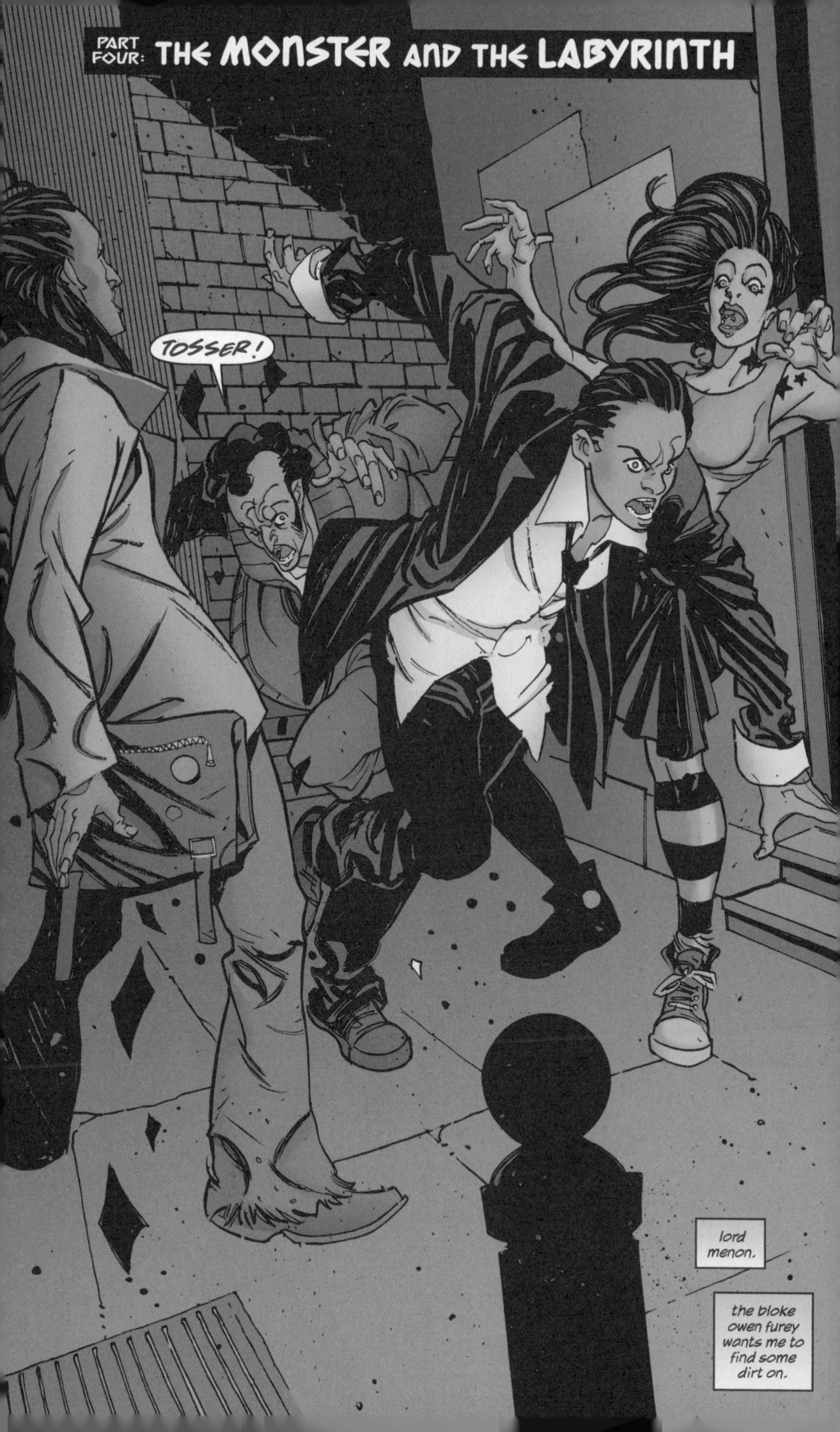
PART FOUR: THE MONSTER AND THE LABYRINTH
TOSSER!
lord menon.
the bloke owen furey wants me to find some dirt on.

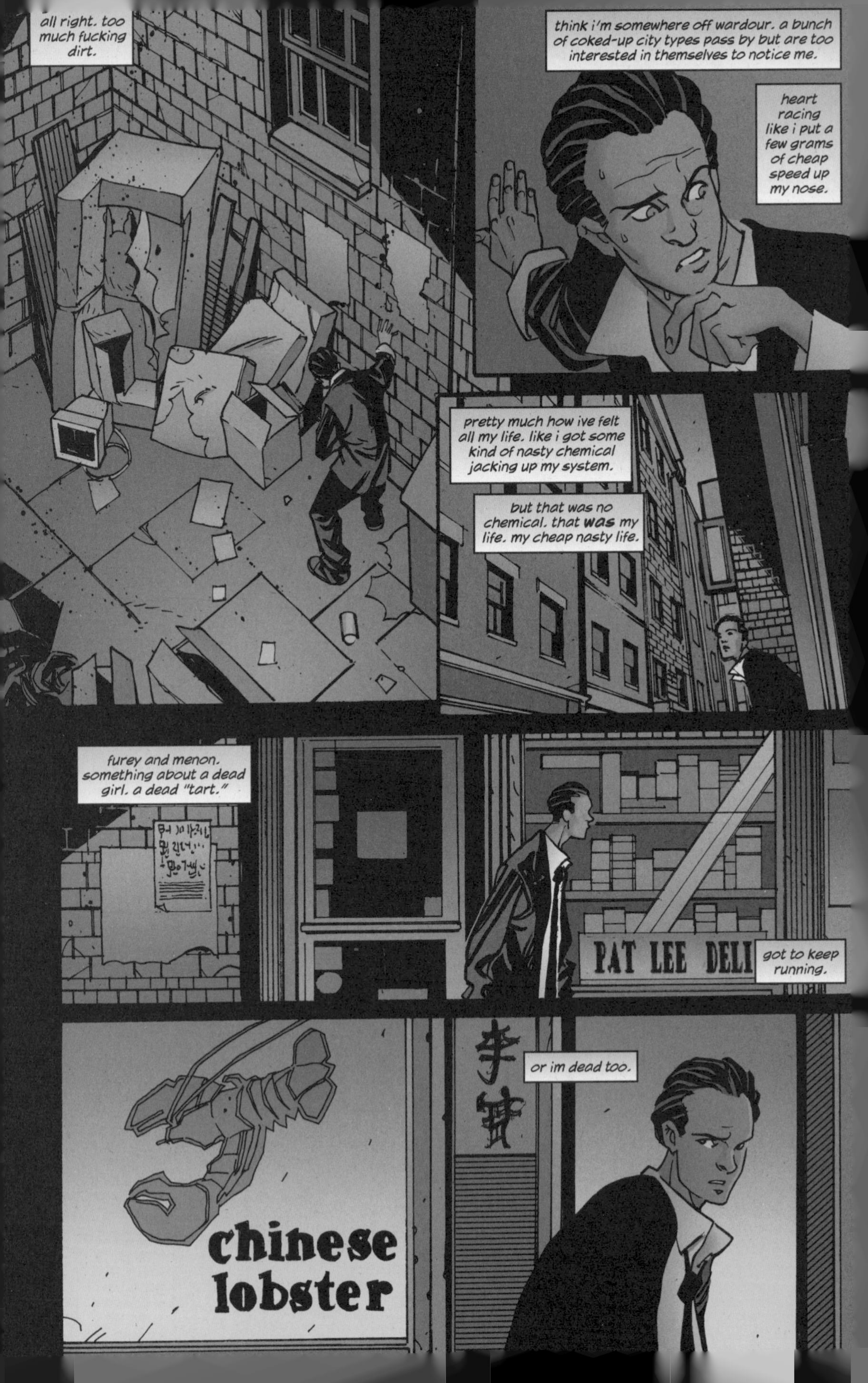

all right. too much fucking dirt.
think i'm somewhere off wardour. a bunch of coked-up city types pass by but are too interested in themselves to notice me.
heart racing like i put a few grams of cheap speed up my nose.
pretty much how ive felt all my life. like i got some kind of nasty chemical jacking up my system.
but that was no chemical. that was my life. my cheap nasty life.
furey and menon. something about a dead girl. a dead "tart."
PAT LEE DELI
got to keep running.
chinese lobster
or im dead too.

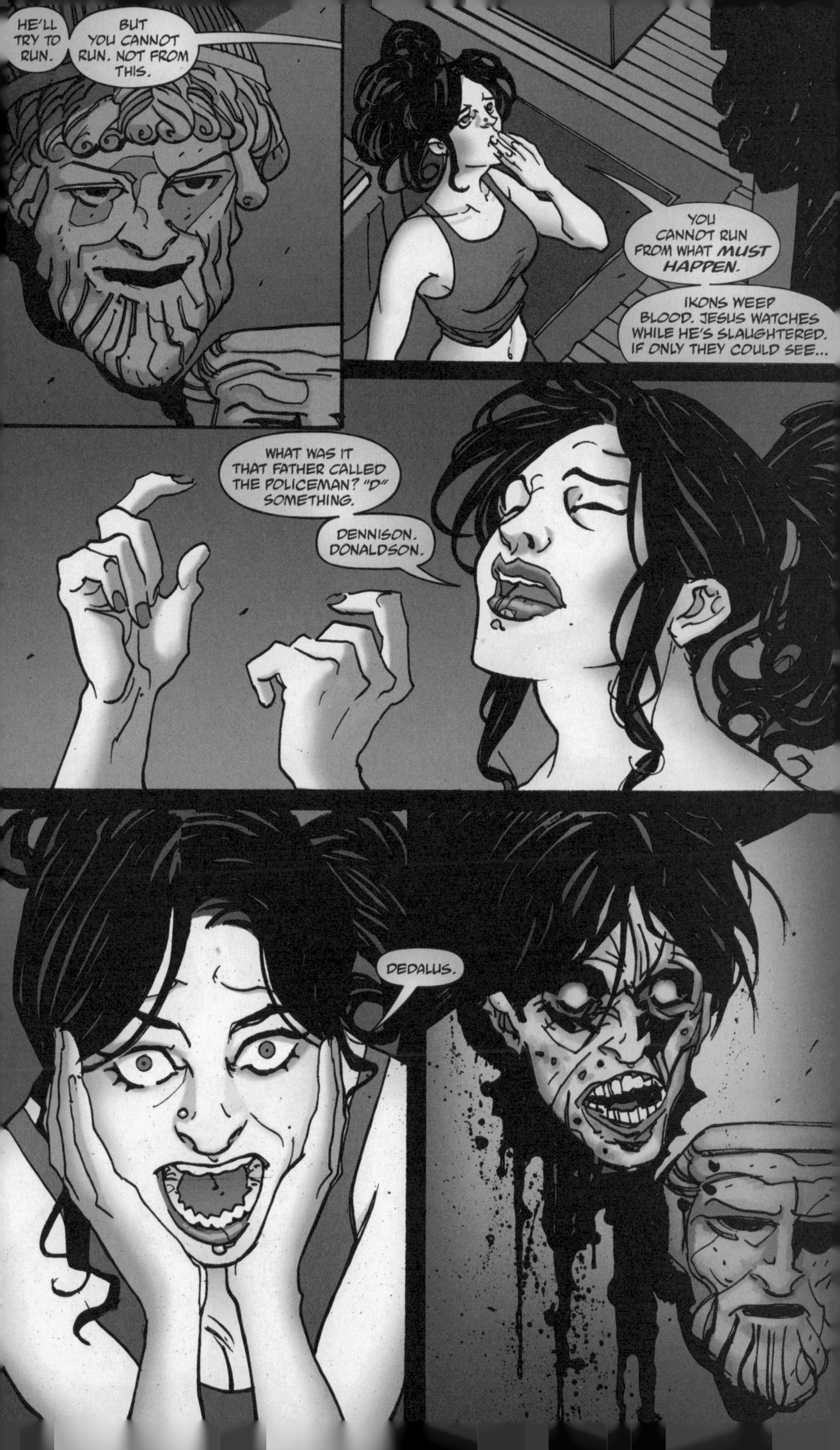
HE'LL TRY TO RUN.
BUT YOU CANNOT RUN. NOT FROM THIS.
YOU CANNOT RUN FROM WHAT MUST HAPPEN.
IKONS WEEP BLOOD. JESUS WATCHES WHILE HE'S SLAUGHTERED. IF ONLY THEY COULD SEE...
WHAT WAS IT THAT FATHER CALLED THE POLICEMAN? "D" SOMETHING.
DENNISON. DONALDSON.
DEDALUS.

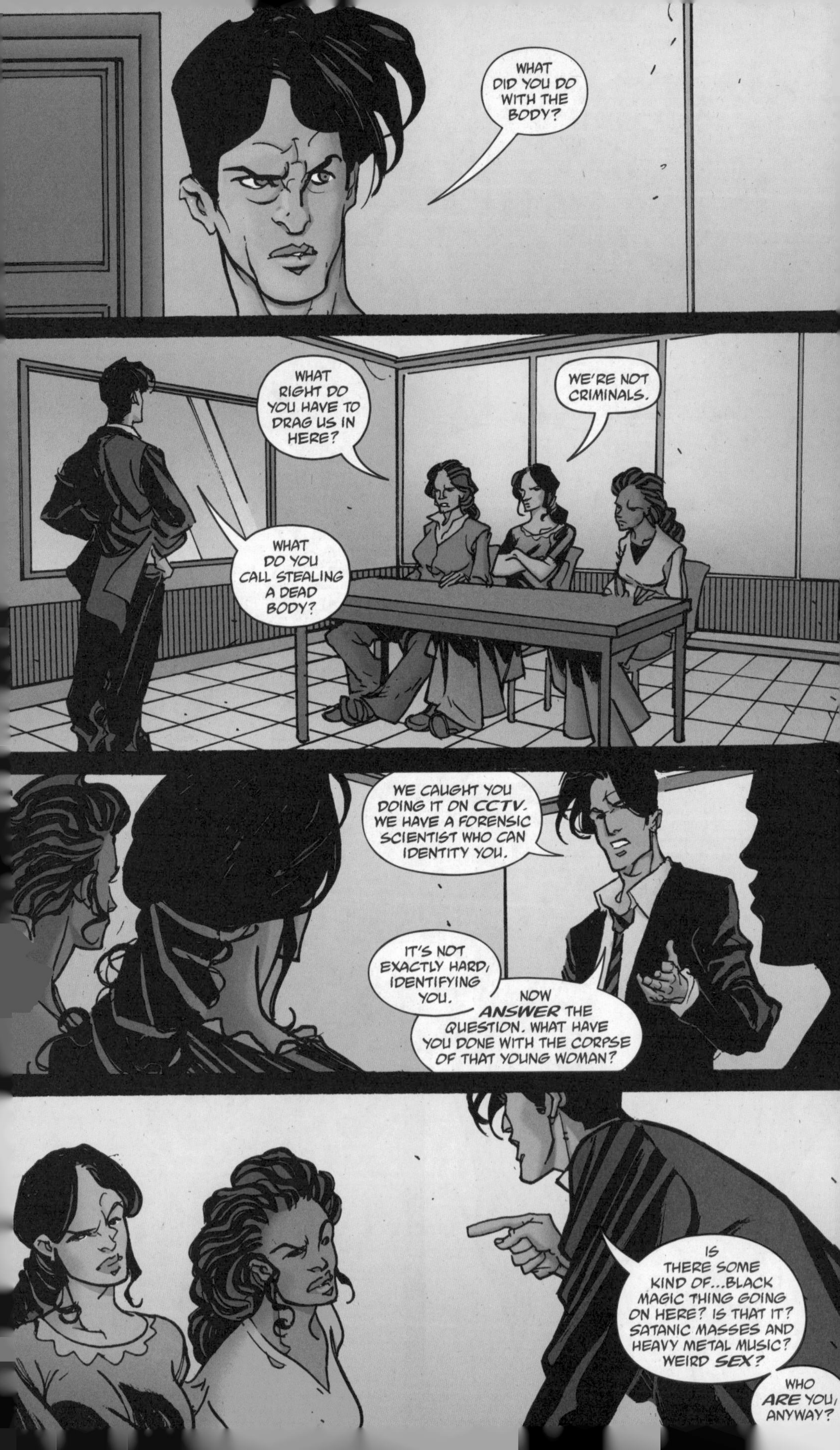
WHAT DID YOU DO WITH THE BODY?
WHAT RIGHT DO YOU HAVE TO DRAG US IN HERE?
WE'RE NOT CRIMINALS.
WHAT DO YOU CALL STEALING A DEAD BODY?
WE CAUGHT YOU DOING IT ON CCTV. WE HAVE A FORENSIC SCIENTIST WHO CAN IDENTITY YOU.
IT'S NOT EXACTLY HARD, IDENTIFYING YOU.
NOW ANSWER THE QUESTION. WHAT HAVE YOU DONE WITH THE CORPSE OF THAT YOUNG WOMAN?
IS THERE SOME KIND OF...BLACK MAGIC THING GOING ON HERE? IS THAT IT? SATANIC MASSES AND HEAVY METAL MUSIC? WEIRD SEX?
WHO ARE YOU, ANYWAY?

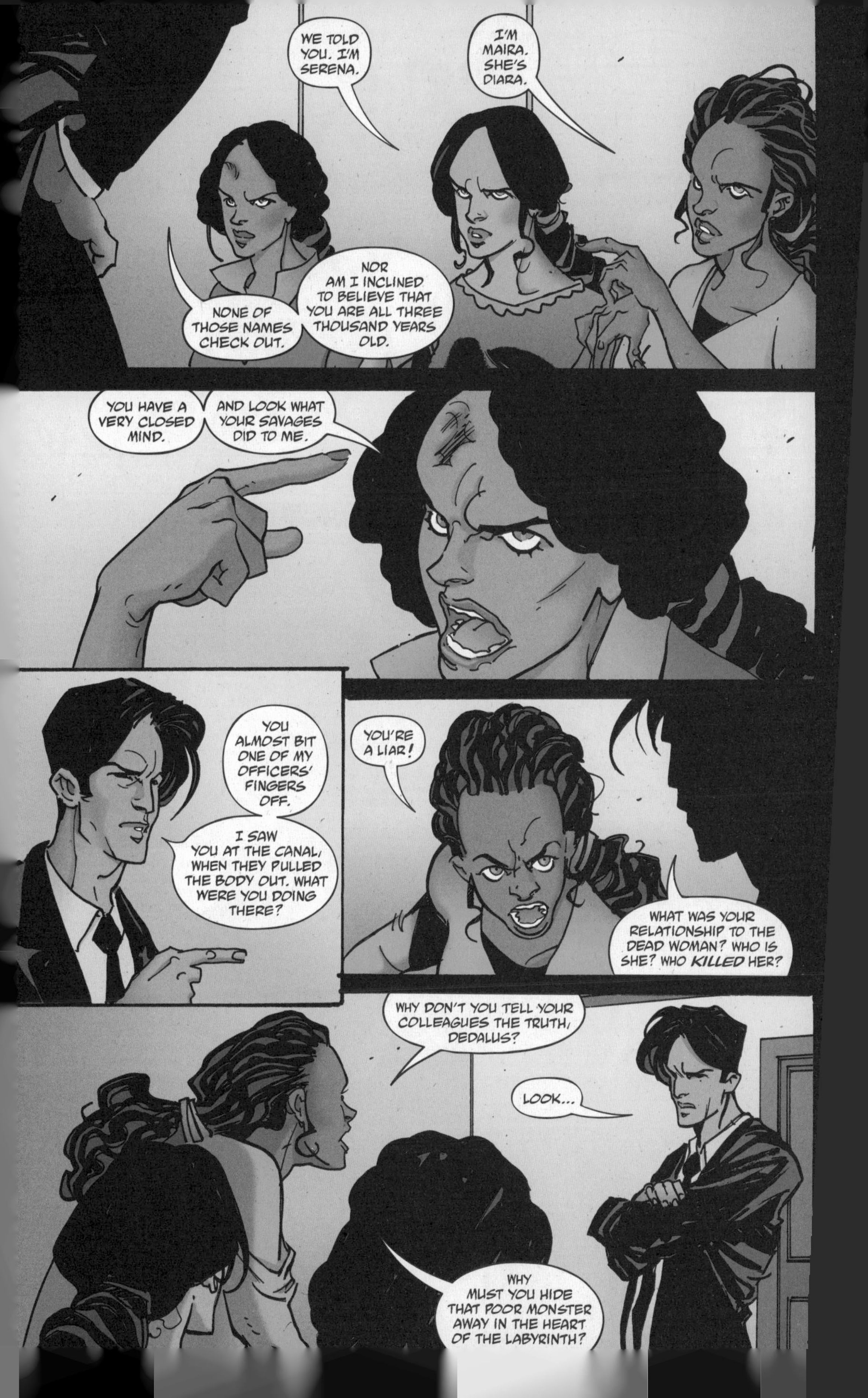
WE TOLD YOU. I'M SERENA.
I'M MAIRA. SHE'S DIARA.
NONE OF THOSE NAMES CHECK OUT.
NOR AM I INCLINED TO BELIEVE THAT YOU ARE ALL THREE THOUSAND YEARS OLD.
YOU HAVE A VERY CLOSED MIND.
AND LOOK WHAT YOUR SAVAGES DID TO ME.
YOU ALMOST BIT ONE OF MY OFFICERS' FINGERS OFF.
I SAW YOU AT THE CANAL, WHEN THEY PULLED THE BODY OUT. WHAT WERE YOU DOING THERE?
YOU'RE A LIAR!
WHAT WAS YOUR RELATIONSHIP TO THE DEAD WOMAN? WHO IS SHE? WHO KILLED HER?
WHY DON'T YOU TELL YOUR COLLEAGUES THE TRUTH, DEDALUS?
LOOK...
WHY MUST YOU HIDE THAT POOR MONSTER AWAY IN THE HEART OF THE LABYRINTH?

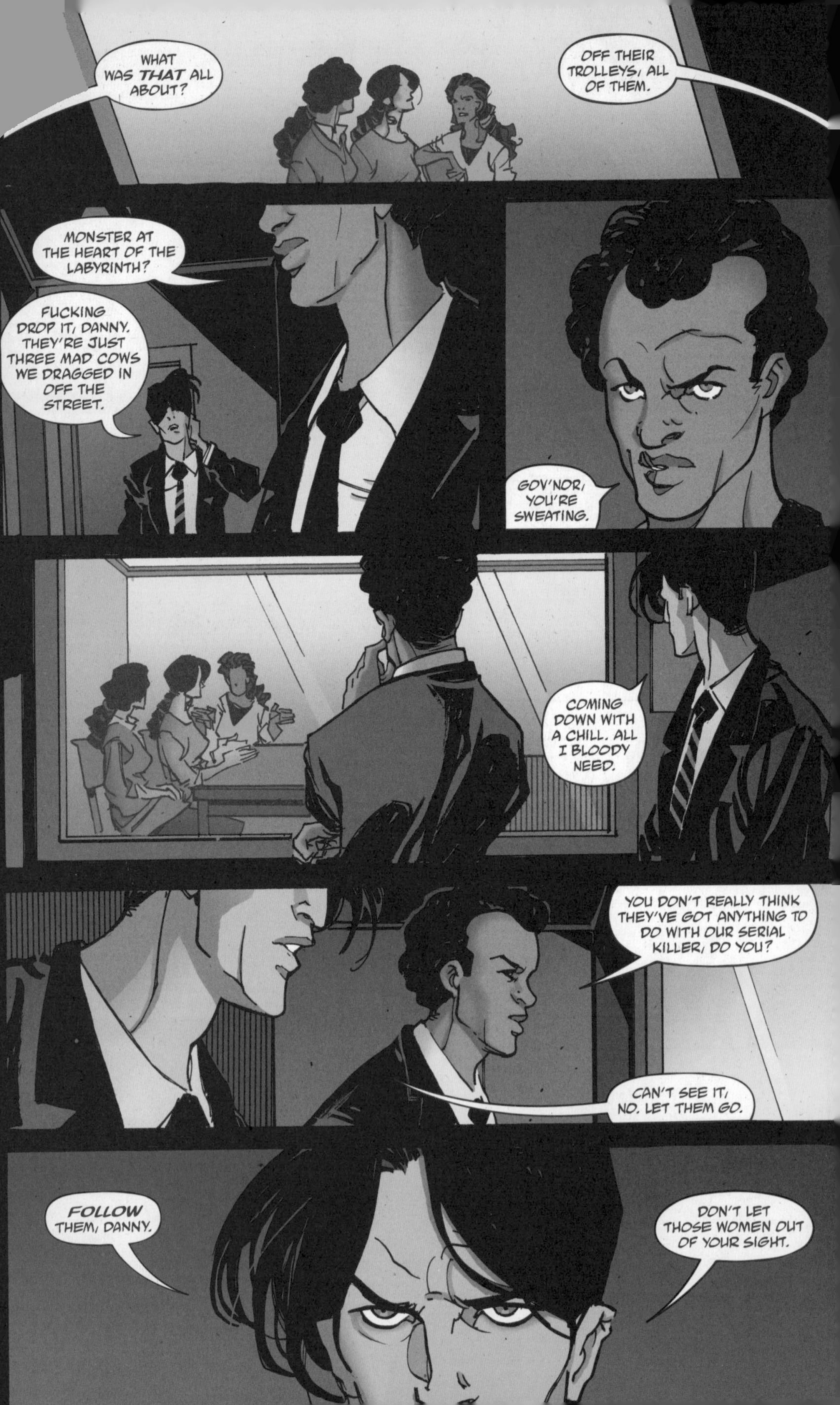
WHAT WAS *THAT* ALL ABOUT?
OFF THEIR TROLLEYS, ALL OF THEM.
MONSTER AT THE HEART OF THE LABYRINTH?
FUCKING DROP IT, DANNY. THEY'RE JUST THREE MAD COWS WE DRAGGED IN OFF THE STREET.
GOV'NOR, YOU'RE SWEATING.
COMING DOWN WITH A CHILL. ALL I BLOODY NEED.
YOU DON'T REALLY THINK THEY'VE GOT ANYTHING TO DO WITH OUR SERIAL KILLER, DO YOU?
CAN'T SEE IT, NO. LET THEM GO.
FOLLOW THEM, DANNY.
DON'T LET THOSE WOMEN OUT OF YOUR SIGHT.

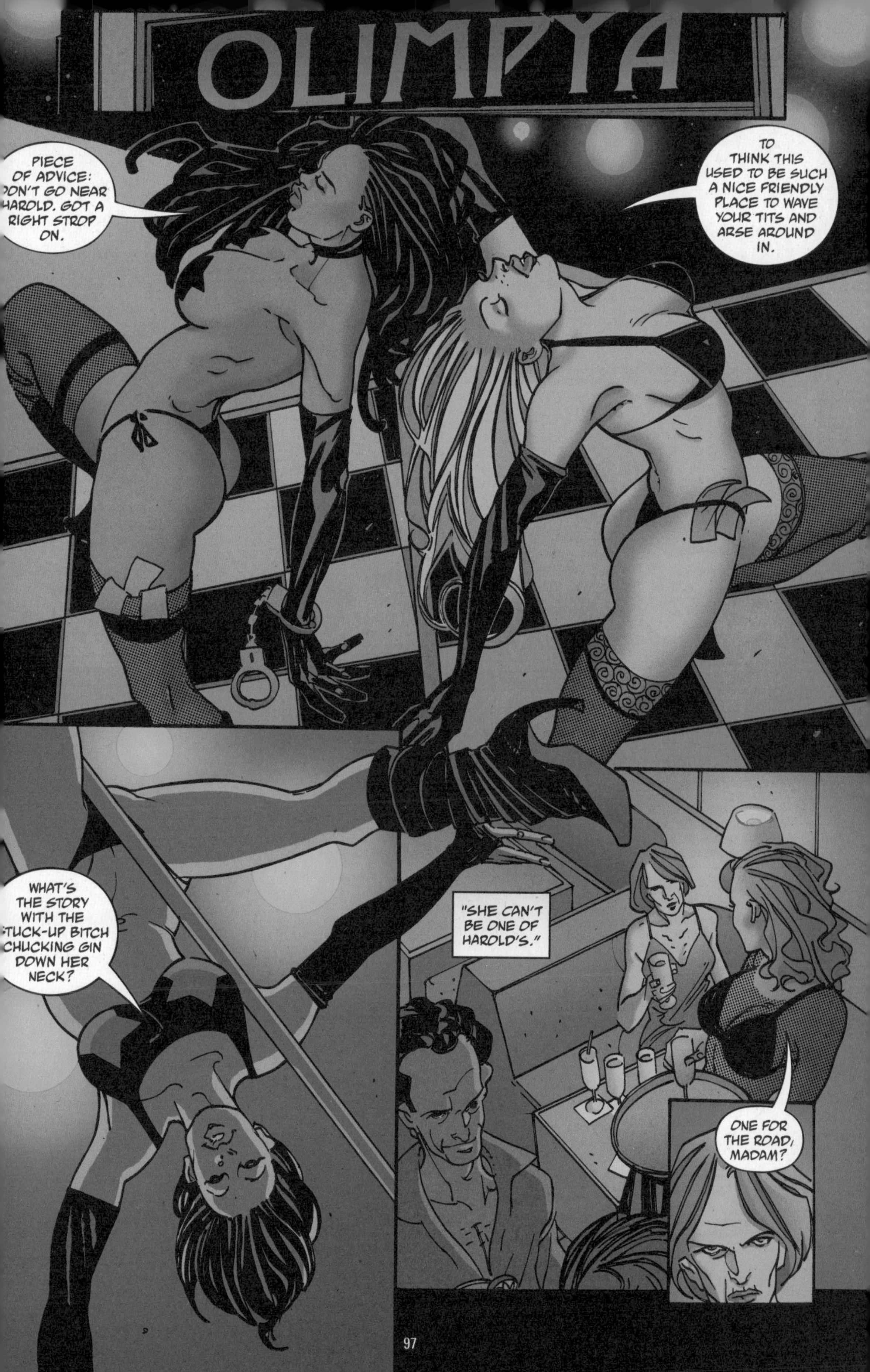
OLIMPYA
PIECE OF ADVICE: DON'T GO NEAR HAROLD. GOT A RIGHT STROP ON.
TO THINK THIS USED TO BE SUCH A NICE FRIENDLY PLACE TO WAVE YOUR TITS AND ARSE AROUND IN.
WHAT'S THE STORY WITH THE STUCK-UP BITCH CHUCKING GIN DOWN HER NECK?
"SHE CAN'T BE ONE OF HAROLD'S."
ONE FOR THE ROAD, MADAM?

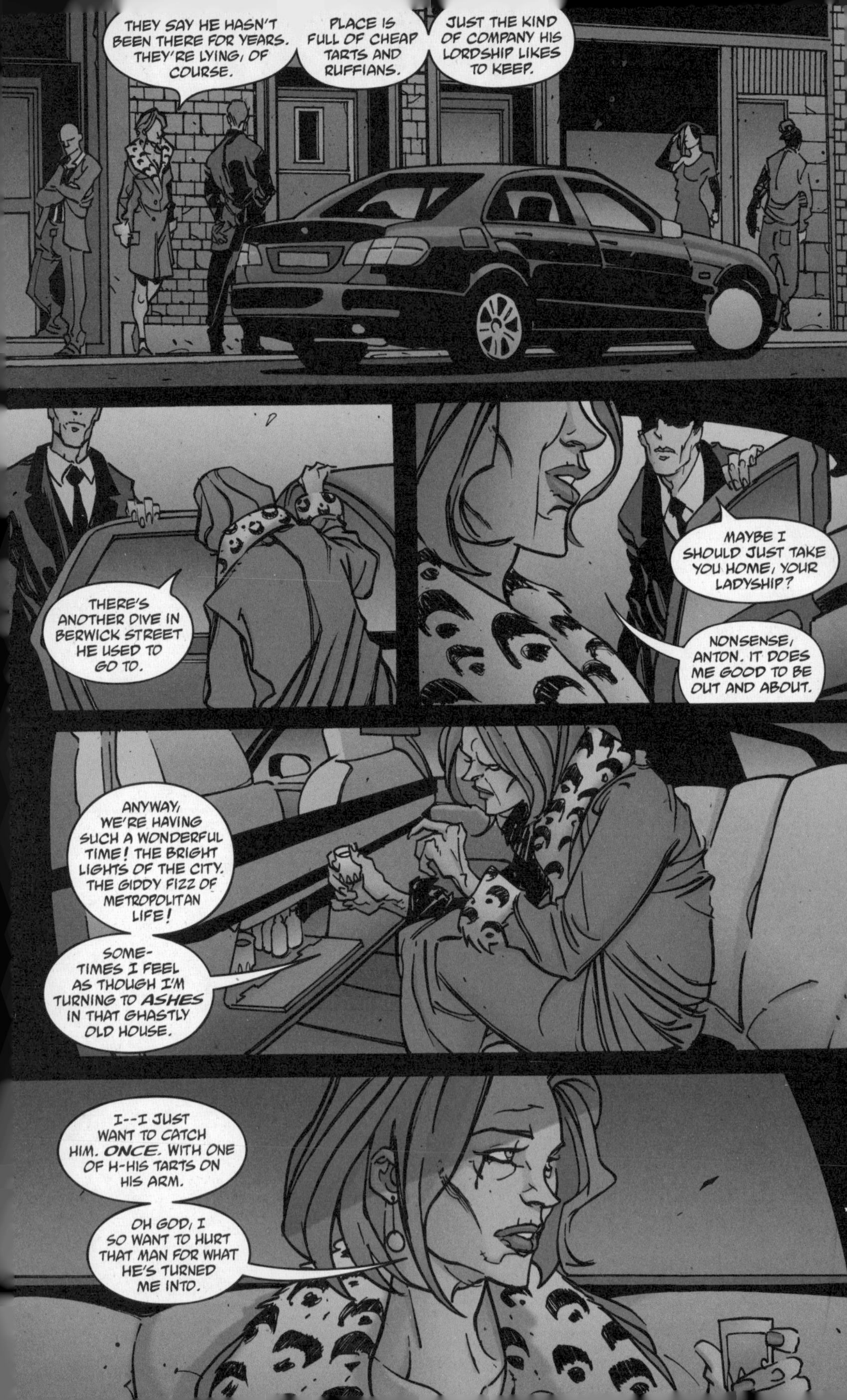
THEY SAY HE HASN'T BEEN THERE FOR YEARS. THEY'RE LYING, OF COURSE.
PLACE IS FULL OF CHEAP TARTS AND RUFFIANS.
JUST THE KIND OF COMPANY HIS LORDSHIP LIKES TO KEEP.
THERE'S ANOTHER DIVE IN BERWICK STREET HE USED TO GO TO.
MAYBE I SHOULD JUST TAKE YOU HOME, YOUR LADYSHIP?
NONSENSE, ANTON. IT DOES ME GOOD TO BE OUT AND ABOUT.
ANYWAY, WE'RE HAVING SUCH A WONDERFUL TIME! THE BRIGHT LIGHTS OF THE CITY. THE GIDDY FIZZ OF METROPOLITAN LIFE!
SOME-TIMES I FEEL AS THOUGH I'M TURNING TO ASHES IN THAT GHASTLY OLD HOUSE.
I--I JUST WANT TO CATCH HIM. ONCE. WITH ONE OF H-HIS TARTS ON HIS ARM.
OH GOD, I SO WANT TO HURT THAT MAN FOR WHAT HE'S TURNED ME INTO.

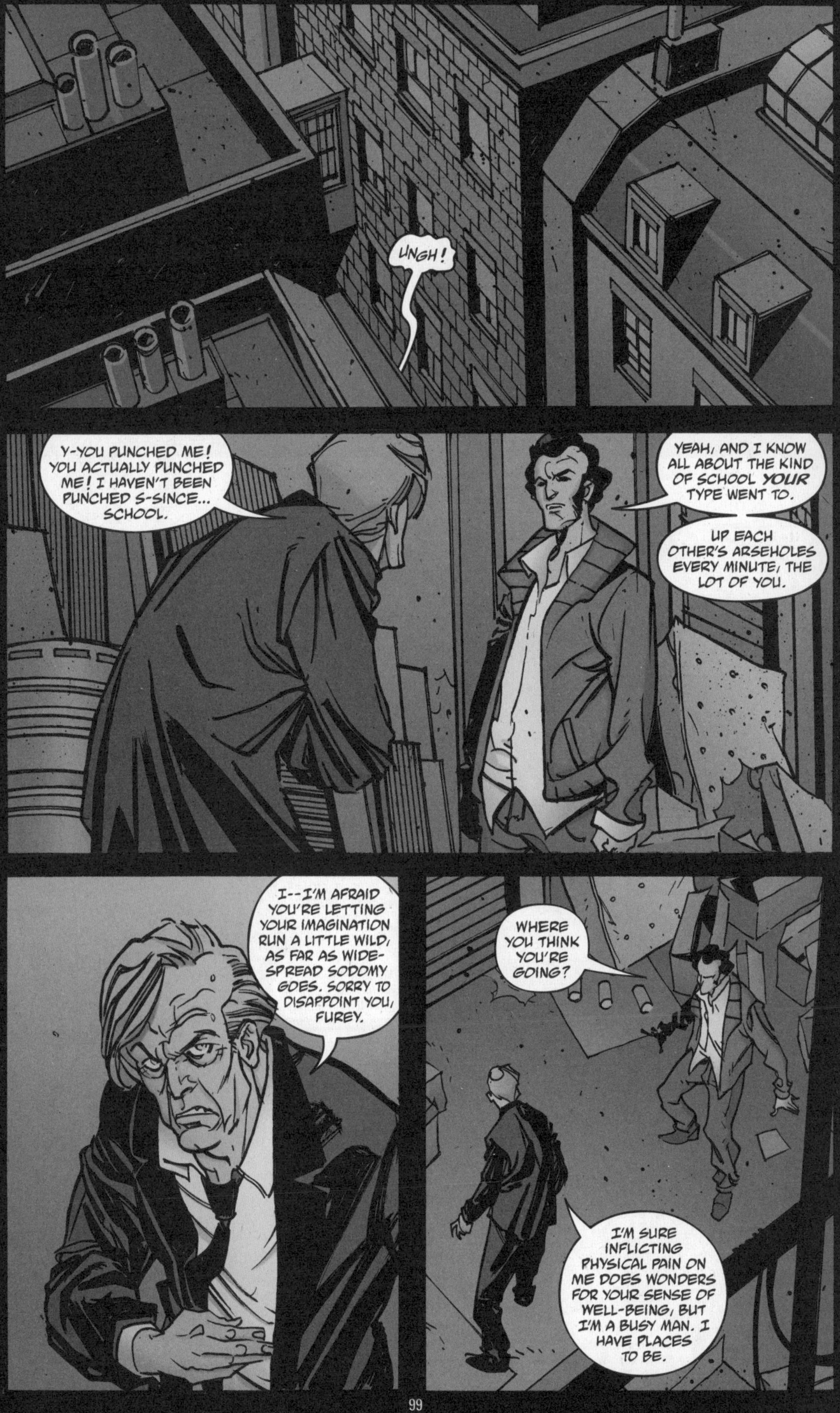
UNGH!
Y-YOU PUNCHED ME! YOU ACTUALLY PUNCHED ME! I HAVEN'T BEEN PUNCHED S-SINCE... SCHOOL.
YEAH, AND I KNOW ALL ABOUT THE KIND OF SCHOOL YOUR TYPE WENT TO.
UP EACH OTHER'S ARSEHOLES EVERY MINUTE, THE LOT OF YOU.
I--I'M AFRAID YOU'RE LETTING YOUR IMAGINATION RUN A LITTLE WILD, AS FAR AS WIDE-SPREAD SODOMY GOES. SORRY TO DISAPPOINT YOU, FUREY.
WHERE YOU THINK YOU'RE GOING?
I'M SURE INFLICTING PHYSICAL PAIN ON ME DOES WONDERS FOR YOUR SENSE OF WELL-BEING, BUT I'M A BUSY MAN. I HAVE PLACES TO BE.

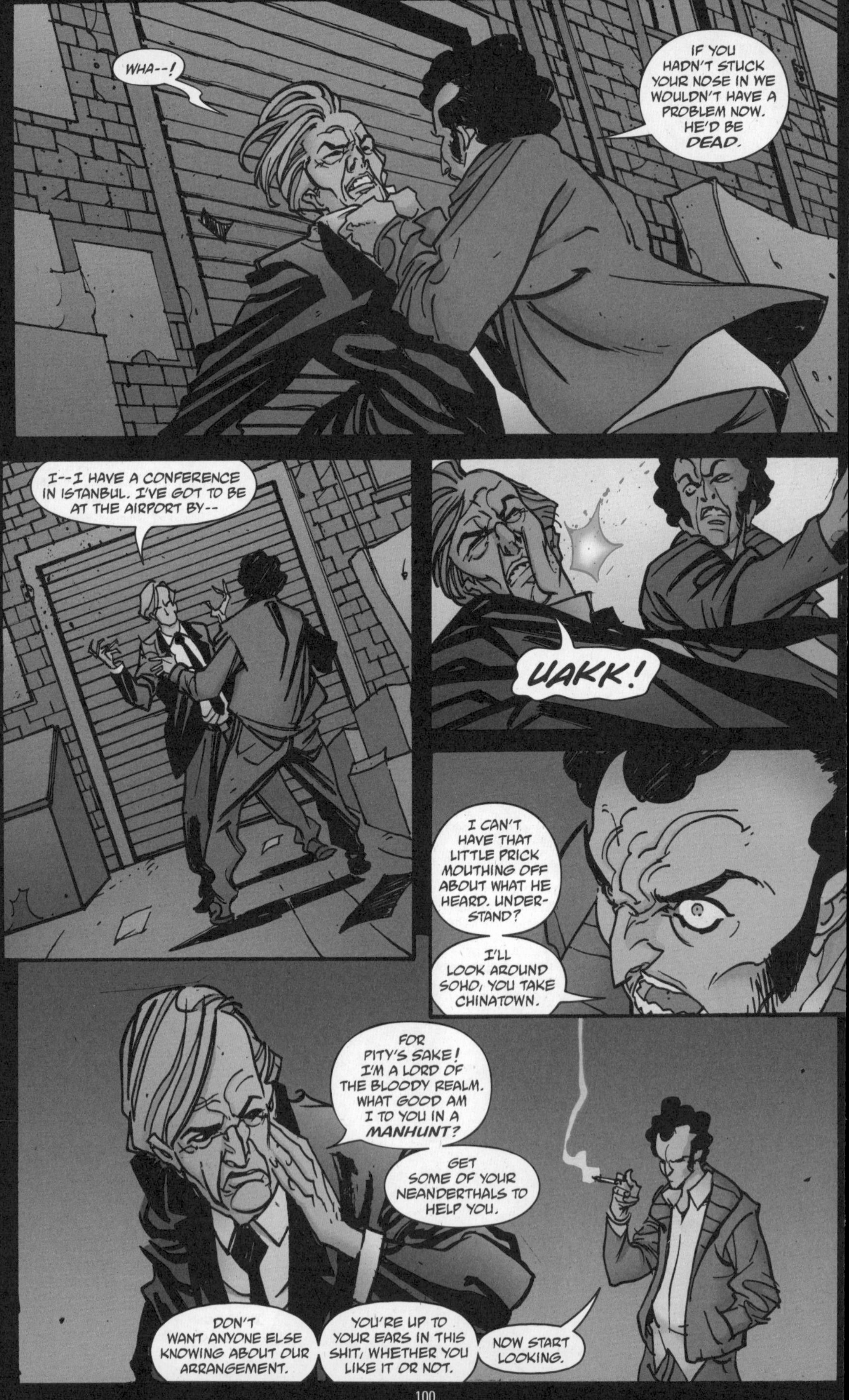
WHA--!
IF YOU HADN'T STUCK YOUR NOSE IN WE WOULDN'T HAVE A PROBLEM NOW. HE'D BE DEAD.
I--I HAVE A CONFERENCE IN ISTANBUL. I'VE GOT TO BE AT THE AIRPORT BY--
UAKK!
I CAN'T HAVE THAT LITTLE PRICK MOUTHING OFF ABOUT WHAT HE HEARD. UNDER-STAND?
I'LL LOOK AROUND SOHO, YOU TAKE CHINATOWN.
FOR PITY'S SAKE! I'M A LORD OF THE BLOODY REALM. WHAT GOOD AM I TO YOU IN A MANHUNT?
GET SOME OF YOUR NEANDERTHALS TO HELP YOU.
DON'T WANT ANYONE ELSE KNOWING ABOUT OUR ARRANGEMENT.
YOU'RE UP TO YOUR EARS IN THIS SHIT, WHETHER YOU LIKE IT OR NOT.
NOW START LOOKING.

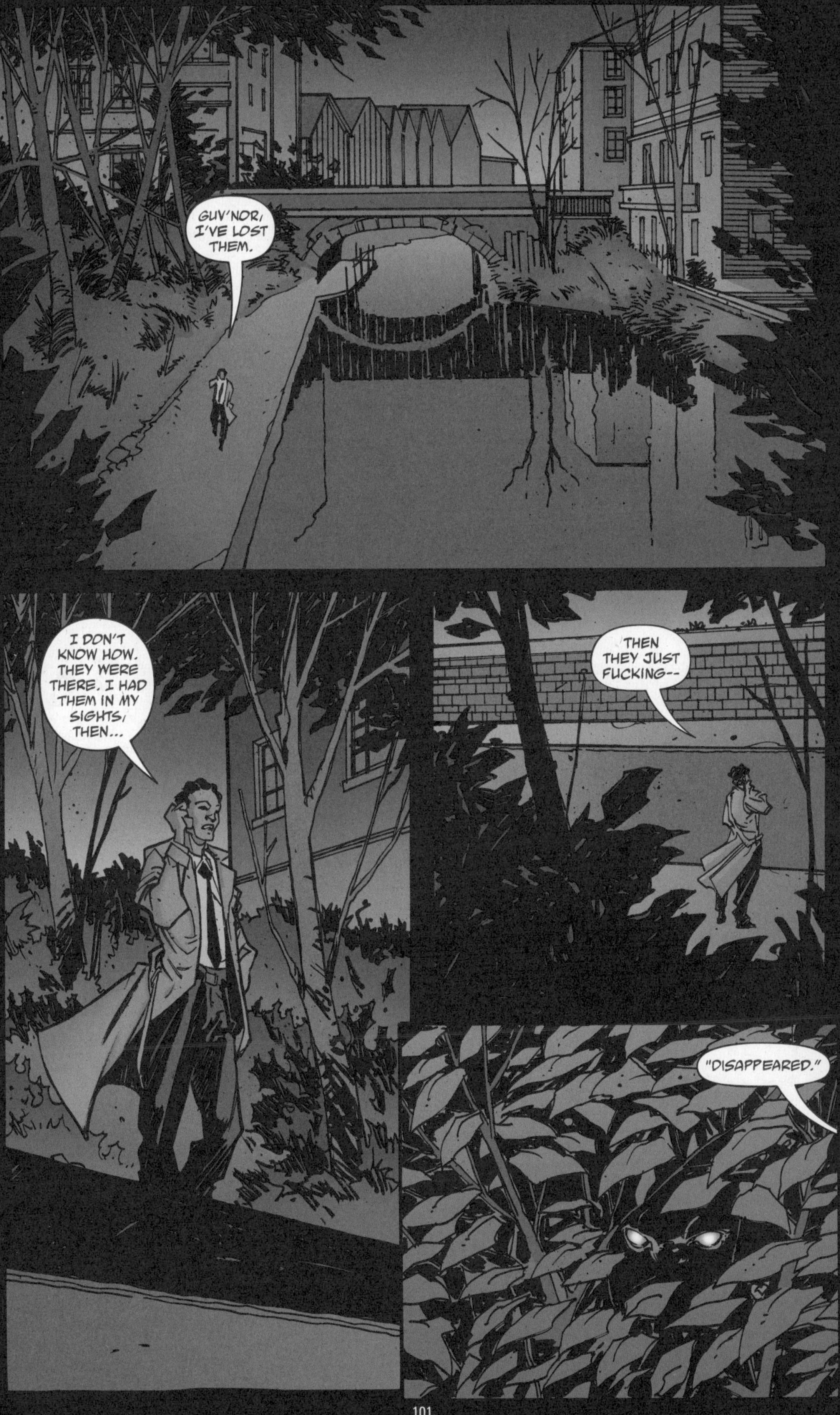
GUV'NOR, I'VE LOST THEM.
I DON'T KNOW HOW. THEY WERE THERE. I HAD THEM IN MY SIGHTS, THEN...
THEN THEY JUST FUCKING--
"DISAPPEARED."

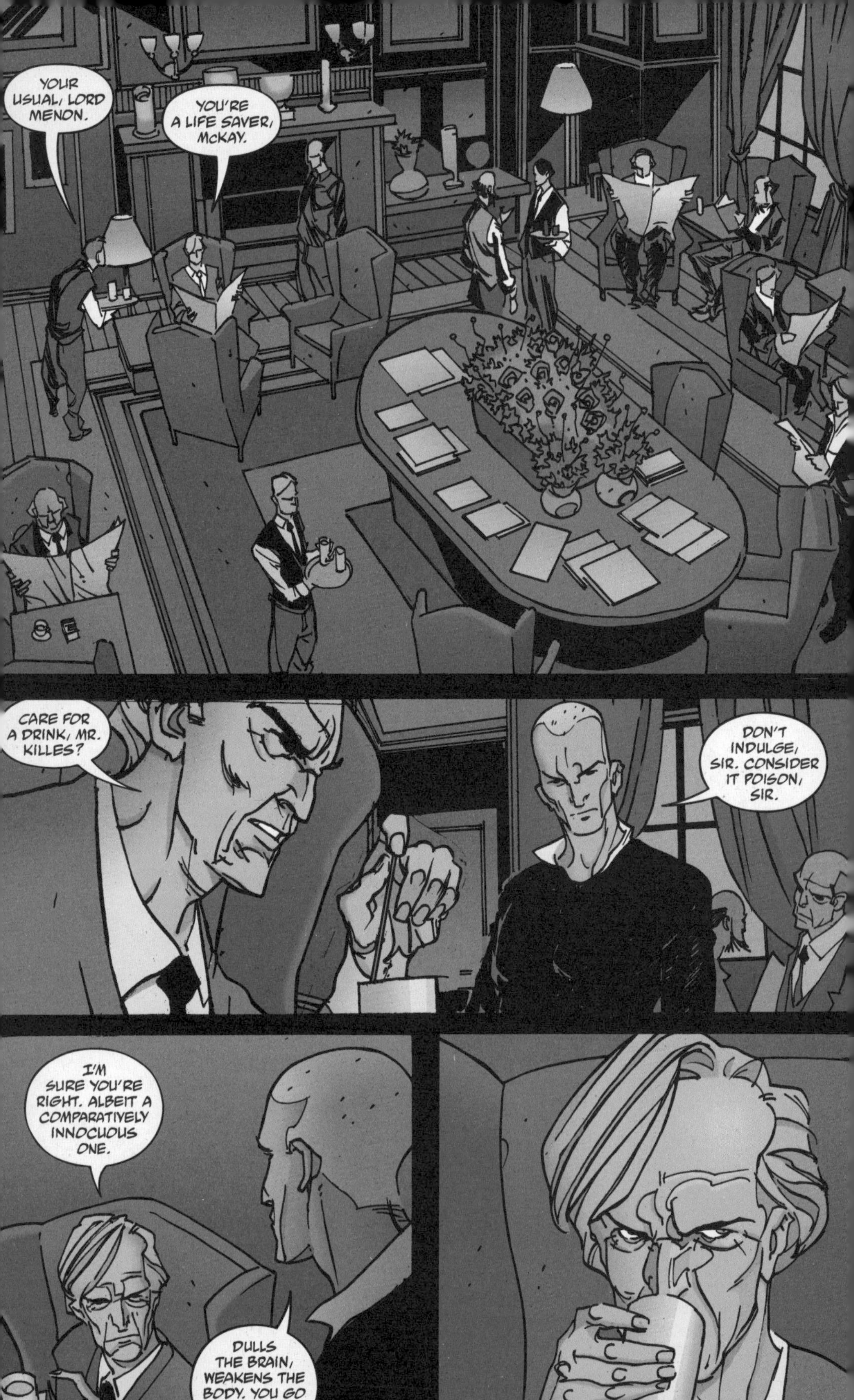
YOUR USUAL, LORD MENON.
YOU'RE A LIFE SAVER, McKAY.
CARE FOR A DRINK, MR. KILLES?
DON'T INDULGE, SIR. CONSIDER IT POISON, SIR.
I'M SURE YOU'RE RIGHT. ALBEIT A COMPARATIVELY INNOCUOUS ONE.
DULLS THE BRAIN, WEAKENS THE BODY. YOU GO AHEAD, SIR.

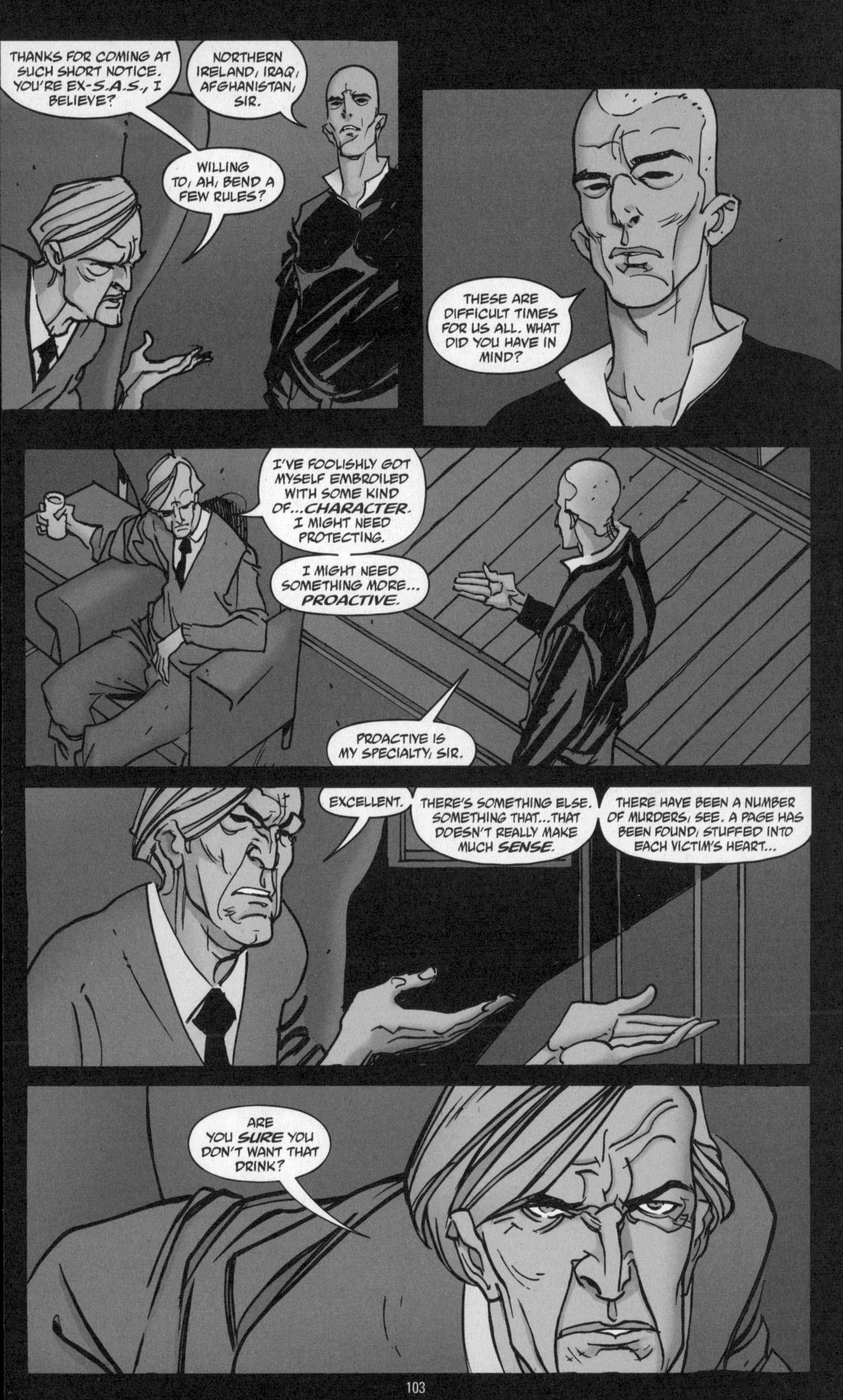
THANKS FOR COMING AT SUCH SHORT NOTICE. YOU'RE EX-S.A.S., I BELIEVE?
NORTHERN IRELAND, IRAQ, AFGHANISTAN, SIR.
WILLING TO, AH, BEND A FEW RULES?
THESE ARE DIFFICULT TIMES FOR US ALL. WHAT DID YOU HAVE IN MIND?
I'VE FOOLISHLY GOT MYSELF EMBROILED WITH SOME KIND OF...CHARACTER. I MIGHT NEED PROTECTING.
I MIGHT NEED SOMETHING MORE... PROACTIVE.
PROACTIVE IS MY SPECIALTY, SIR.
EXCELLENT.
THERE'S SOMETHING ELSE. SOMETHING THAT...THAT DOESN'T REALLY MAKE MUCH SENSE.
THERE HAVE BEEN A NUMBER OF MURDERS, SEE. A PAGE HAS BEEN FOUND, STUFFED INTO EACH VICTIM'S HEART...
ARE YOU SURE YOU DON'T WANT THAT DRINK?

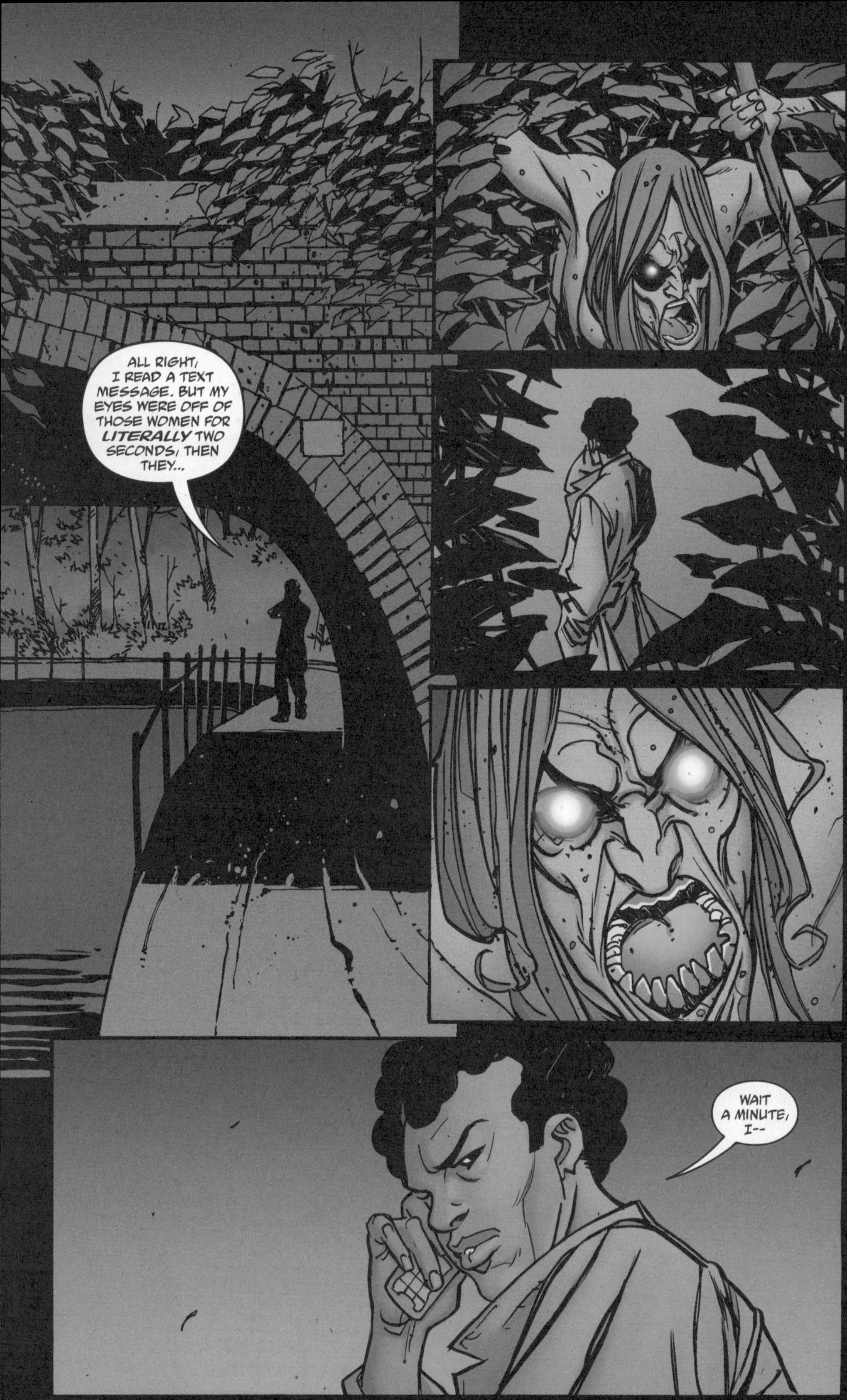
ALL RIGHT, I READ A TEXT MESSAGE. BUT MY EYES WERE OFF OF THOSE WOMEN FOR *LITERALLY* TWO SECONDS, THEN THEY...
WAIT A MINUTE, I--

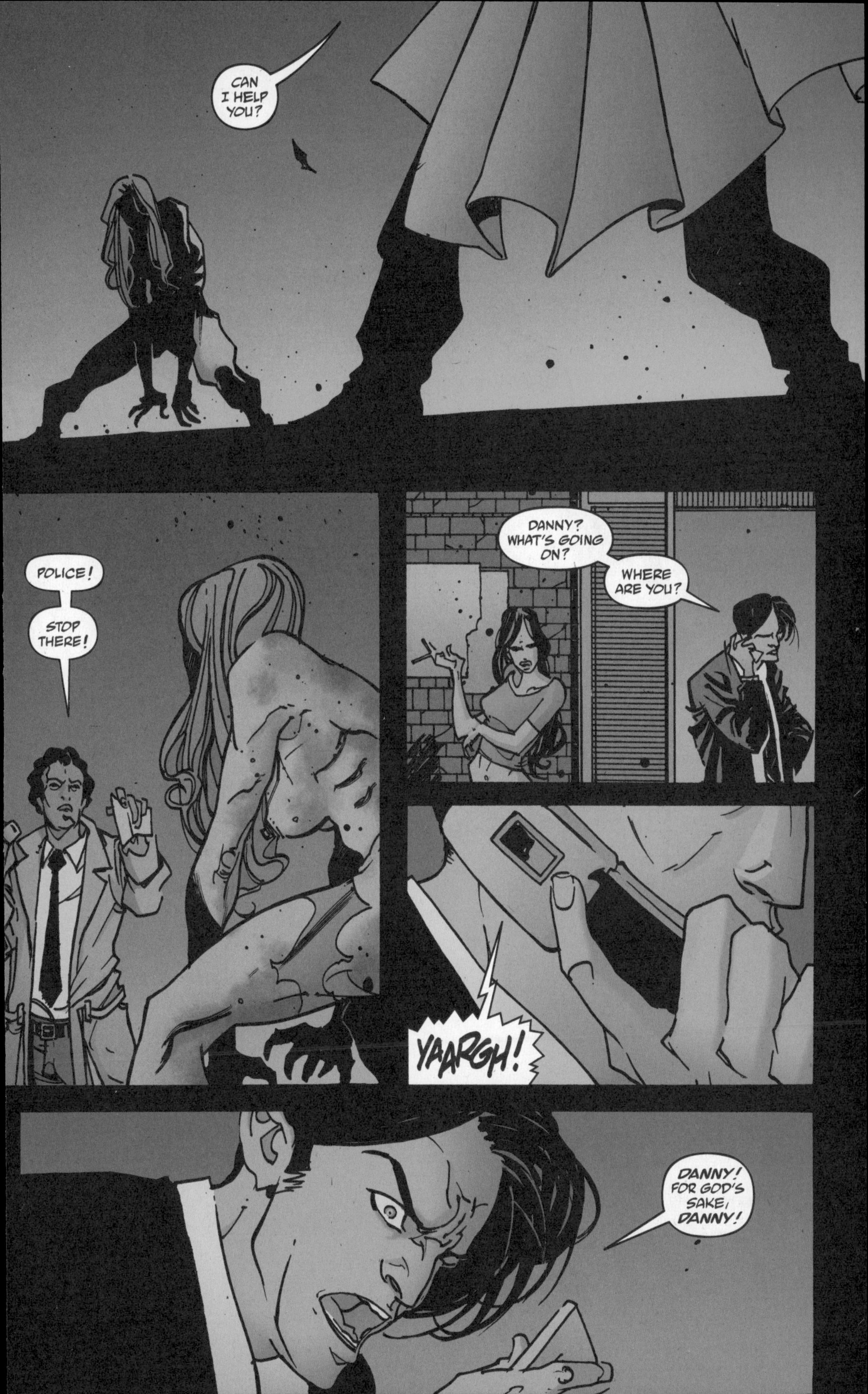

CAN I HELP YOU?
POLICE!
STOP THERE!
DANNY? WHAT'S GOING ON?
WHERE ARE YOU?
YAARGH!
DANNY! FOR GOD'S SAKE, DANNY!

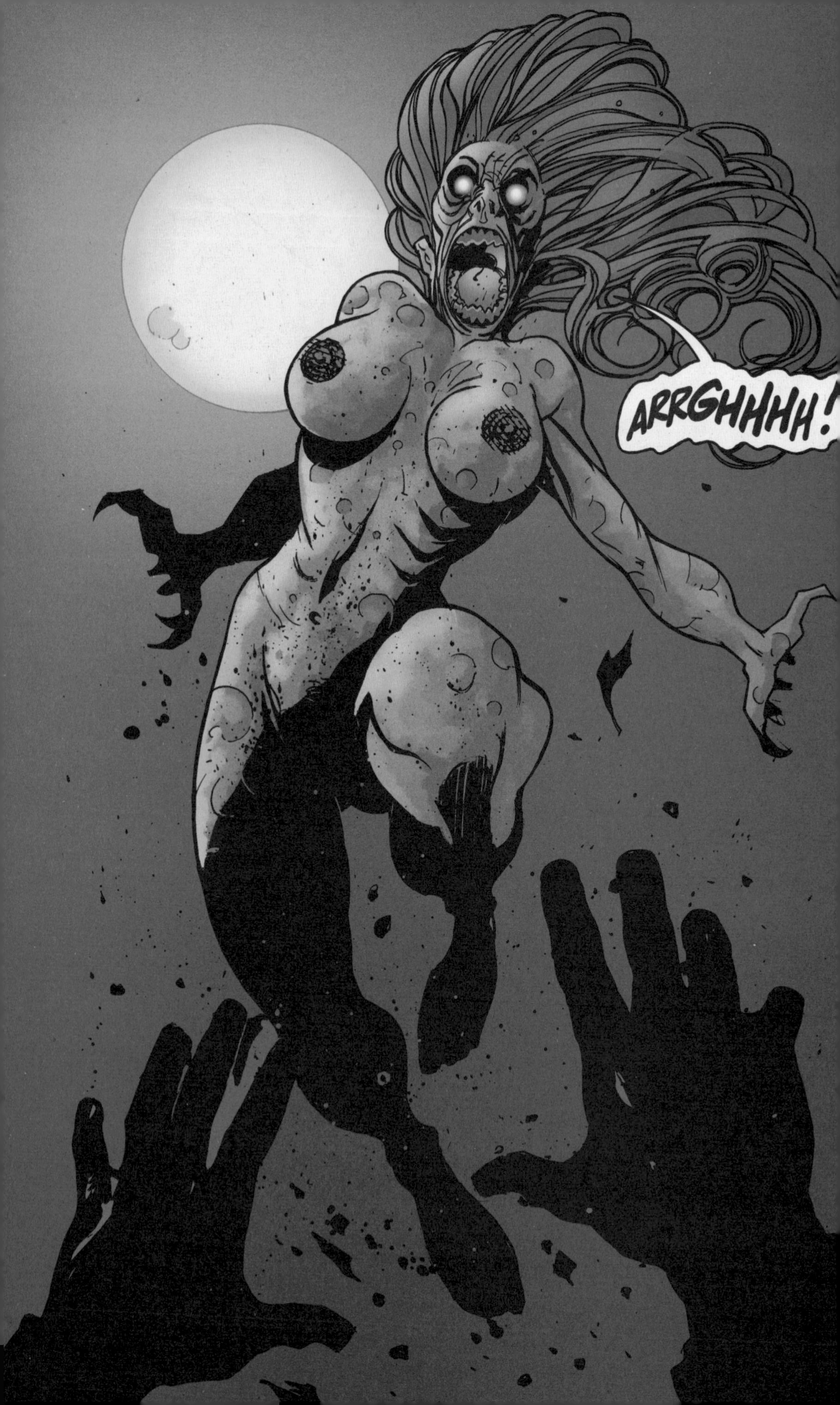
ARRGHHHH!

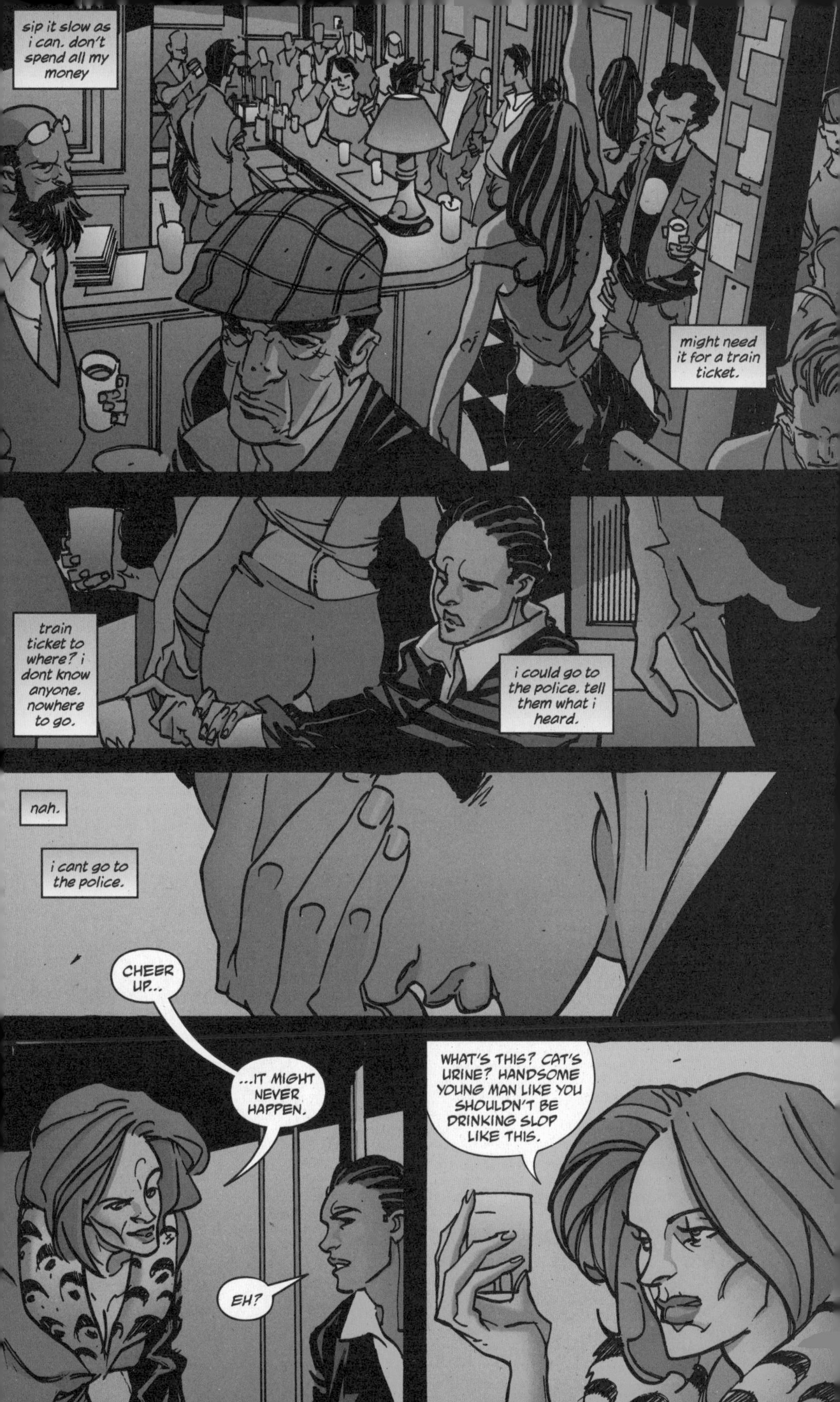
sip it slow as i can. don't spend all my money
might need it for a train ticket.
train ticket to where? i dont know anyone. nowhere to go.
i could go to the police. tell them what i heard.
nah.
i cant go to the police.
CHEER UP...
...IT MIGHT NEVER HAPPEN.
EH?
WHAT'S THIS? CAT'S URINE? HANDSOME YOUNG MAN LIKE YOU SHOULDN'T BE DRINKING SLOP LIKE THIS.

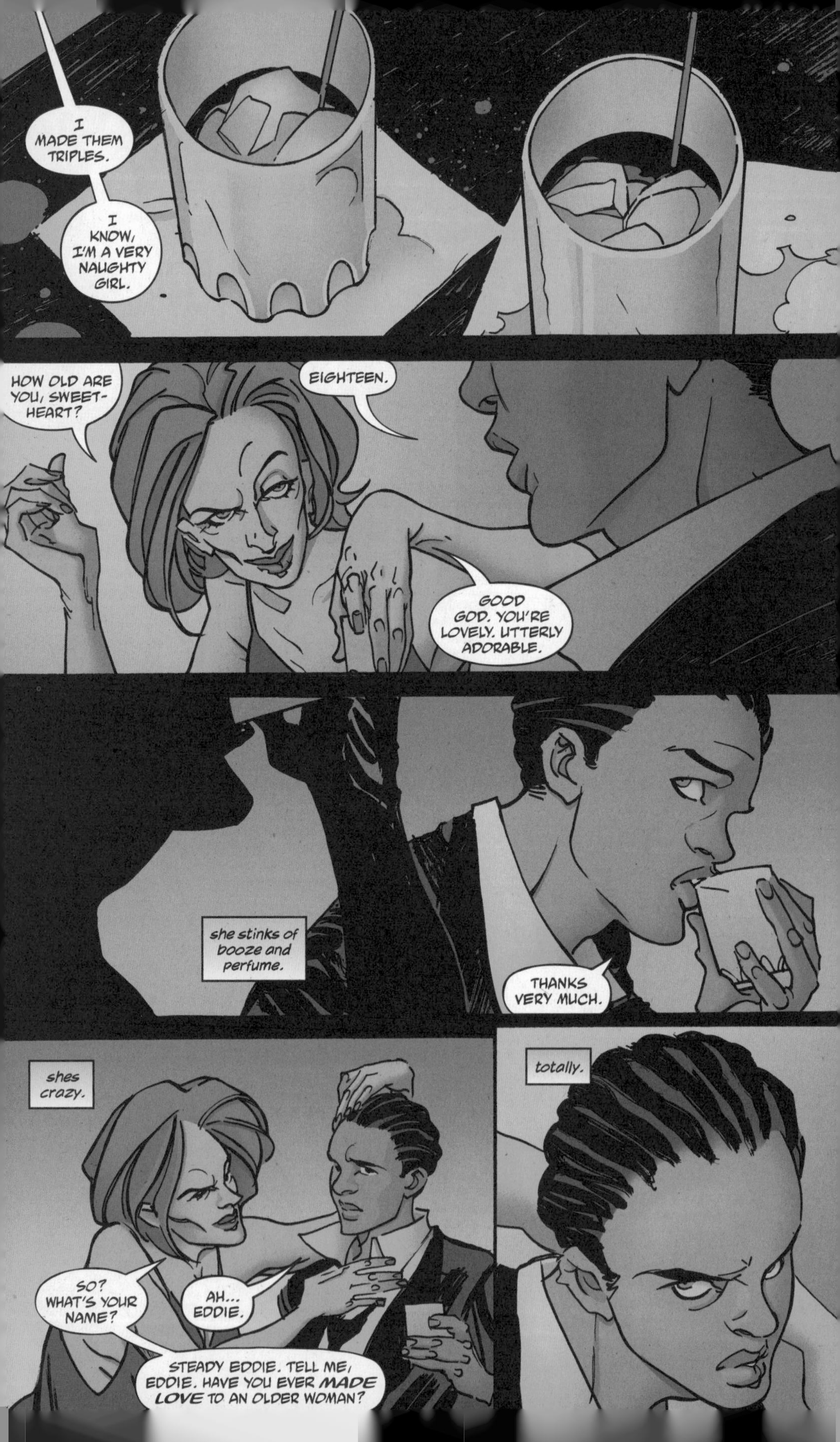

I MADE THEM TRIPLES.
I KNOW, I'M A VERY NAUGHTY GIRL.
HOW OLD ARE YOU, SWEET-HEART?
EIGHTEEN.
GOOD GOD. YOU'RE LOVELY. UTTERLY ADORABLE.
she stinks of booze and perfume.
THANKS VERY MUCH.
shes crazy.
SO? WHAT'S YOUR NAME?
AH... EDDIE.
STEADY EDDIE. TELL ME, EDDIE. HAVE YOU EVER MADE LOVE TO AN OLDER WOMAN?
totally.

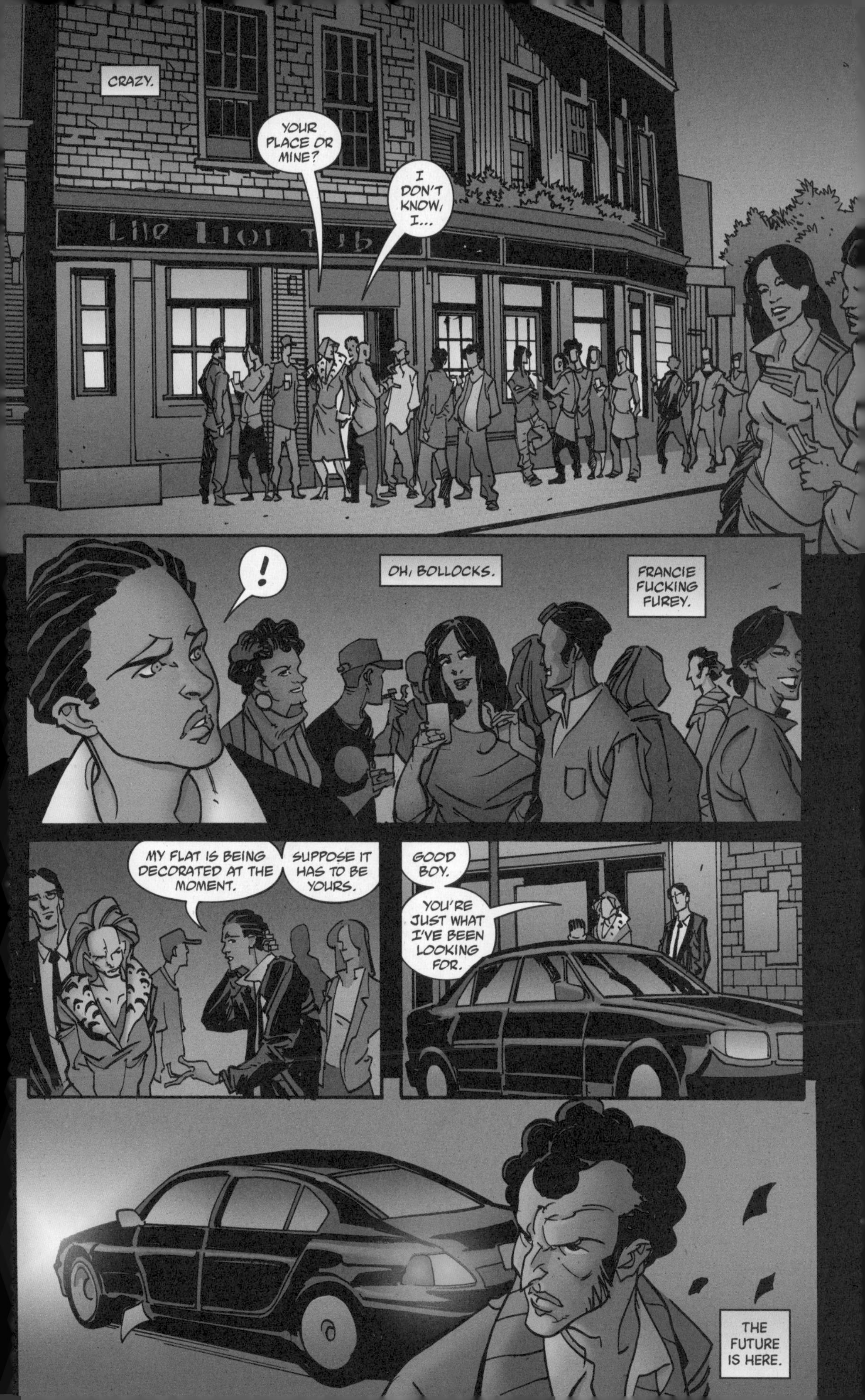
CRAZY.
YOUR PLACE OR MINE?
I DON'T KNOW, I...
!
OH, BOLLOCKS.
FRANCIE FUCKING FUREY.
MY FLAT IS BEING DECORATED AT THE MOMENT.
SUPPOSE IT HAS TO BE YOURS.
GOOD BOY.
YOU'RE JUST WHAT I'VE BEEN LOOKING FOR.
THE FUTURE IS HERE.

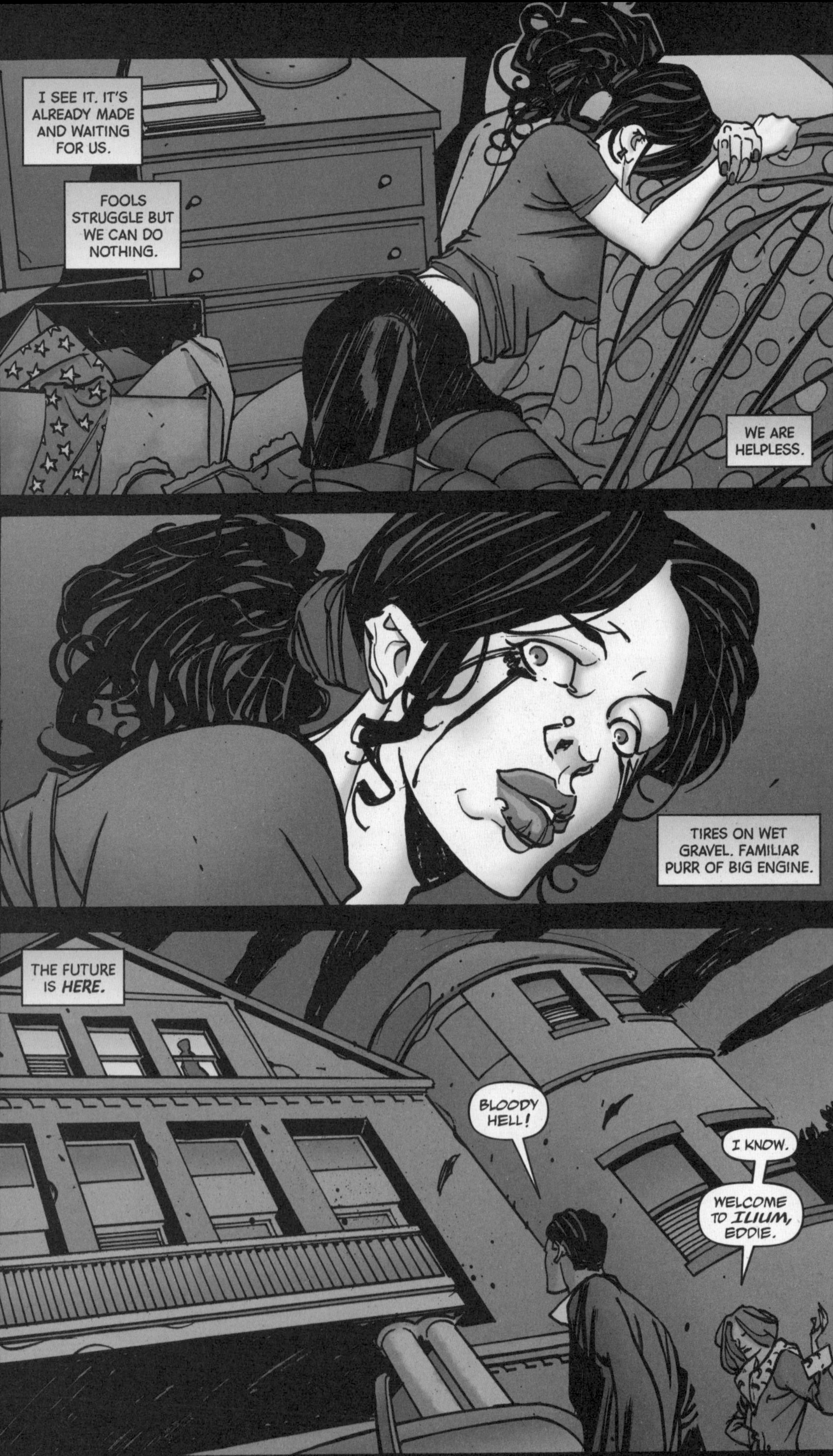
I SEE IT. IT'S ALREADY MADE AND WAITING FOR US.
FOOLS STRUGGLE BUT WE CAN DO NOTHING.
WE ARE HELPLESS.
TIRES ON WET GRAVEL. FAMILIAR PURR OF BIG ENGINE.
THE FUTURE IS *HERE.*
BLOODY HELL!
I KNOW.
WELCOME TO *ILIUM,* EDDIE.

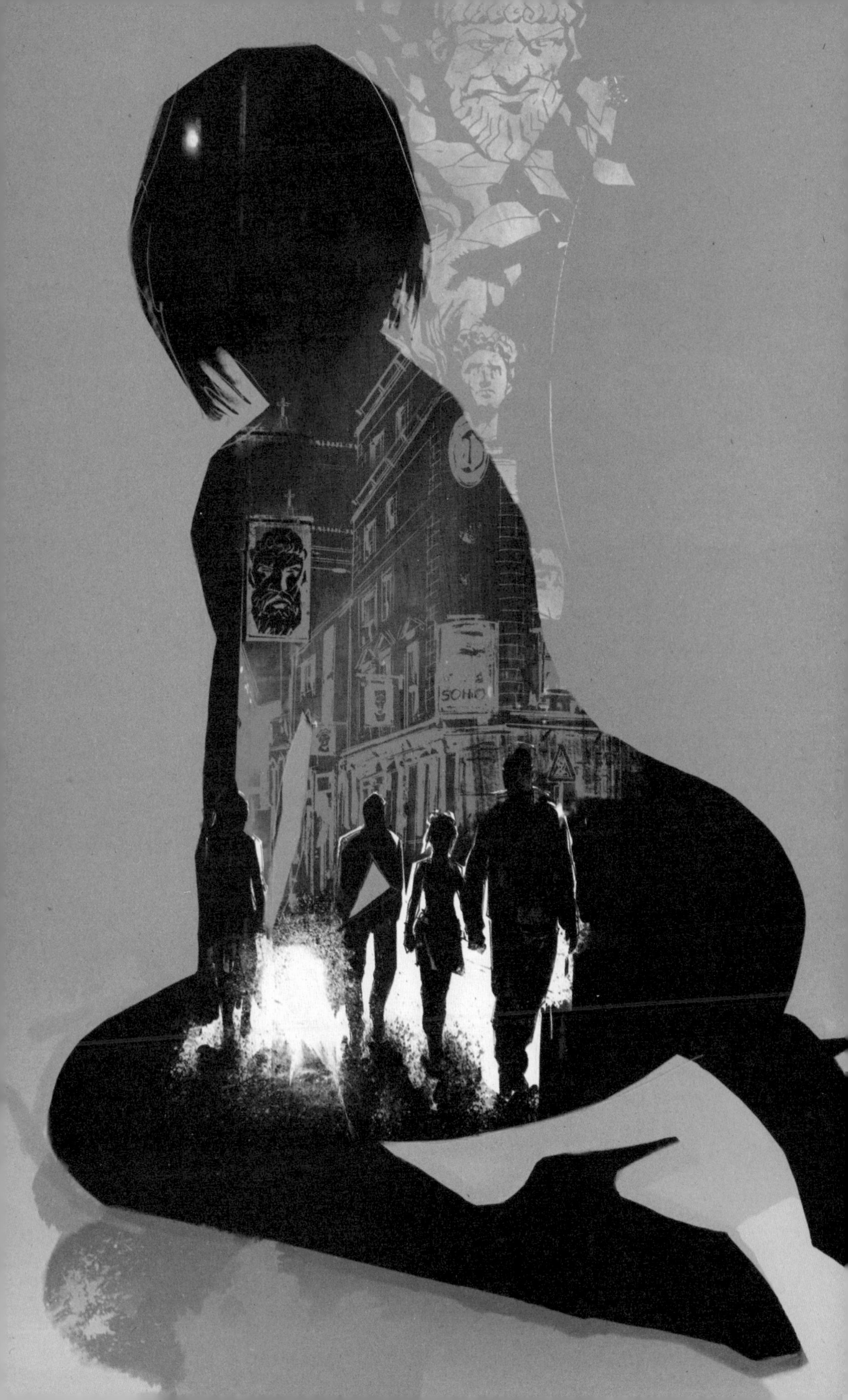
SOHO

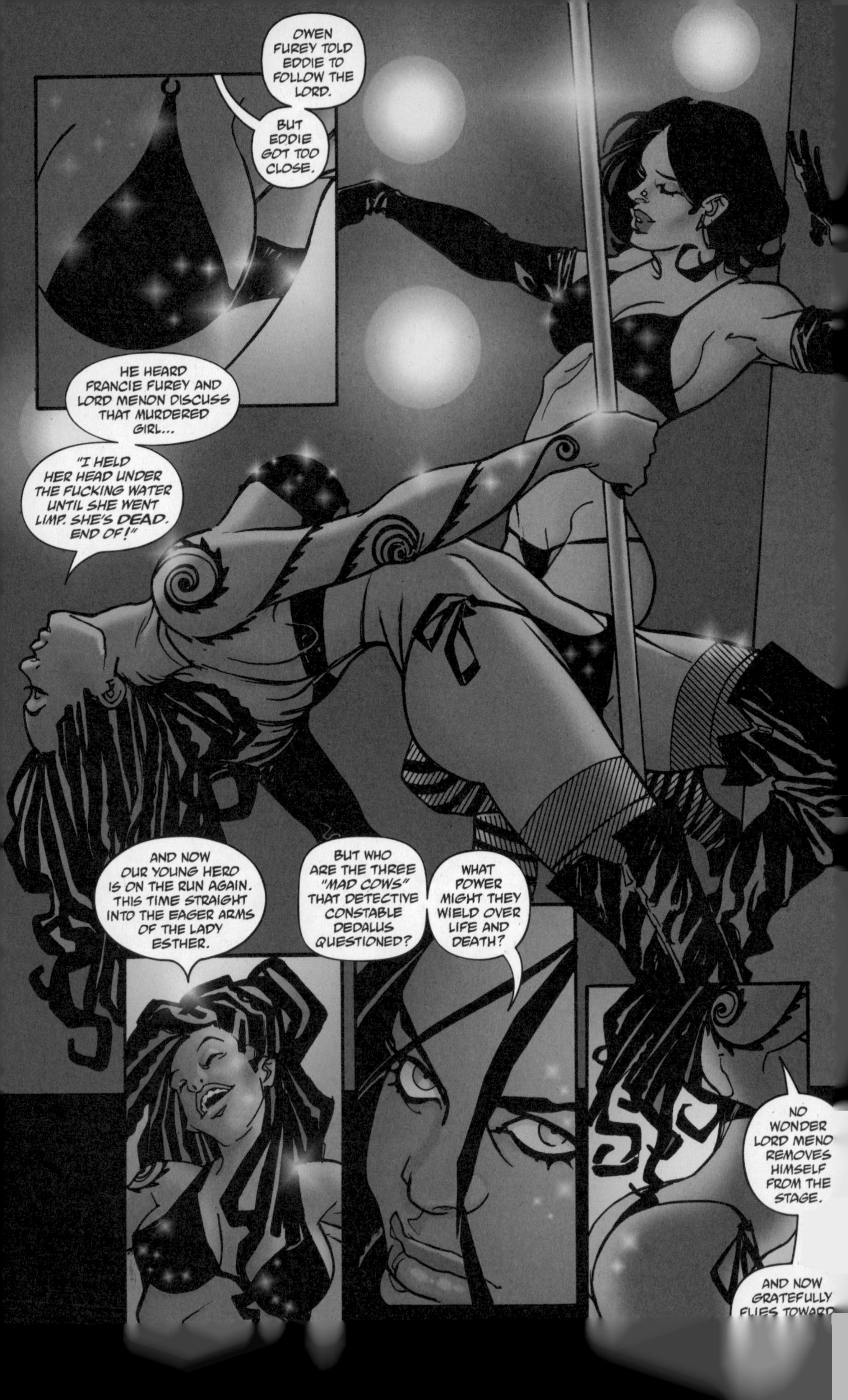
OWEN FUREY TOLD EDDIE TO FOLLOW THE LORD.
BUT EDDIE GOT TOO CLOSE.
HE HEARD FRANCIE FUREY AND LORD MENON DISCUSS THAT MURDERED GIRL...
"I HELD HER HEAD UNDER THE FUCKING WATER UNTIL SHE WENT LIMP. SHE'S *DEAD*. END OF!"
AND NOW OUR YOUNG HERO IS ON THE RUN AGAIN. THIS TIME STRAIGHT INTO THE EAGER ARMS OF THE LADY ESTHER.
BUT WHO ARE THE THREE *"MAD COWS"* THAT DETECTIVE CONSTABLE DEDALUS QUESTIONED?
WHAT POWER MIGHT THEY WIELD OVER LIFE AND DEATH?
NO WONDER LORD MENO REMOVES HIMSELF FROM THE STAGE.
AND NOW GRATEFULLY

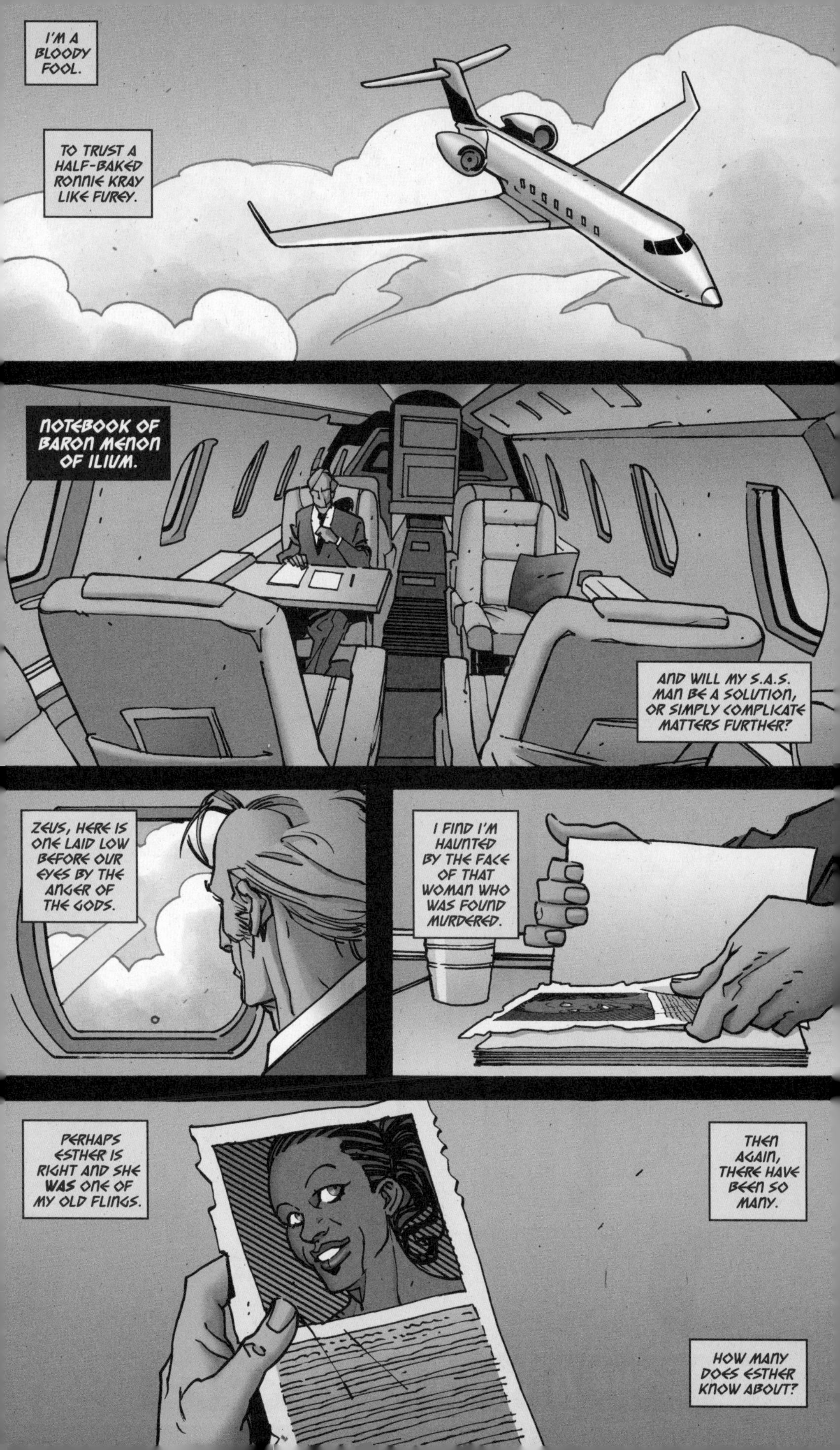
I'M A BLOODY FOOL.
TO TRUST A HALF-BAKED RONNIE KRAY LIKE FUREY.
NOTEBOOK OF BARON MENON OF ILIUM.
AND WILL MY S.A.S. MAN BE A SOLUTION, OR SIMPLY COMPLICATE MATTERS FURTHER?
ZEUS, HERE IS ONE LAID LOW BEFORE OUR EYES BY THE ANGER OF THE GODS.
I FIND I'M HAUNTED BY THE FACE OF THAT WOMAN WHO WAS FOUND MURDERED.
PERHAPS ESTHER IS RIGHT AND SHE WAS ONE OF MY OLD FLINGS.
THEN AGAIN, THERE HAVE BEEN SO MANY.
HOW MANY DOES ESTHER KNOW ABOUT?

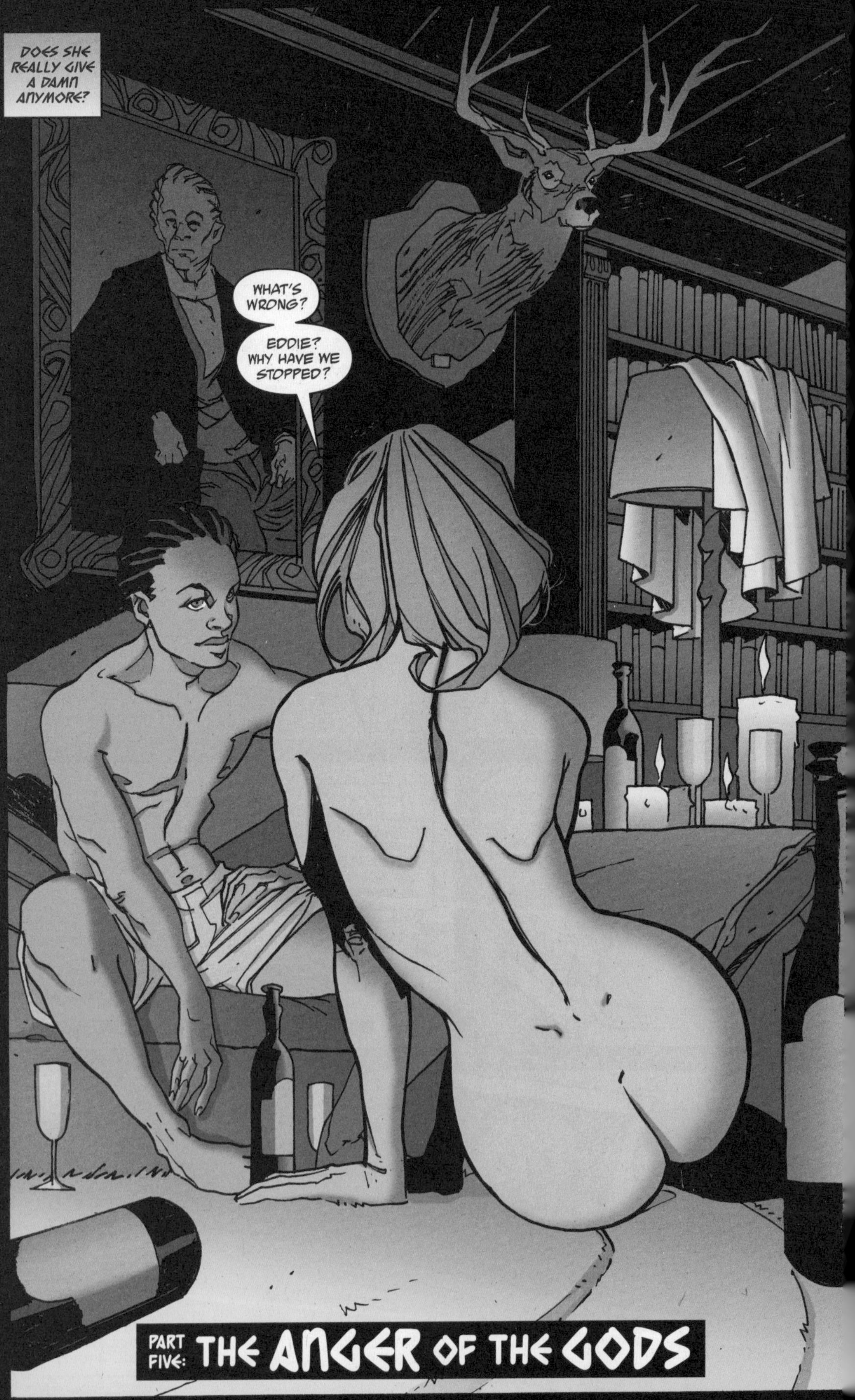
DOES SHE REALLY GIVE A DAMN ANYMORE?
WHAT'S WRONG?
EDDIE? WHY HAVE WE STOPPED?
PART FIVE: THE ANGER OF THE GODS

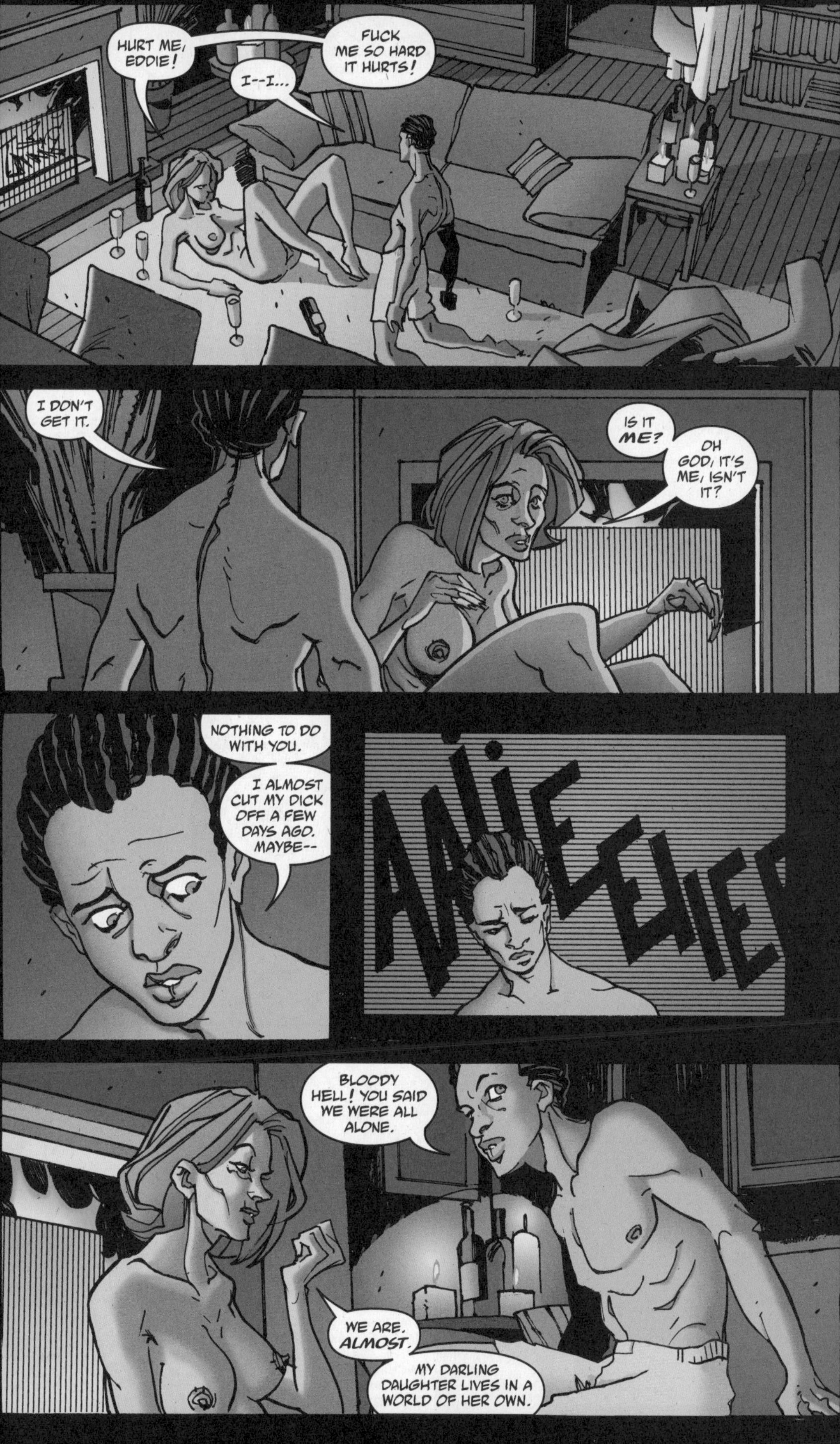
HURT ME, EDDIE!
FUCK ME SO HARD IT HURTS!
I--I...
I DON'T GET IT.
IS IT ME?
OH GOD, IT'S ME, ISN'T IT?
NOTHING TO DO WITH YOU.
I ALMOST CUT MY DICK OFF A FEW DAYS AGO. MAYBE--
BLOODY HELL! YOU SAID WE WERE ALL ALONE.
WE ARE. ALMOST.
MY DARLING DAUGHTER LIVES IN A WORLD OF HER OWN.

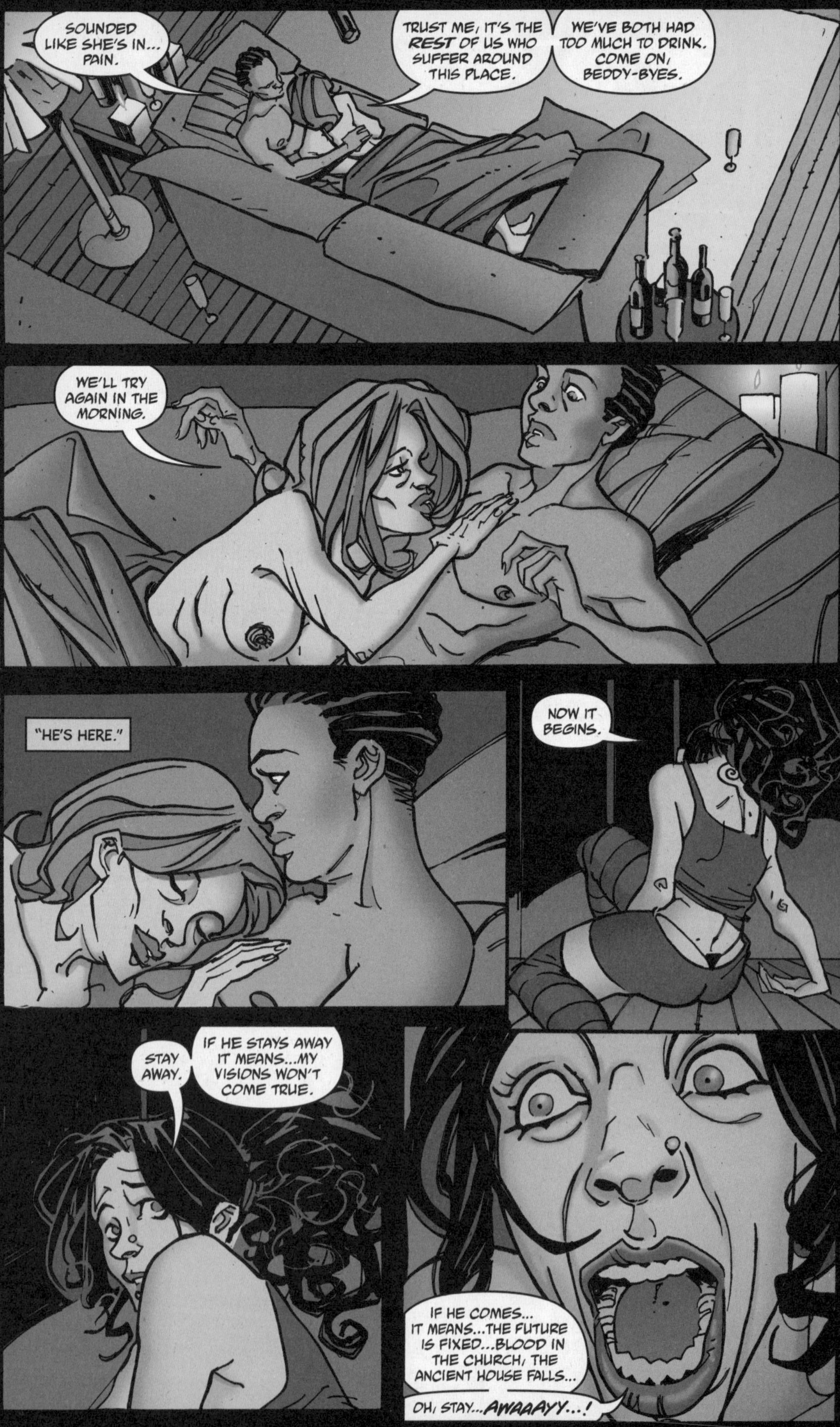
SOUNDED LIKE SHE'S IN... PAIN.
TRUST ME, IT'S THE REST OF US WHO SUFFER AROUND THIS PLACE.
WE'VE BOTH HAD TOO MUCH TO DRINK. COME ON, BEDDY-BYES.
WE'LL TRY AGAIN IN THE MORNING.
"HE'S HERE."
NOW IT BEGINS.
STAY AWAY.
IF HE STAYS AWAY IT MEANS...MY VISIONS WON'T COME TRUE.
IF HE COMES... IT MEANS...THE FUTURE IS FIXED...BLOOD IN THE CHURCH, THE ANCIENT HOUSE FALLS...
OH, STAY...AWAAAYY...!

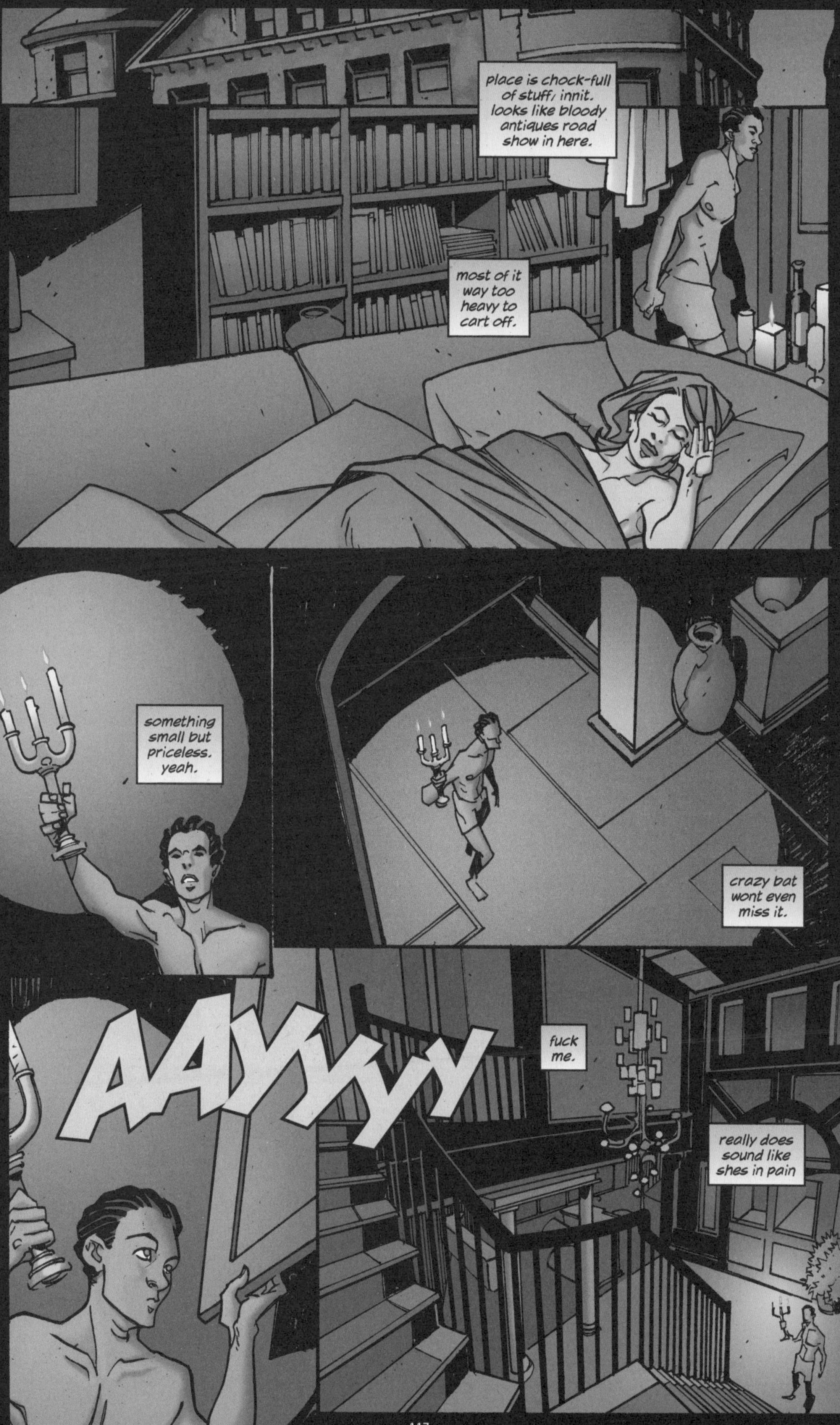

place is chock-full of stuff, innit. looks like bloody antiques road show in here.
most of it way too heavy to cart off.
something small but priceless. yeah.
crazy bat wont even miss it.
AAYYYY
fuck me.
really does sound like shes in pain

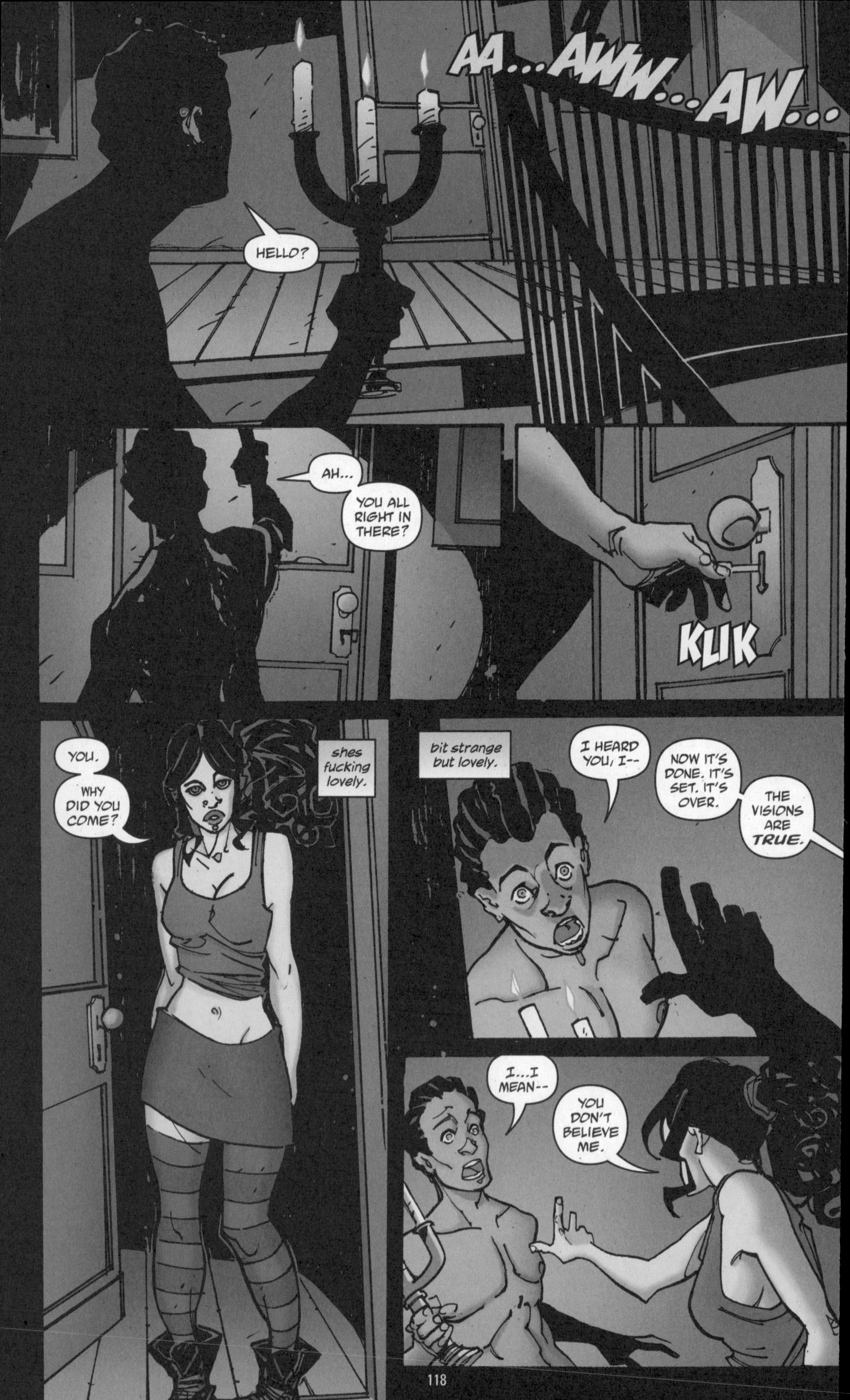

AA...AWW...AW...
HELLO?
AH...
YOU ALL RIGHT IN THERE?
KLIK
YOU.
WHY DID YOU COME?
shes fucking lovely.
bit strange but lovely.
I HEARD YOU, I--
NOW IT'S DONE. IT'S SET. IT'S OVER.
THE VISIONS ARE TRUE.
I...I MEAN--
YOU DON'T BELIEVE ME.

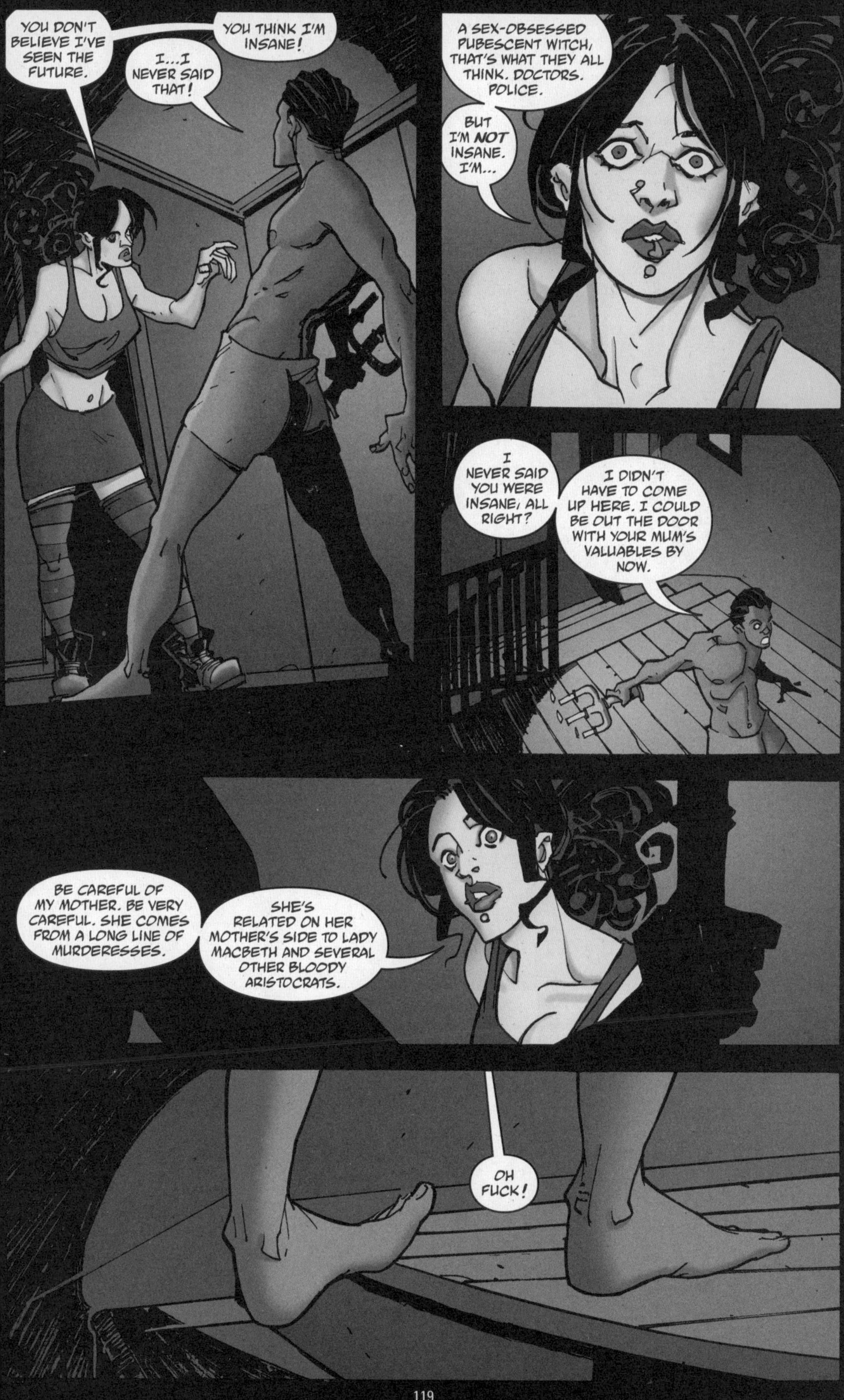
YOU DON'T BELIEVE I'VE SEEN THE FUTURE.
YOU THINK I'M INSANE!
I...I NEVER SAID THAT!
A SEX-OBSESSED PUBESCENT WITCH, THAT'S WHAT THEY ALL THINK. DOCTORS. POLICE.
BUT I'M NOT INSANE. I'M...
I NEVER SAID YOU WERE INSANE, ALL RIGHT?
I DIDN'T HAVE TO COME UP HERE. I COULD BE OUT THE DOOR WITH YOUR MUM'S VALUABLES BY NOW.
BE CAREFUL OF MY MOTHER. BE VERY CAREFUL. SHE COMES FROM A LONG LINE OF MURDERESSES.
SHE'S RELATED ON HER MOTHER'S SIDE TO LADY MACBETH AND SEVERAL OTHER BLOODY ARISTOCRATS.
OH FUCK!

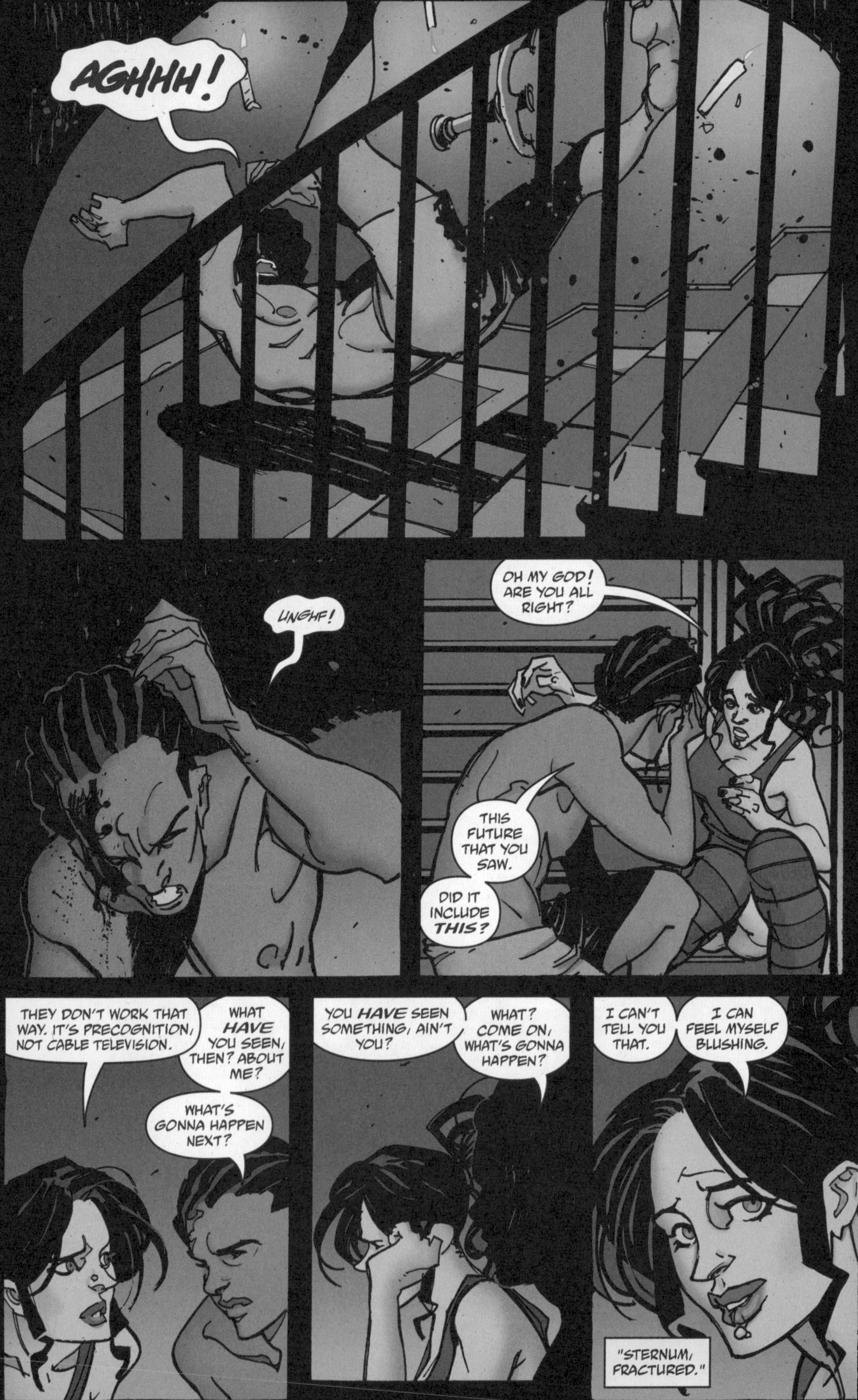
AGHHH!
UNGHF!
OH MY GOD! ARE YOU ALL RIGHT?
THIS FUTURE THAT YOU SAW.
DID IT INCLUDE **THIS**?
THEY DON'T WORK THAT WAY. IT'S PRECOGNITION, NOT CABLE TELEVISION.
WHAT **HAVE** YOU SEEN, THEN? ABOUT ME?
WHAT'S GONNA HAPPEN NEXT?
YOU **HAVE** SEEN SOMETHING, AIN'T YOU?
WHAT? COME ON, WHAT'S GONNA HAPPEN?
I CAN'T TELL YOU THAT.
I CAN FEEL MYSELF BLUSHING.
"STERNUM, FRACTURED."

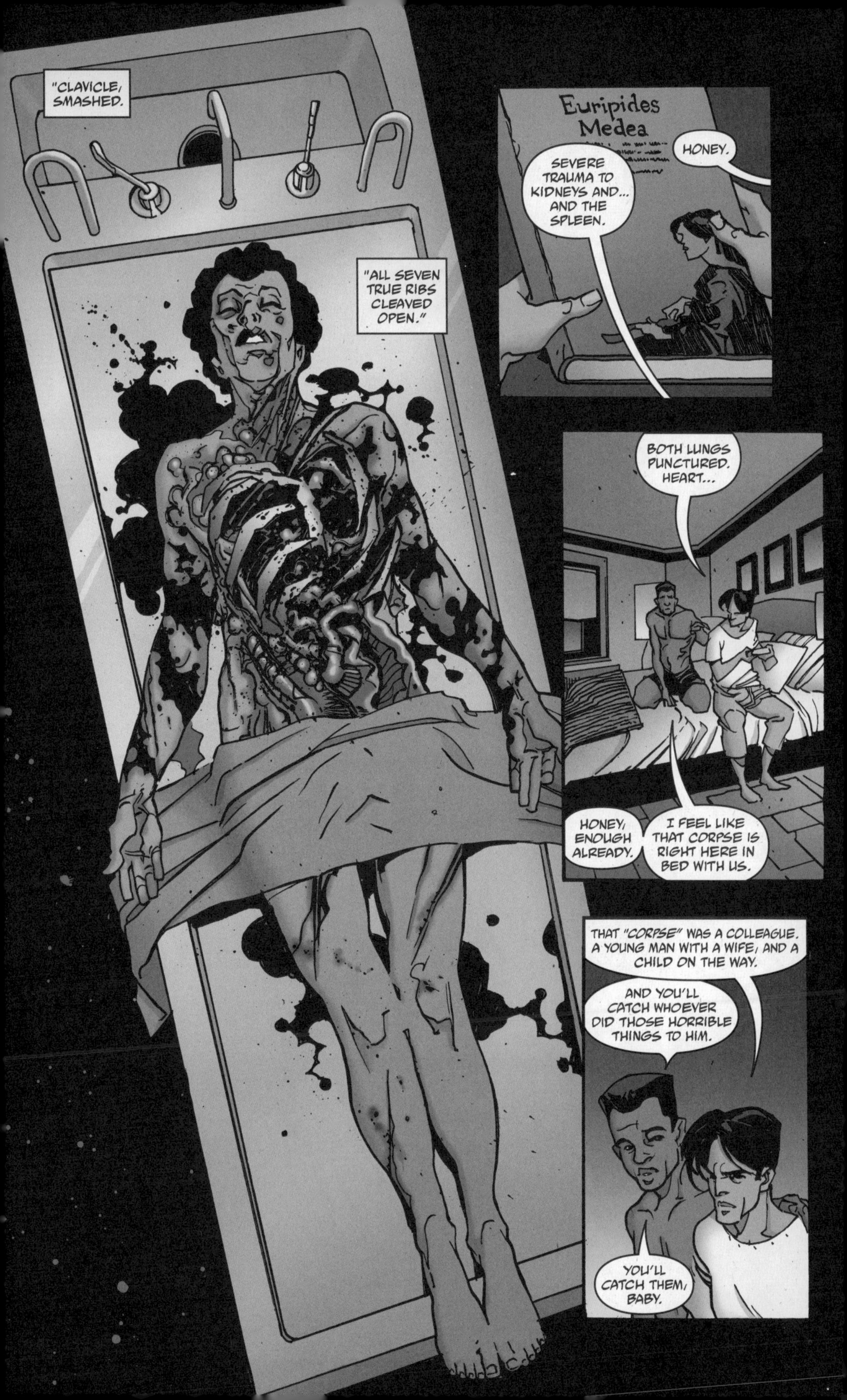
"CLAVICLE, SMASHED.
"ALL SEVEN TRUE RIBS CLEAVED OPEN."
Euripides Medea
SEVERE TRAUMA TO KIDNEYS AND... AND THE SPLEEN.
HONEY.
BOTH LUNGS PUNCTURED. HEART...
HONEY, ENOUGH ALREADY.
I FEEL LIKE THAT CORPSE IS RIGHT HERE IN BED WITH US.
THAT "CORPSE" WAS A COLLEAGUE. A YOUNG MAN WITH A WIFE, AND A CHILD ON THE WAY.
AND YOU'LL CATCH WHOEVER DID THOSE HORRIBLE THINGS TO HIM.
YOU'LL CATCH THEM, BABY.

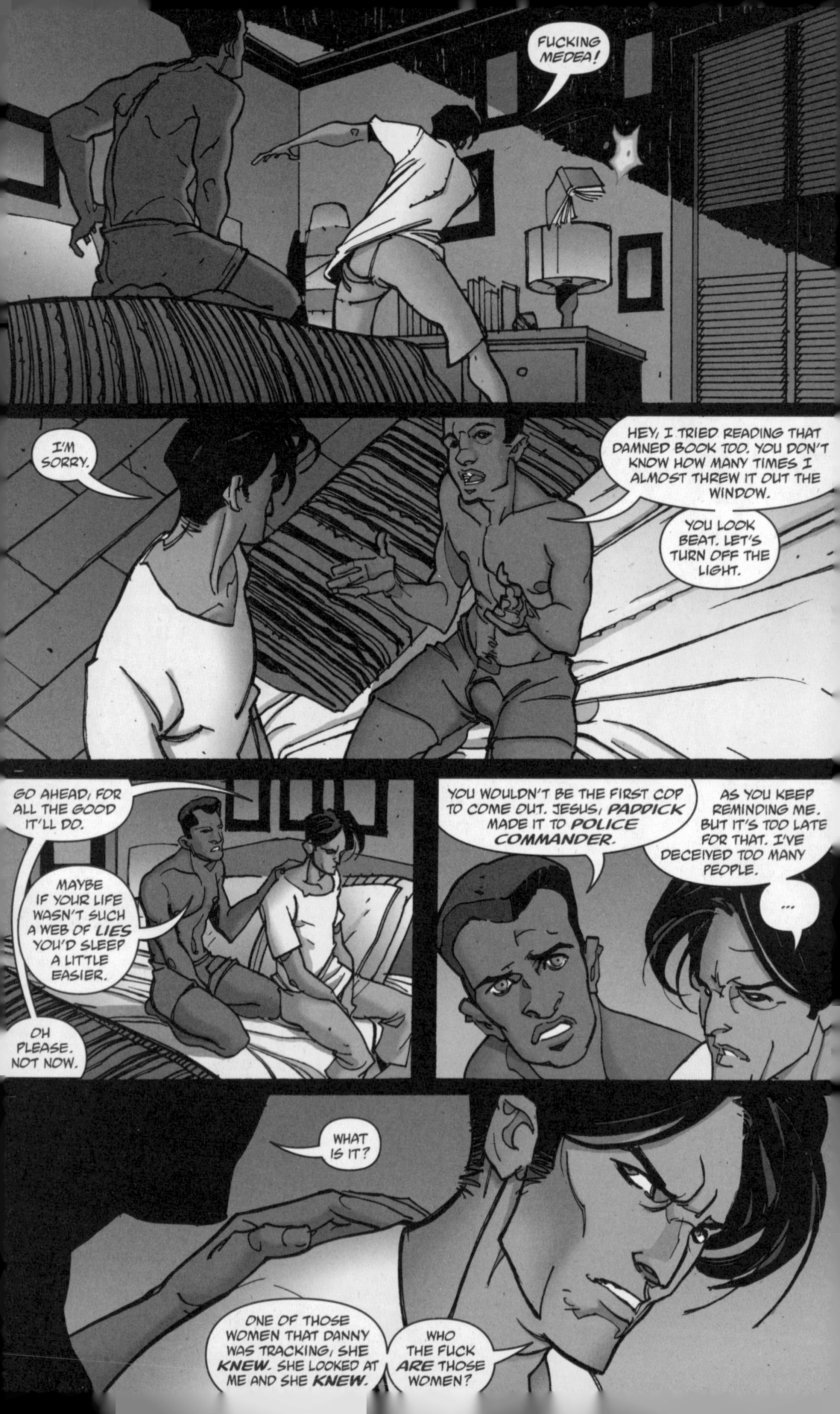
FUCKING MEDEA!
I'M SORRY.
HEY, I TRIED READING THAT DAMNED BOOK TOO. YOU DON'T KNOW HOW MANY TIMES I ALMOST THREW IT OUT THE WINDOW.
YOU LOOK BEAT. LET'S TURN OFF THE LIGHT.
GO AHEAD, FOR ALL THE GOOD IT'LL DO.
MAYBE IF YOUR LIFE WASN'T SUCH A WEB OF LIES YOU'D SLEEP A LITTLE EASIER.
OH PLEASE. NOT NOW.
YOU WOULDN'T BE THE FIRST COP TO COME OUT. JESUS, PADDICK MADE IT TO POLICE COMMANDER.
AS YOU KEEP REMINDING ME. BUT IT'S TOO LATE FOR THAT. I'VE DECEIVED TOO MANY PEOPLE.
...
WHAT IS IT?
ONE OF THOSE WOMEN THAT DANNY WAS TRACKING, SHE KNEW. SHE LOOKED AT ME AND SHE KNEW.
WHO THE FUCK ARE THOSE WOMEN?

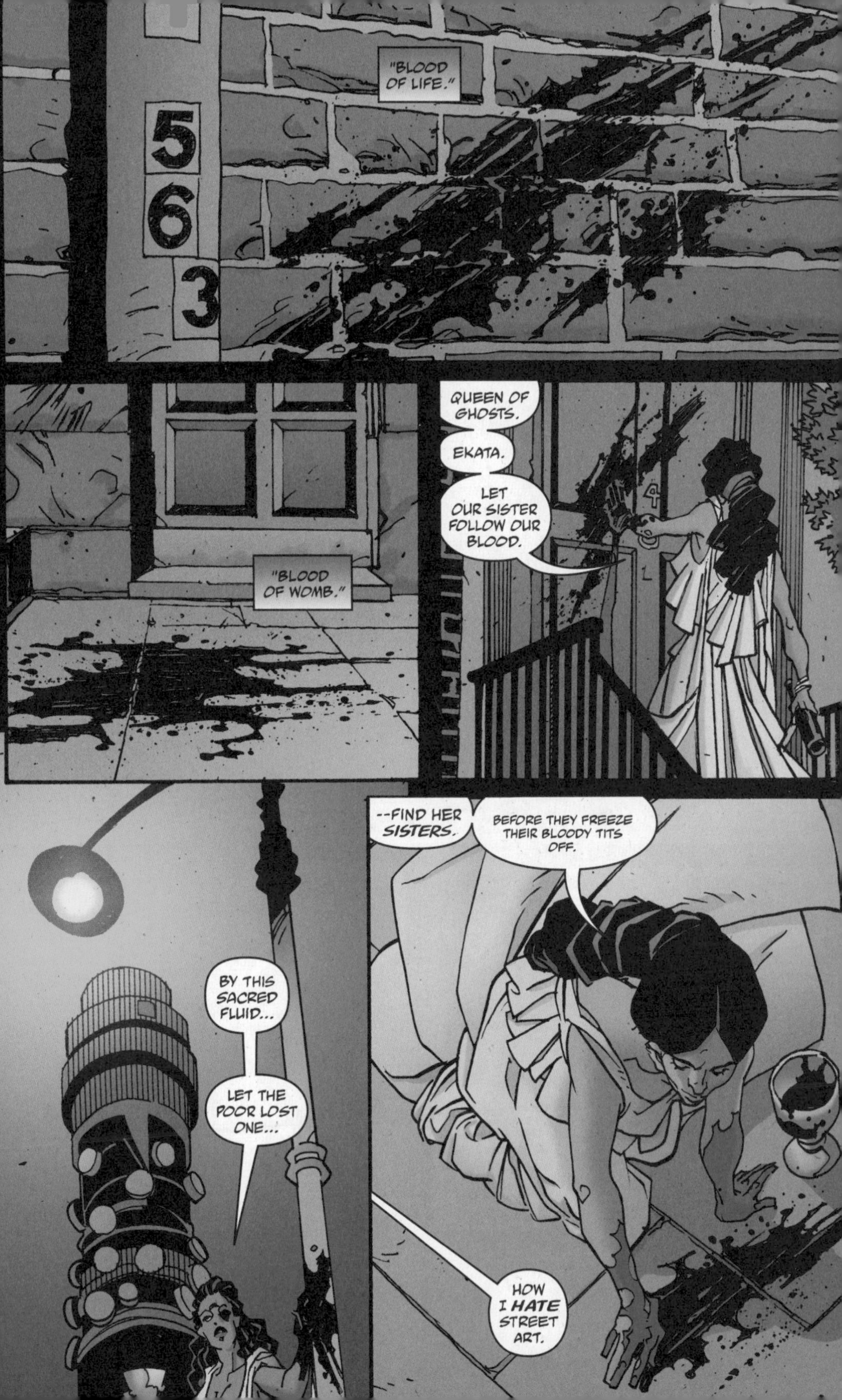
"BLOOD OF LIFE."
"BLOOD OF WOMB."
QUEEN OF GHOSTS.
EKATA.
LET OUR SISTER FOLLOW OUR BLOOD.
BY THIS SACRED FLUID...
LET THE POOR LOST ONE...
--FIND HER SISTERS.
BEFORE THEY FREEZE THEIR BLOODY TITS OFF.
HOW I HATE STREET ART.

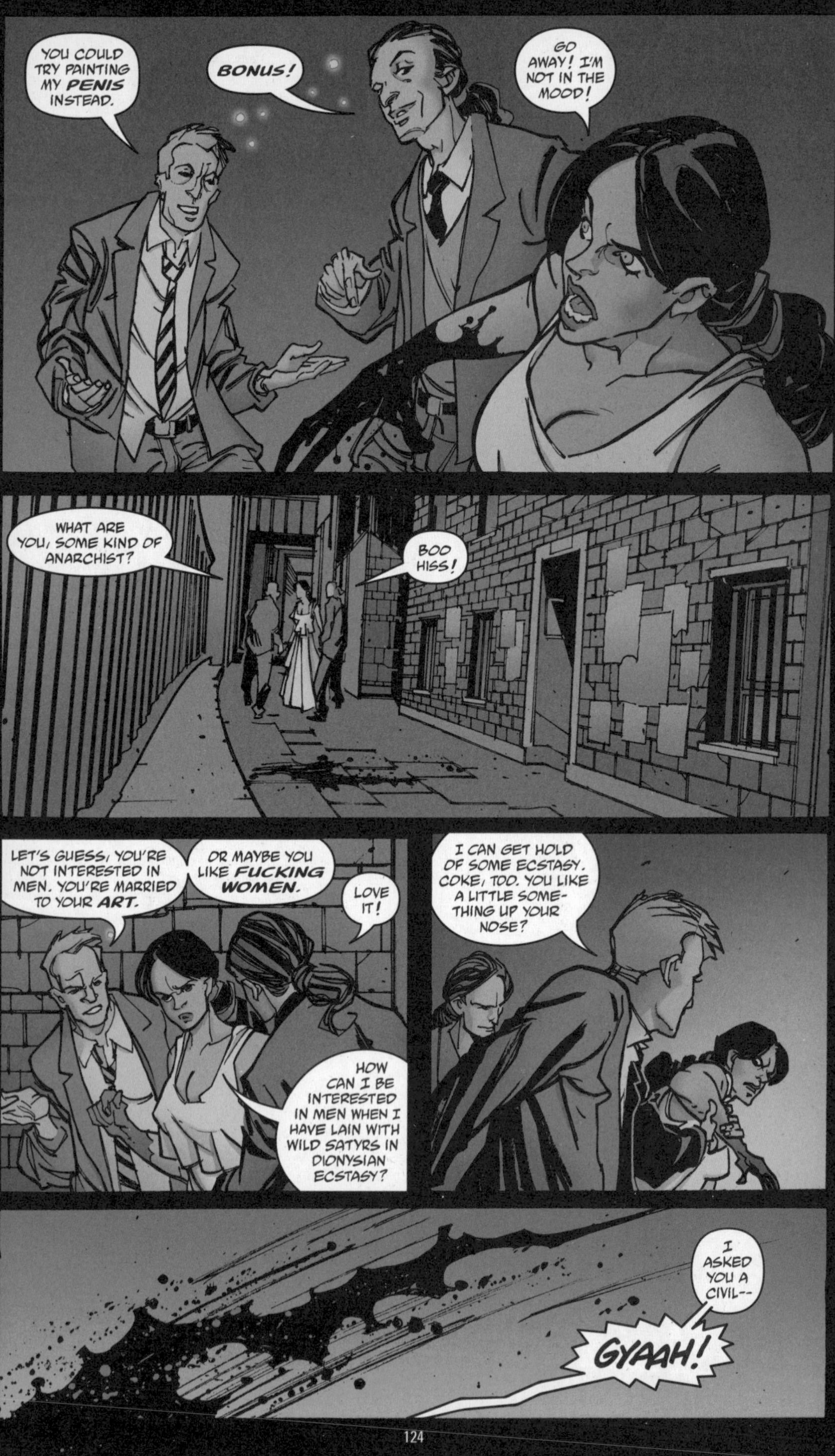

YOU COULD TRY PAINTING MY PENIS INSTEAD.
BONUS!
GO AWAY! I'M NOT IN THE MOOD!
WHAT ARE YOU, SOME KIND OF ANARCHIST?
BOO HISS!
LET'S GUESS, YOU'RE NOT INTERESTED IN MEN. YOU'RE MARRIED TO YOUR ART.
OR MAYBE YOU LIKE FUCKING WOMEN.
LOVE IT!
HOW CAN I BE INTERESTED IN MEN WHEN I HAVE LAIN WITH WILD SATYRS IN DIONYSIAN ECSTASY?
I CAN GET HOLD OF SOME ECSTASY. COKE, TOO. YOU LIKE A LITTLE SOME-THING UP YOUR NOSE?
I ASKED YOU A CIVIL--
GYAAH!

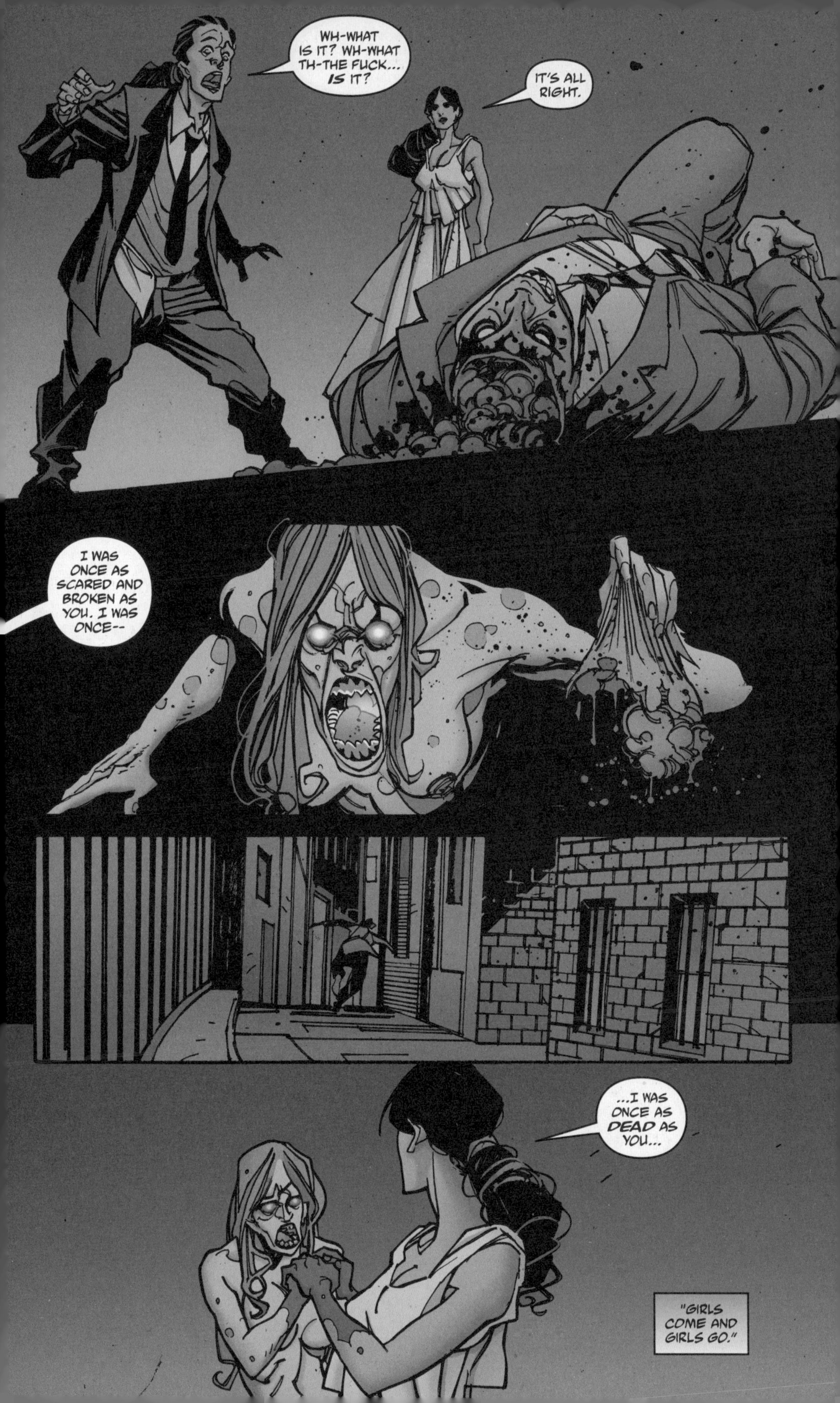

WH-WHAT IS IT? WH-WHAT TH-THE FUCK... IS IT?
IT'S ALL RIGHT.
I WAS ONCE AS SCARED AND BROKEN AS YOU. I WAS ONCE--
...I WAS ONCE AS DEAD AS YOU...
"GIRLS COME AND GIRLS GO."

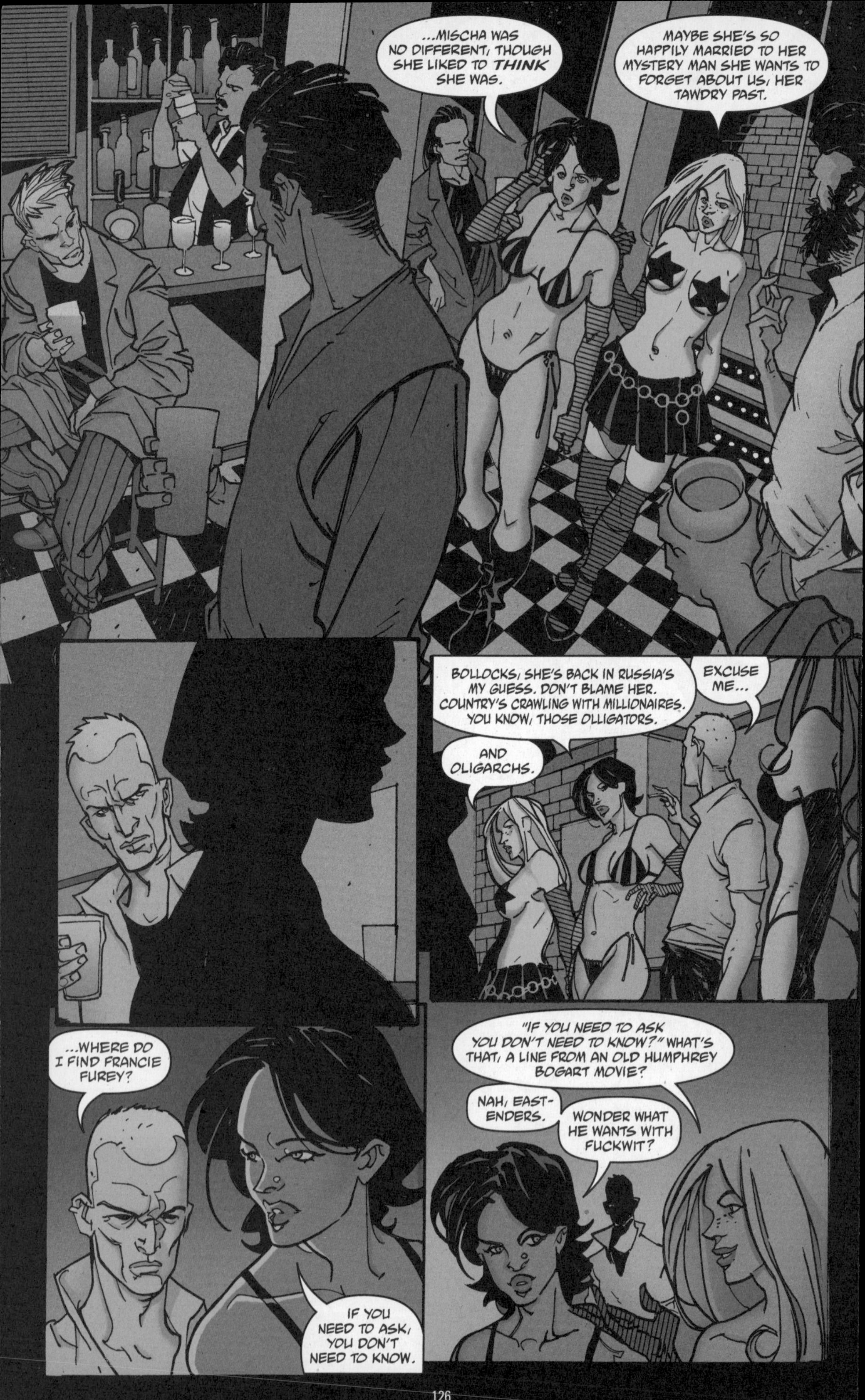
...MISCHA WAS NO DIFFERENT, THOUGH SHE LIKED TO THINK SHE WAS.
MAYBE SHE'S SO HAPPILY MARRIED TO HER MYSTERY MAN SHE WANTS TO FORGET ABOUT US, HER TAWDRY PAST.
BOLLOCKS, SHE'S BACK IN RUSSIA'S MY GUESS. DON'T BLAME HER. COUNTRY'S CRAWLING WITH MILLIONAIRES. YOU KNOW, THOSE OLLIGATORS.
AND OLIGARCHS.
EXCUSE ME...
...WHERE DO I FIND FRANCIE FUREY?
IF YOU NEED TO ASK, YOU DON'T NEED TO KNOW.
"IF YOU NEED TO ASK YOU DON'T NEED TO KNOW?" WHAT'S THAT, A LINE FROM AN OLD HUMPHREY BOGART MOVIE?
NAH, EAST-ENDERS.
WONDER WHAT HE WANTS WITH FUCKWIT?

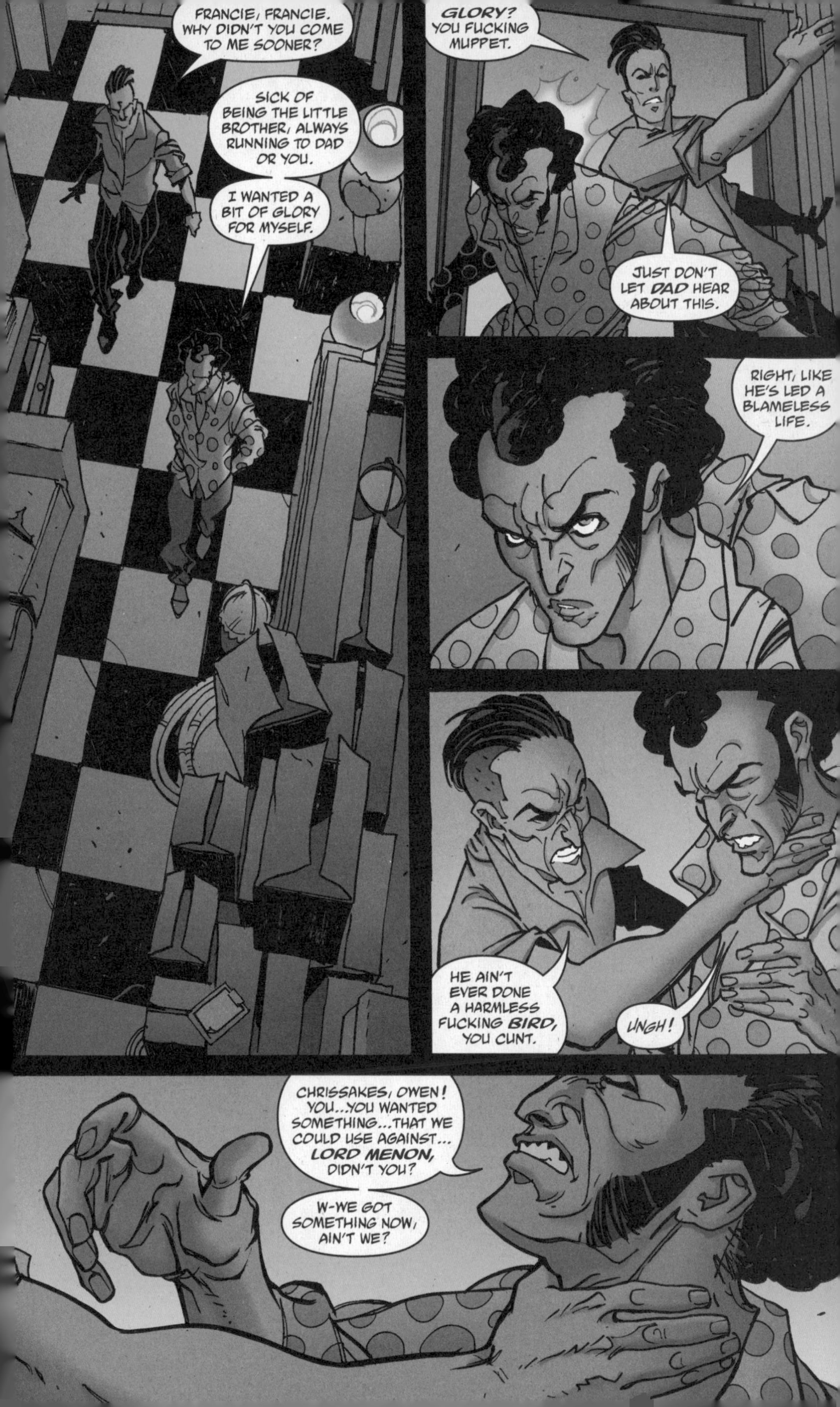
FRANCIE, FRANCIE. WHY DIDN'T YOU COME TO ME SOONER?
SICK OF BEING THE LITTLE BROTHER, ALWAYS RUNNING TO DAD OR YOU.
I WANTED A BIT OF GLORY FOR MYSELF.
GLORY? YOU FUCKING MUPPET.
JUST DON'T LET DAD HEAR ABOUT THIS.
RIGHT, LIKE HE'S LED A BLAMELESS LIFE.
HE AIN'T EVER DONE A HARMLESS FUCKING BIRD, YOU CUNT.
UNGH!
CHRISSAKES, OWEN! YOU...YOU WANTED SOMETHING...THAT WE COULD USE AGAINST... LORD MENON, DIDN'T YOU?
W-WE GOT SOMETHING NOW, AIN'T WE?

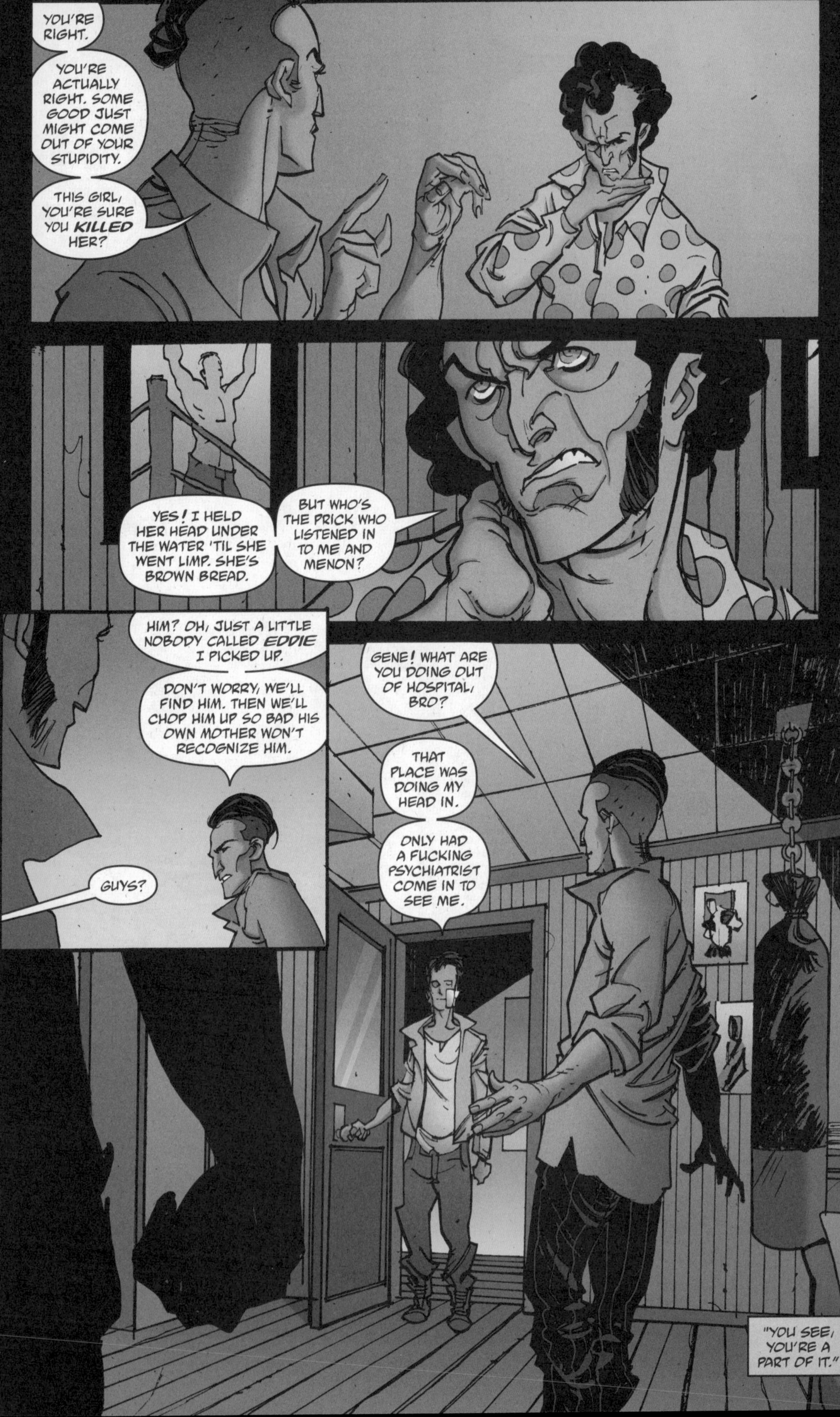
YOU'RE RIGHT.
YOU'RE ACTUALLY RIGHT. SOME GOOD JUST MIGHT COME OUT OF YOUR STUPIDITY.
THIS GIRL, YOU'RE SURE YOU **KILLED** HER?
YES! I HELD HER HEAD UNDER THE WATER 'TIL SHE WENT LIMP. SHE'S BROWN BREAD.
BUT WHO'S THE PRICK WHO LISTENED IN TO ME AND MENON?
HIM? OH, JUST A LITTLE NOBODY CALLED *EDDIE* I PICKED UP.
DON'T WORRY, WE'LL FIND HIM. THEN WE'LL CHOP HIM UP SO BAD HIS OWN MOTHER WON'T RECOGNIZE HIM.
GUYS?
GENE! WHAT ARE YOU DOING OUT OF HOSPITAL, BRO?
THAT PLACE WAS DOING MY HEAD IN.
ONLY HAD A FUCKING PSYCHIATRIST COME IN TO SEE ME.
"YOU SEE, YOU'RE A PART OF IT."

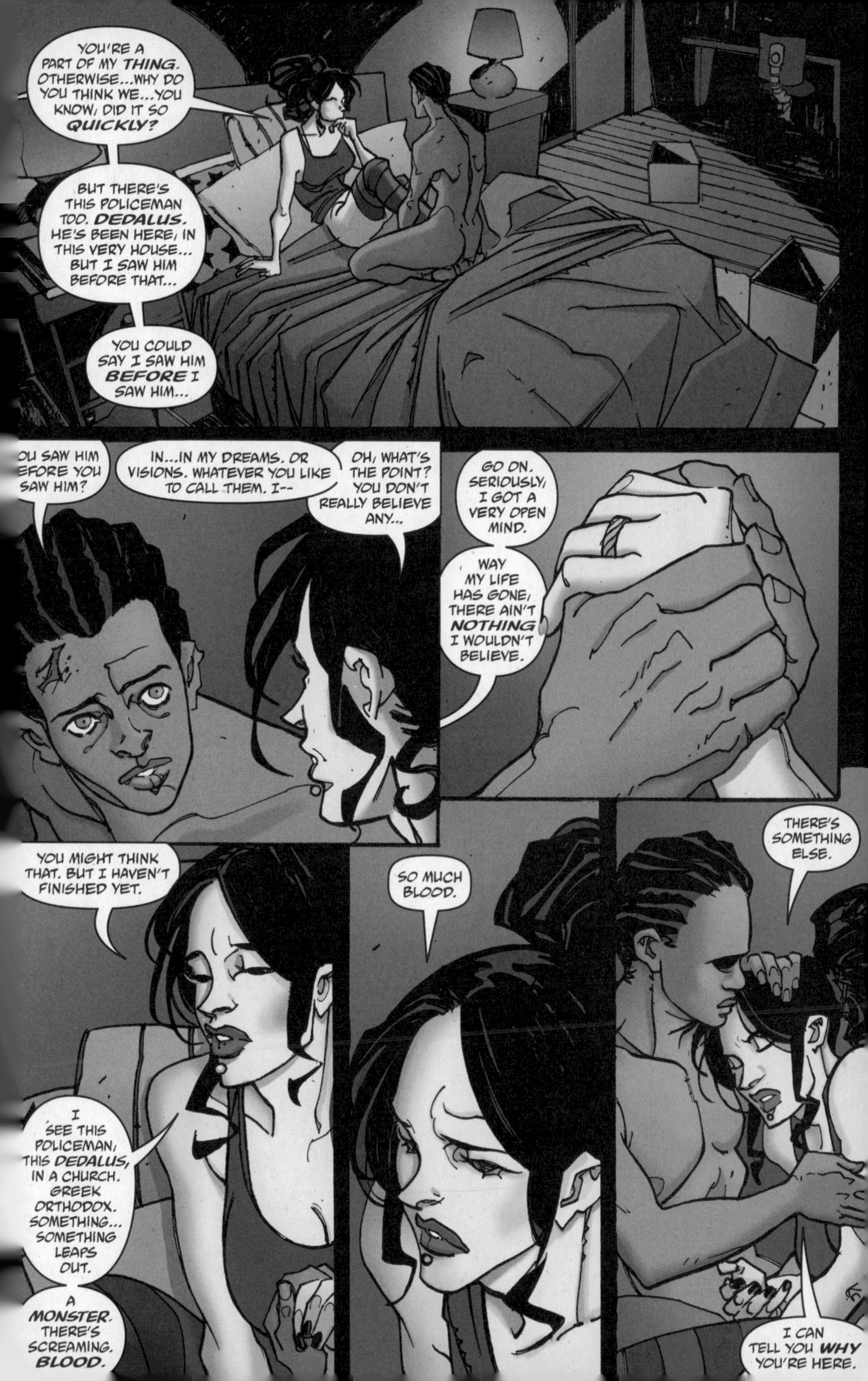
YOU'RE A PART OF MY THING. OTHERWISE...WHY DO YOU THINK WE...YOU KNOW, DID IT SO QUICKLY?
BUT THERE'S THIS POLICEMAN TOO. DEDALUS. HE'S BEEN HERE, IN THIS VERY HOUSE... BUT I SAW HIM BEFORE THAT...
YOU COULD SAY I SAW HIM BEFORE I SAW HIM...
OU SAW HIM EFORE YOU SAW HIM?
IN...IN MY DREAMS. OR VISIONS. WHATEVER YOU LIKE TO CALL THEM. I--
OH, WHAT'S THE POINT? YOU DON'T REALLY BELIEVE ANY...
GO ON. SERIOUSLY, I GOT A VERY OPEN MIND.
WAY MY LIFE HAS GONE, THERE AIN'T NOTHING I WOULDN'T BELIEVE.
YOU MIGHT THINK THAT. BUT I HAVEN'T FINISHED YET.
I SEE THIS POLICEMAN, THIS DEDALUS, IN A CHURCH. GREEK ORTHODOX. SOMETHING... SOMETHING LEAPS OUT.
A MONSTER. THERE'S SCREAMING. BLOOD.
SO MUCH BLOOD.
THERE'S SOMETHING ELSE.
I CAN TELL YOU WHY YOU'RE HERE.

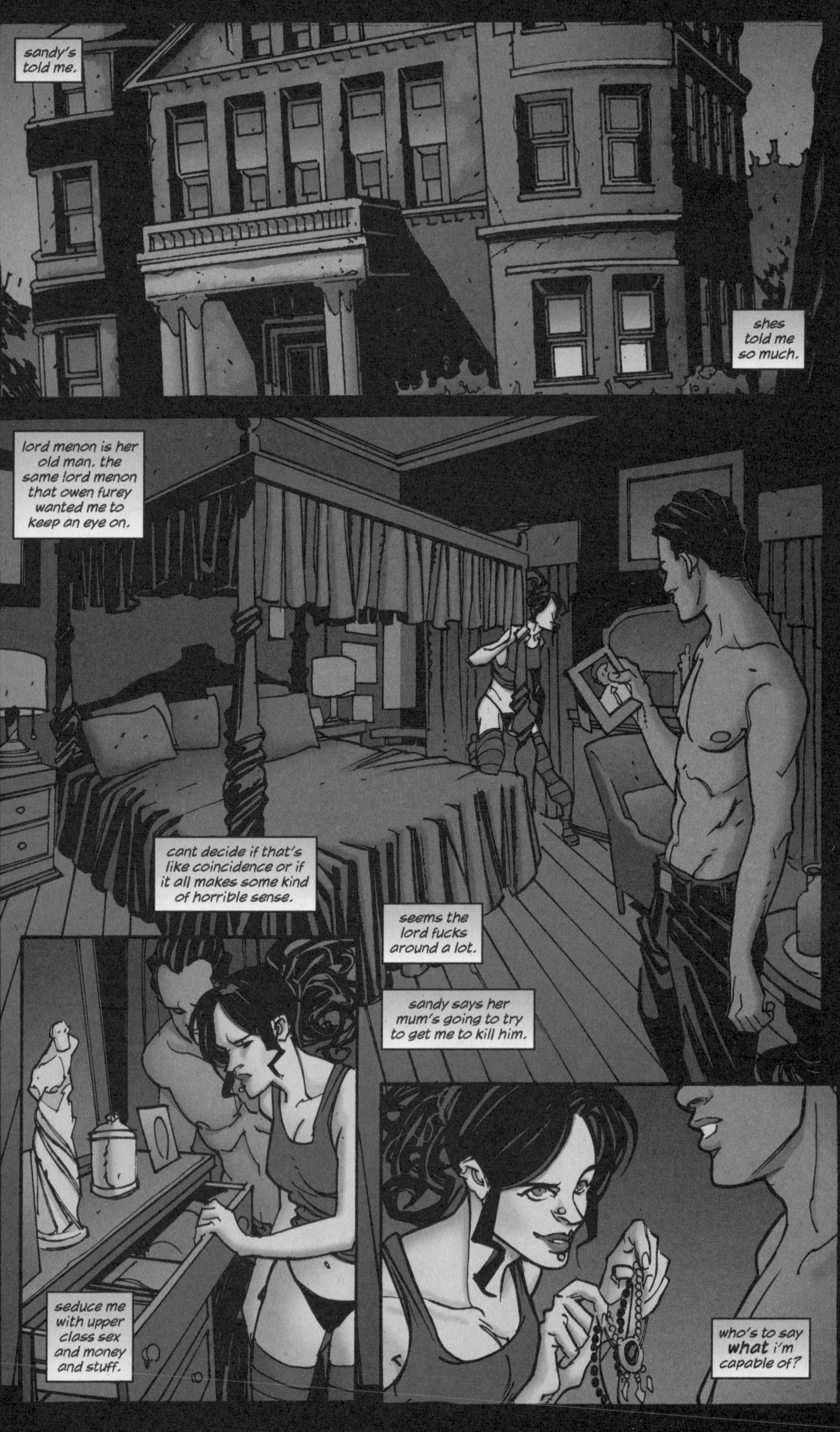
sandy's told me.
shes told me so much.
lord menon is her old man. the same lord menon that owen furey wanted me to keep an eye on.
cant decide if that's like coincidence or if it all makes some kind of horrible sense.
seems the lord fucks around a lot.
sandy says her mum's going to try to get me to kill him.
seduce me with upper class sex and money and stuff.
who's to say **what** i'm capable of?

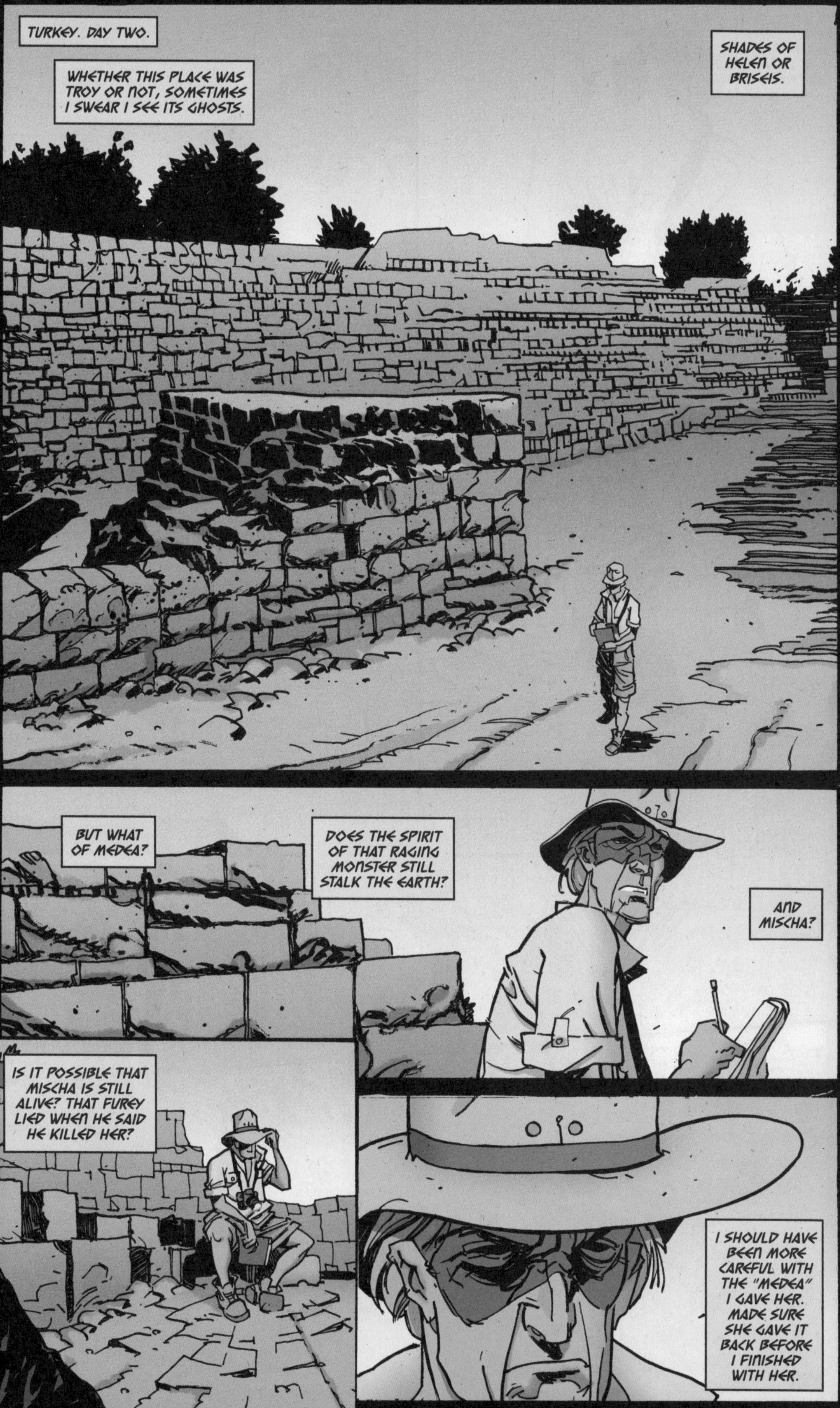
TURKEY. DAY TWO.
WHETHER THIS PLACE WAS TROY OR NOT, SOMETIMES I SWEAR I SEE ITS GHOSTS.
SHADES OF HELEN OR BRISEIS.
BUT WHAT OF MEDEA?
DOES THE SPIRIT OF THAT RAGING MONSTER STILL STALK THE EARTH?
AND MISCHA?
IS IT POSSIBLE THAT MISCHA IS STILL ALIVE? THAT FUREY LIED WHEN HE SAID HE KILLED HER?
I SHOULD HAVE BEEN MORE CAREFUL WITH THE "MEDEA" I GAVE HER. MADE SURE SHE GAVE IT BACK BEFORE I FINISHED WITH HER.

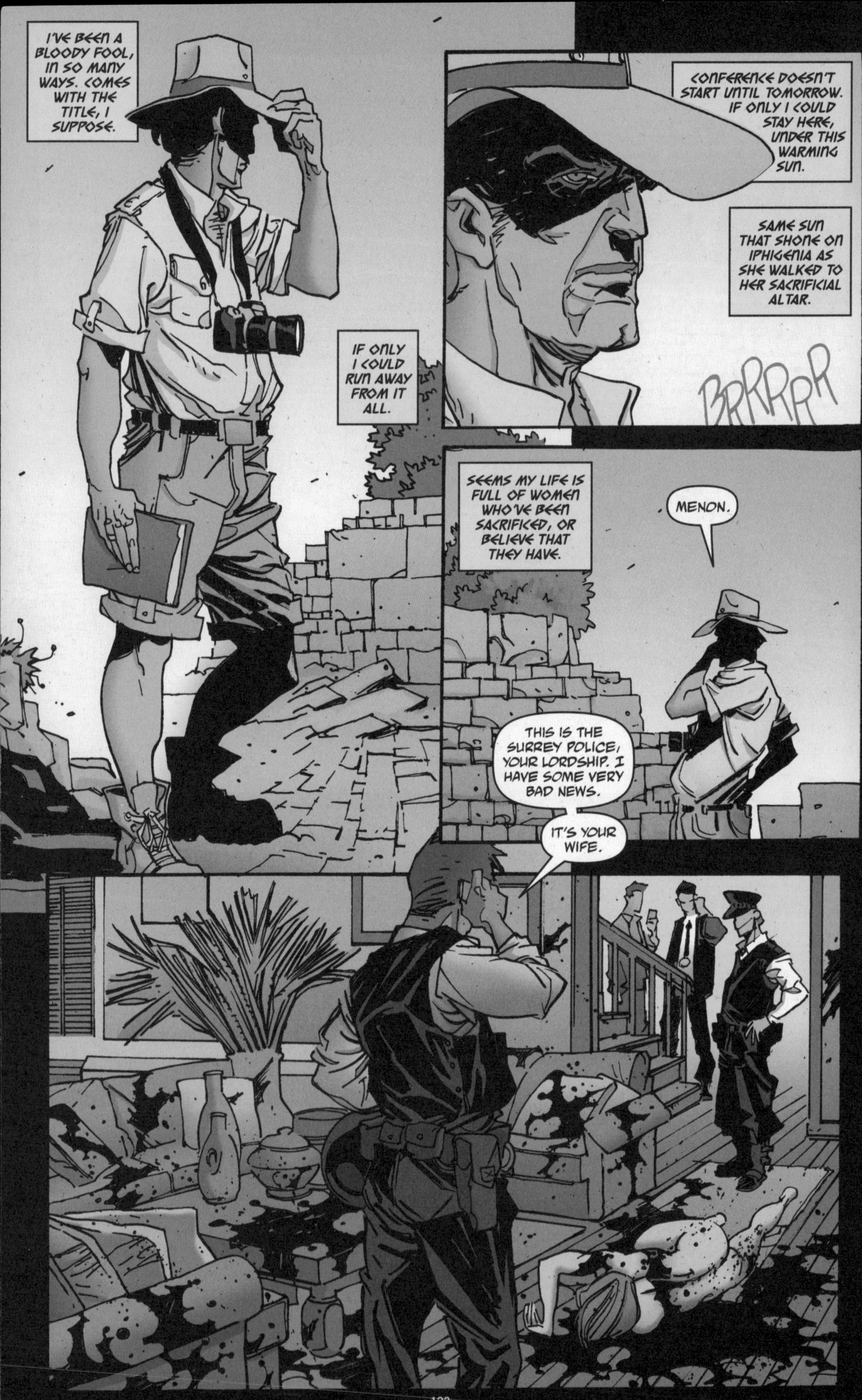
I'VE BEEN A BLOODY FOOL, IN SO MANY WAYS. COMES WITH THE TITLE, I SUPPOSE.
CONFERENCE DOESN'T START UNTIL TOMORROW. IF ONLY I COULD STAY HERE, UNDER THIS WARMING SUN.
SAME SUN THAT SHONE ON IPHIGENIA AS SHE WALKED TO HER SACRIFICIAL ALTAR.
IF ONLY I COULD RUN AWAY FROM IT ALL.
BRRRRR
SEEMS MY LIFE IS FULL OF WOMEN WHO'VE BEEN SACRIFICED, OR BELIEVE THAT THEY HAVE.
MENON.
THIS IS THE SURREY POLICE, YOUR LORDSHIP. I HAVE SOME VERY BAD NEWS.
IT'S YOUR WIFE.

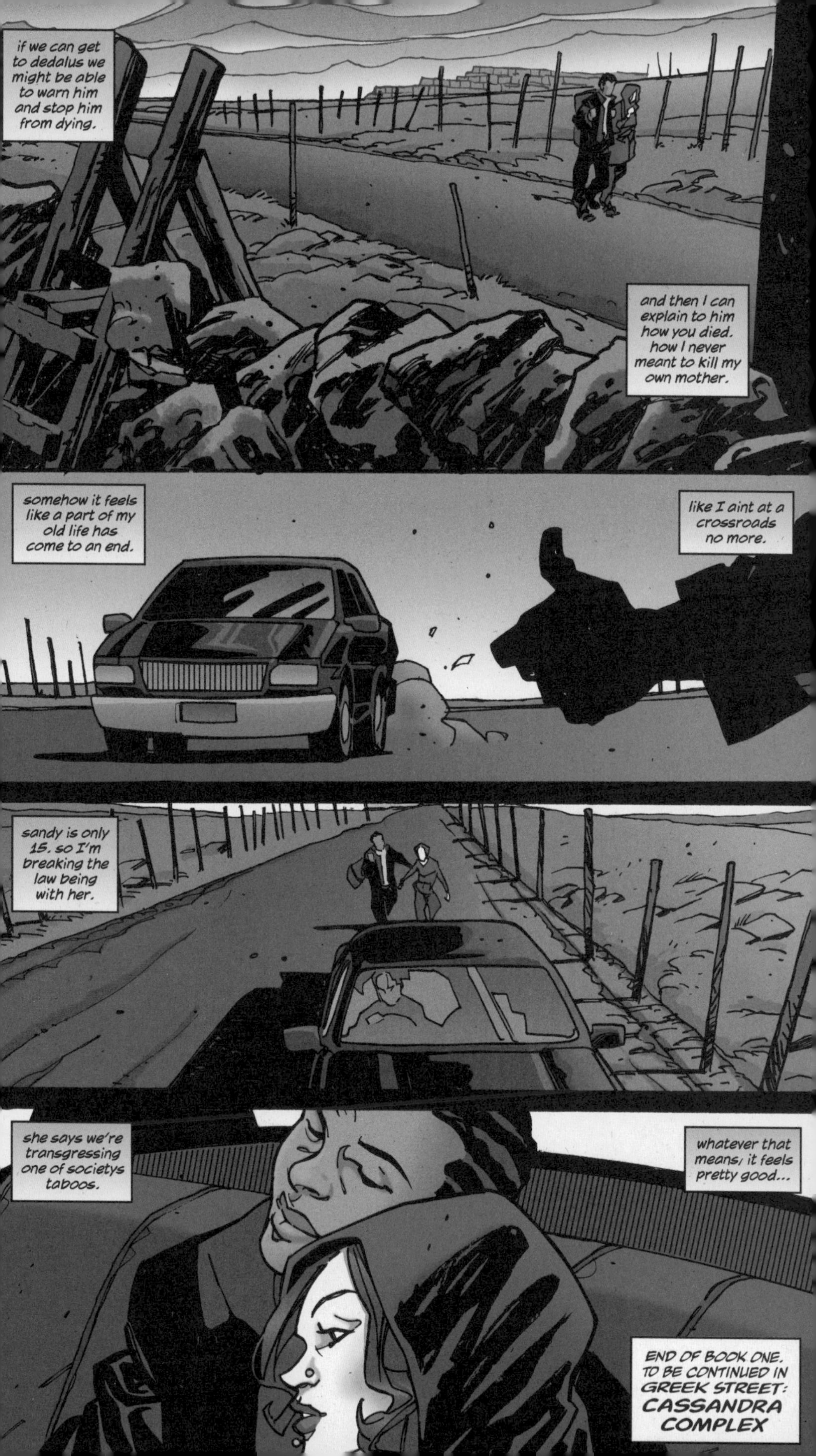
if we can get to dedalus we might be able to warn him and stop him from dying.
and then I can explain to him how you died. how I never meant to kill my own mother.
somehow it feels like a part of my old life has come to an end.
like I aint at a crossroads no more.
sandy is only 15. so I'm breaking the law being with her.
she says we're transgressing one of societys taboos.
whatever that means, it feels pretty good...
END OF BOOK ONE. TO BE CONTINUED IN GREEK STREET: CASSANDRA COMPLEX

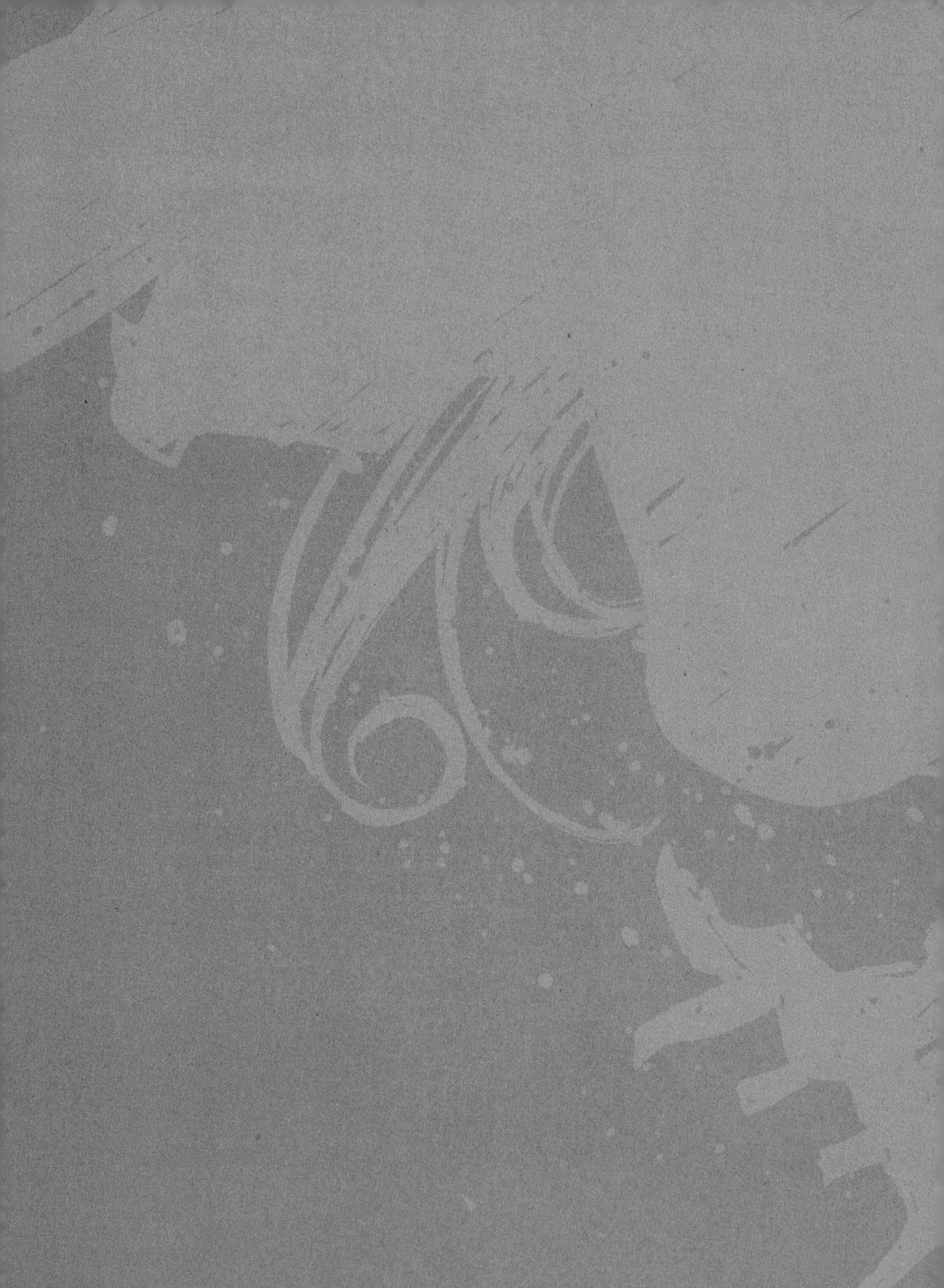

MORTAL CLAY

SKETCHES, CHARACTER DESIGNS AND PRELIMINARY ART BY DAVIDE GIANFELICE

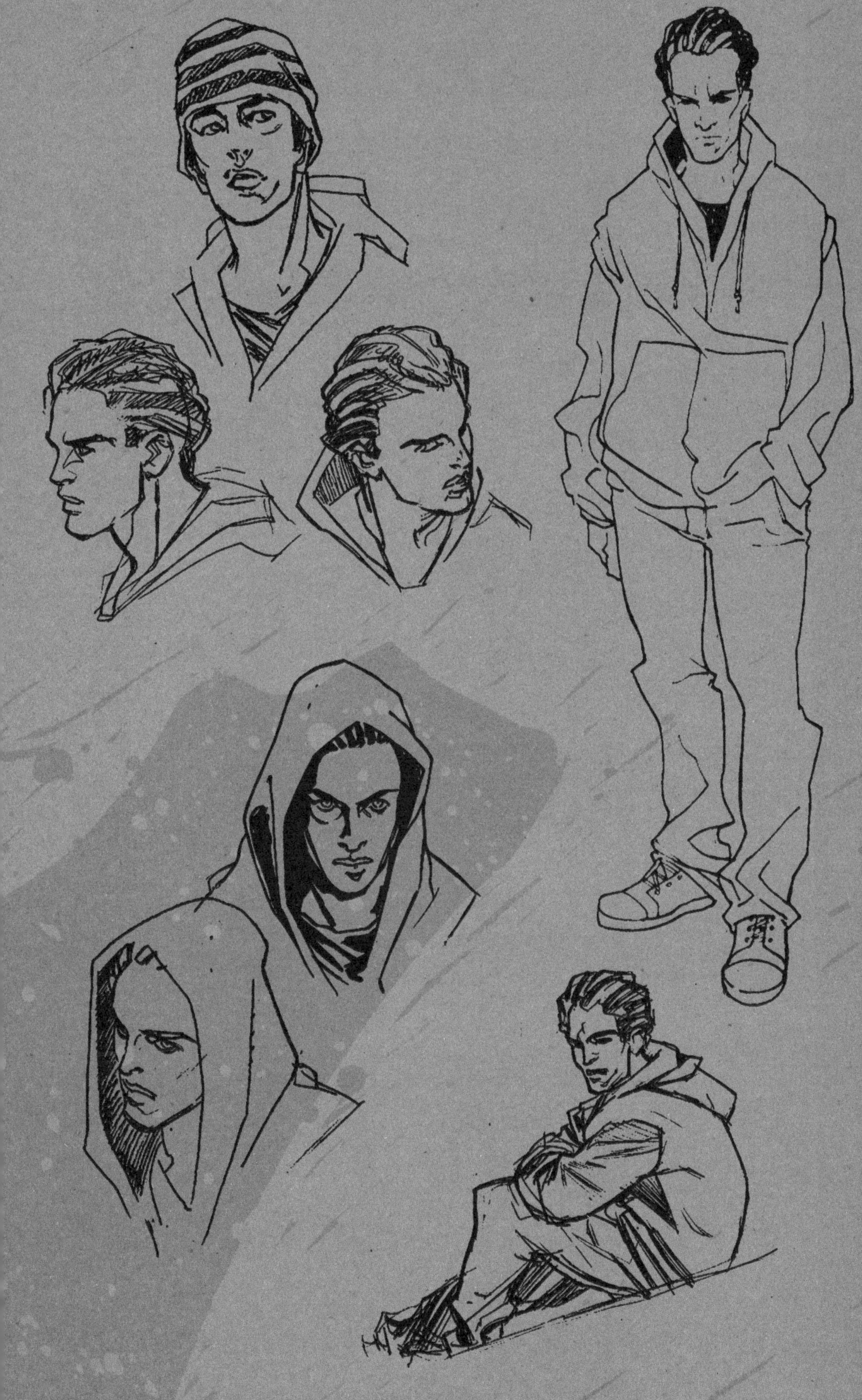

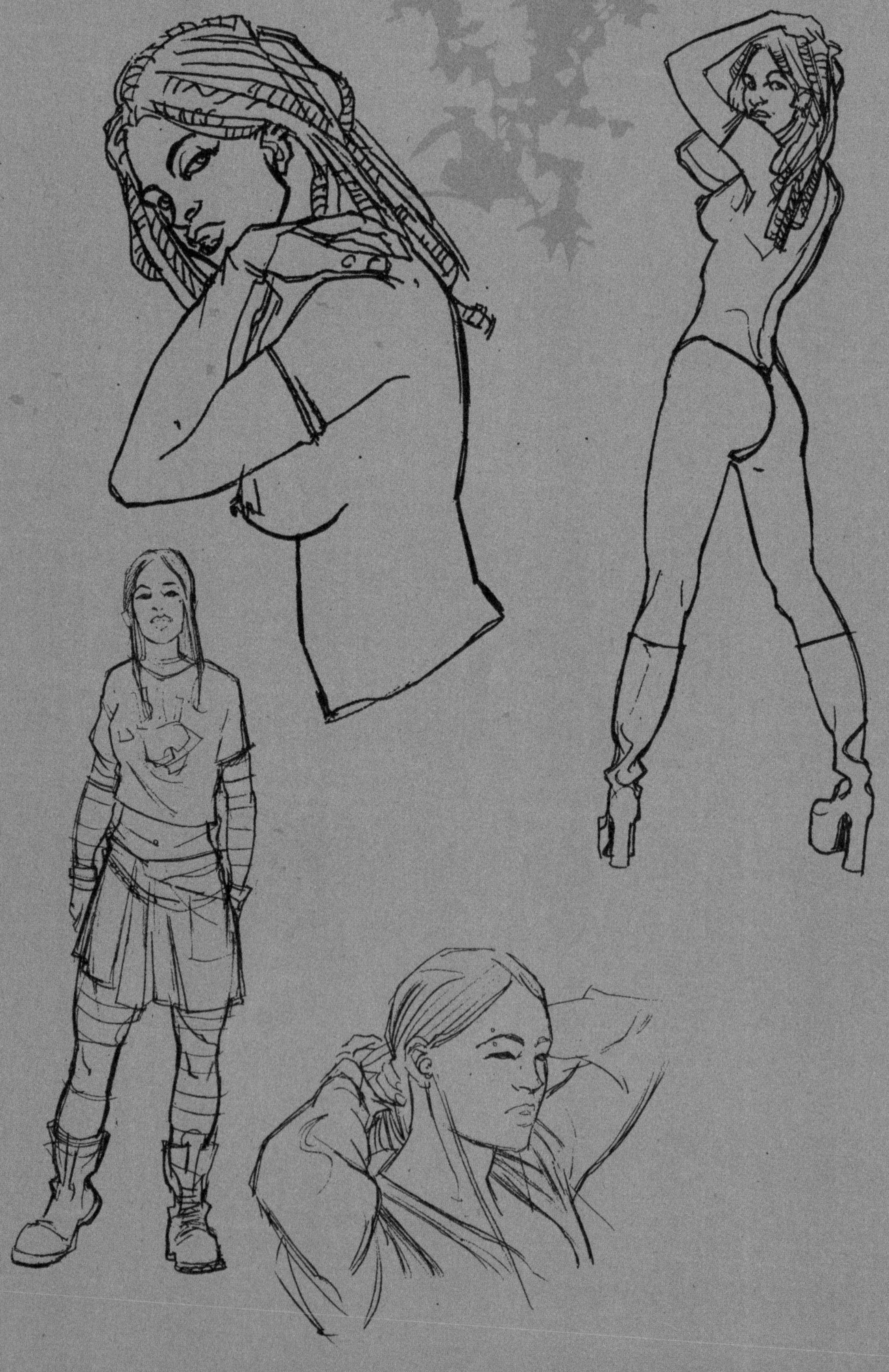

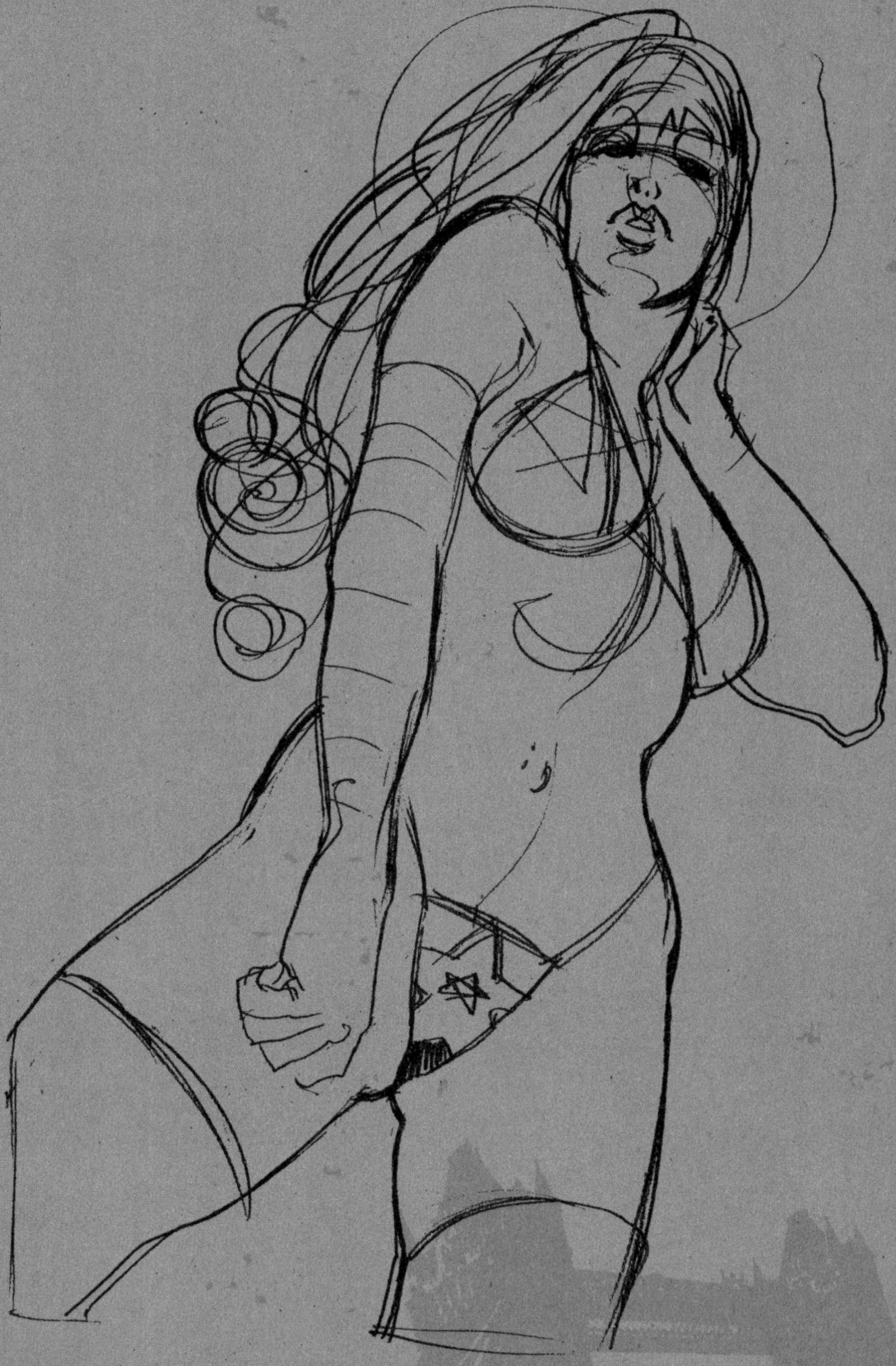

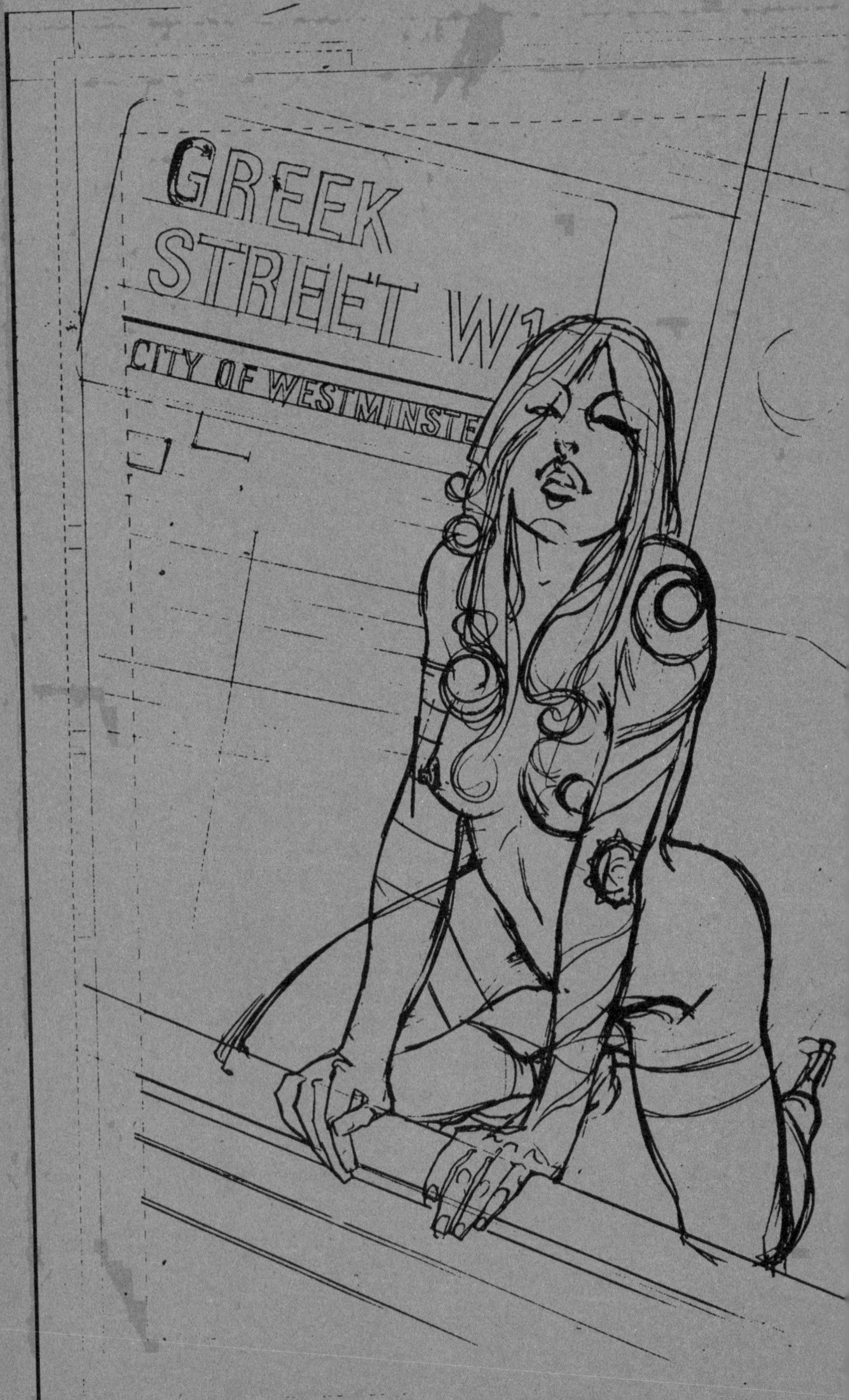
GREEK
STREET W1
CITY OF WESTMINSTE

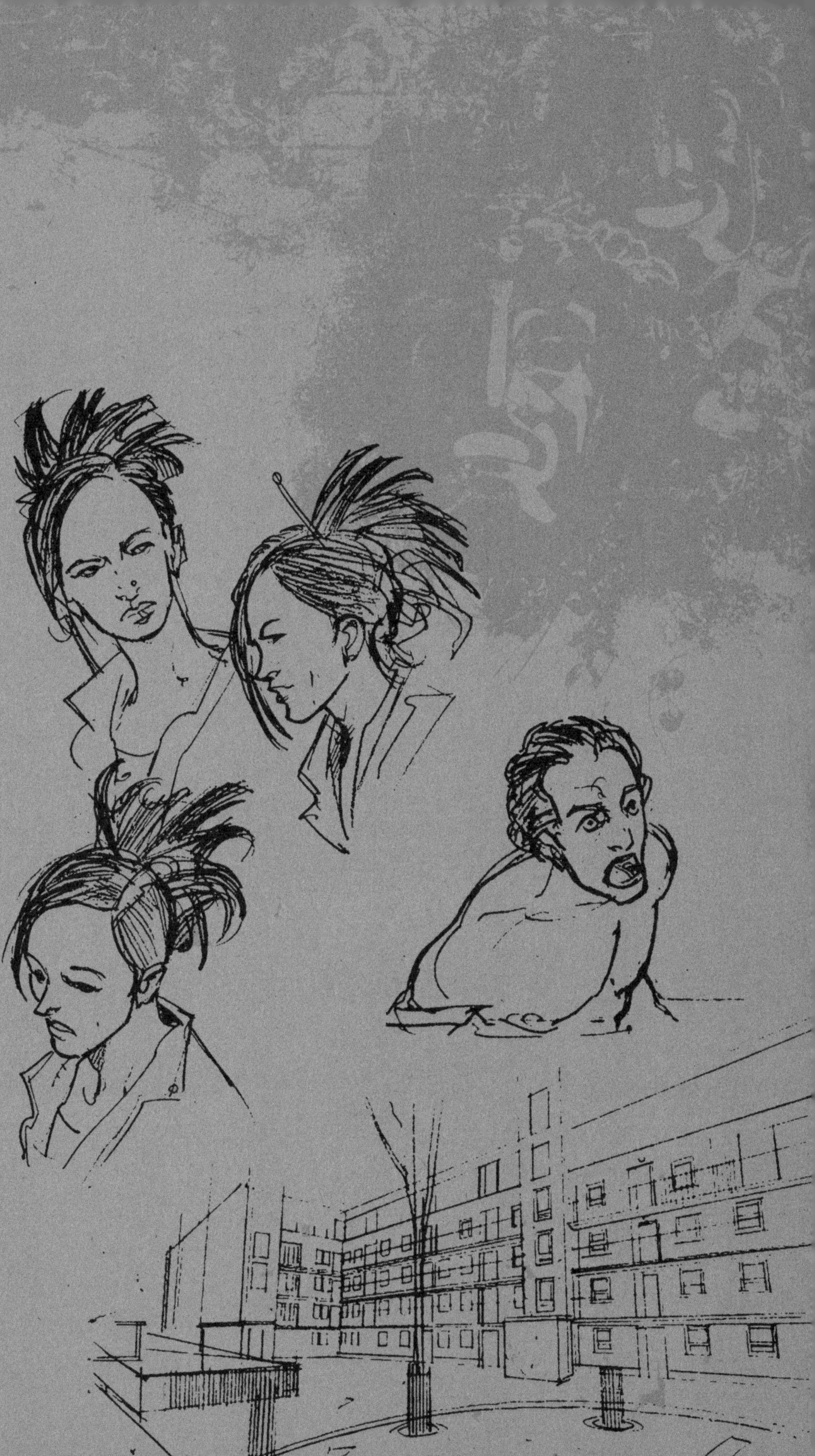

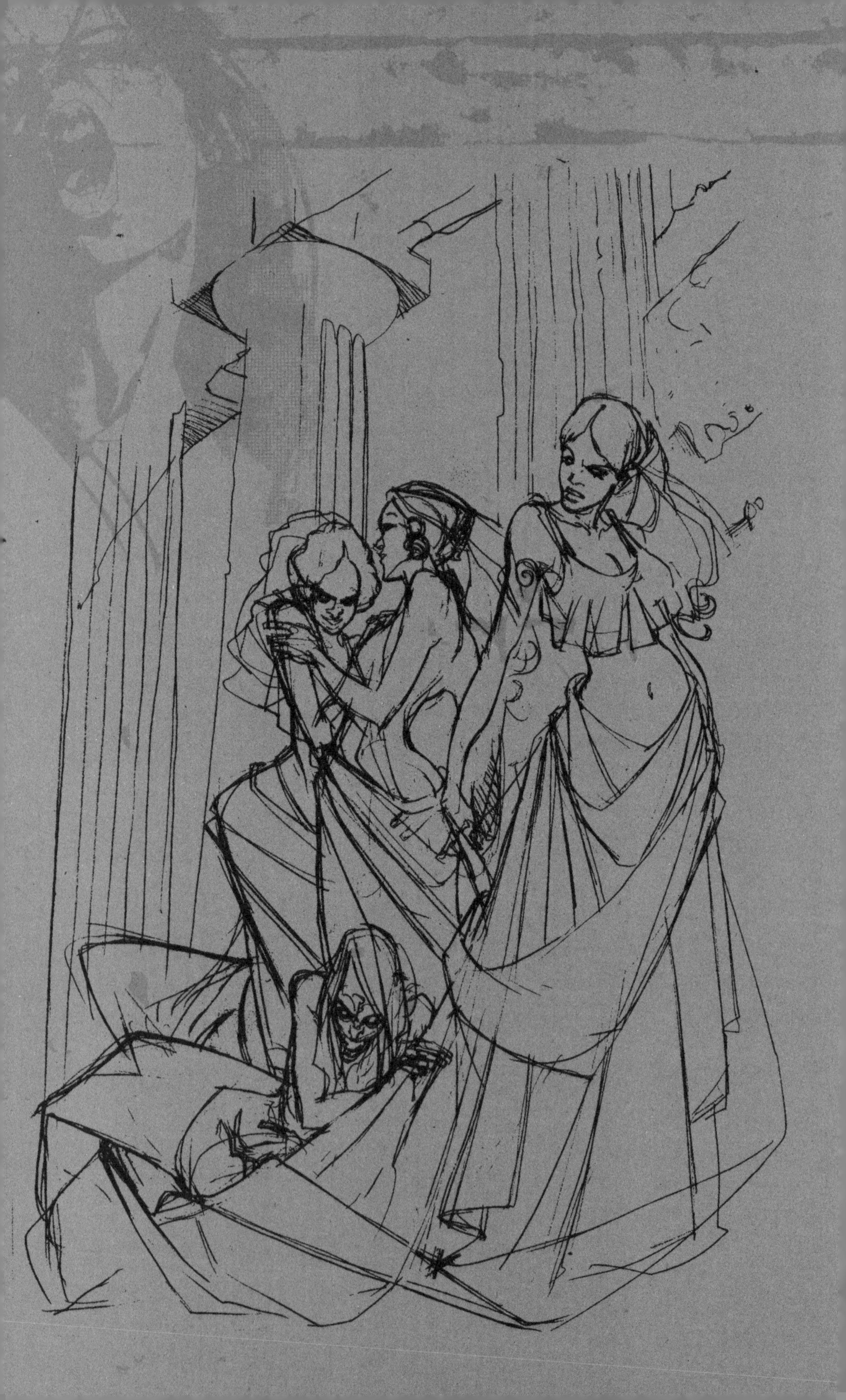

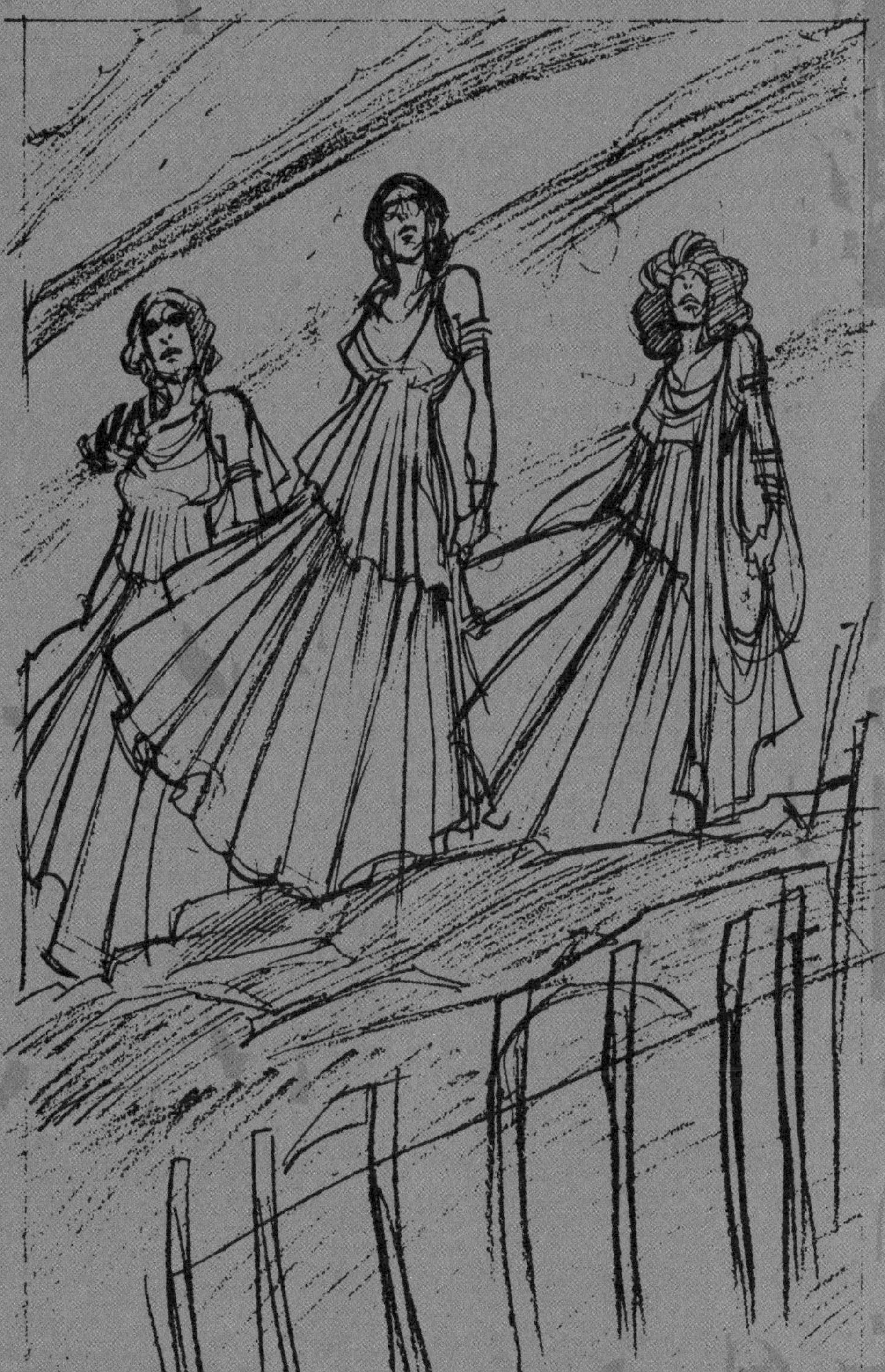

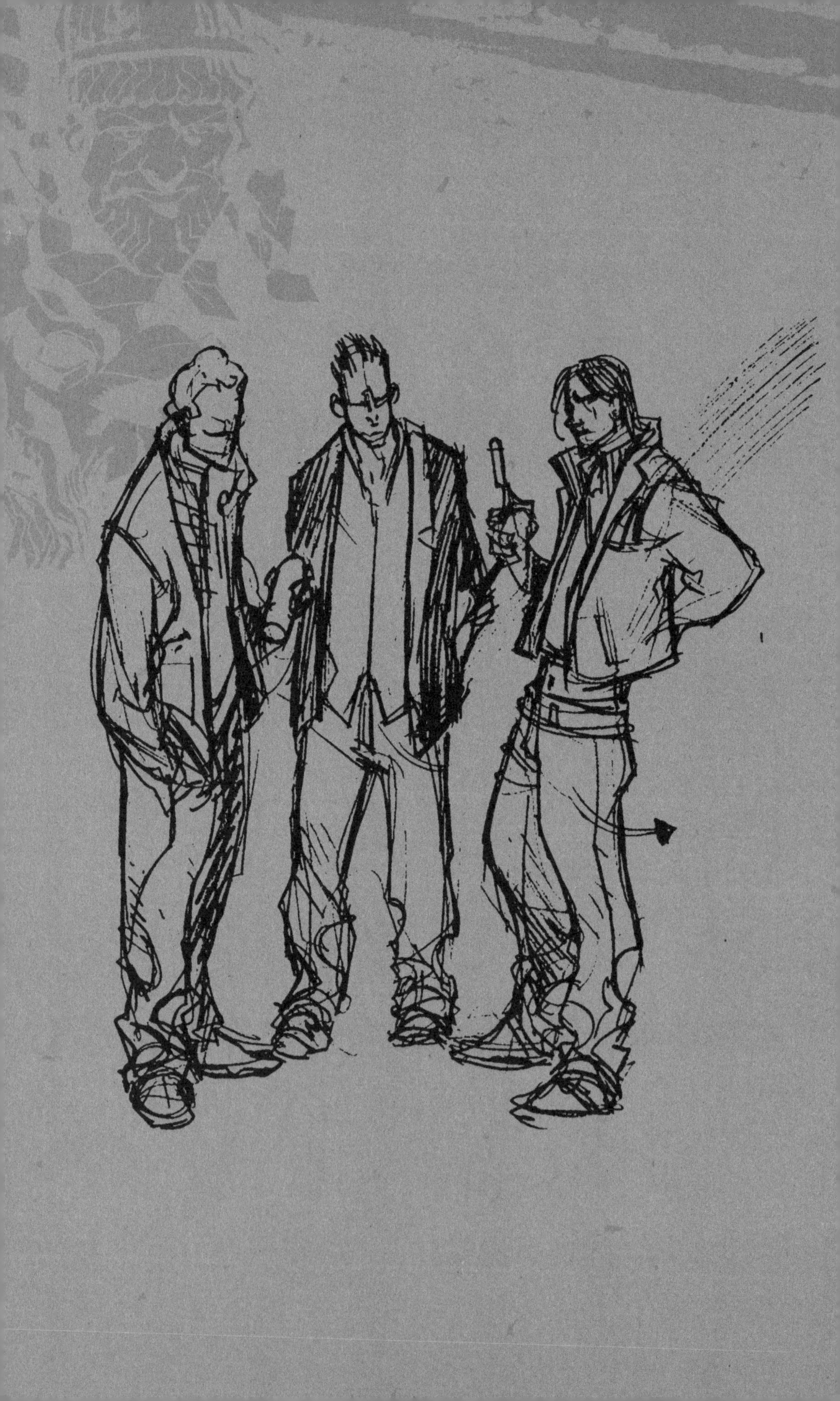